New Currents, Ancient Rivers

Contemporary African Artists in a Generation of Change

Jean Kennedy

Smithsonian Institution Press

Washington and London

98 97 96 95 94 93 92   5 4 3 2 1

Library of Congress Cataloging-in-Publication Data
Kennedy, Jean
New currents, ancient rivers : contemporary
African artists in a generation of change /
Jean Kennedy.
p.   cm.
Includes bibliographical references (p.)
and index.
ISBN 1-56098-037-0 (cloth). —
1. Art, Black—Africa, Sub-Saharan. 2. Art,
Modern—20th century—Africa, Sub-Saharan.
3. Artists—Africa, Sub-Saharan—Biography—
History and criticism. I. Title.
N7391.65.K46   1991
709'.67'09045—dc20   90-10314

Jenifer Blakemore, editor
Alan Carter, designer

Color plates printed in Hong Kong. Text and all
other elements printed in the United States of
America.
The paper in this book meets the requirements of
the American National Standard for Permanence
of Paper for Printed Materials Z39.48-1984.

For permission to reproduce illustrations
appearing in this book, please correspond directly
with the author's daughter, Mimi Wolford. The
Smithsonian Institution Press does not retain
reproduction rights for these illustrations or
maintain a file of addresses for photo sources.

Jean Kennedy died on 30 November 1991,
while this book was still in production. The
Smithsonian Institution Press has made every
effort, with the guidance of Ms. Kennedy's family
and friends, to complete the book as she would
have wished.

Cover: Bruce Onobrakpeya, *Forms in a Landscape*,
1973, deep etching, 24 × 18⅛ in. Photograph by
Richard Wolford.

To the artists of Africa

Contents

Illustrations

Foreword

For many years Jean Kennedy has devoted mind and spirit to the cause of modern African sculpture and painting. Here, at last, is a culminating work that I am sure will be referred to for as long as scholars and persons interested in the vitality of art made and painted south of the Sahara seek some sense of what is going on in a critical cockpit of world creativity.

The world conquest of African modern-traditional music, the songs of Sunny Ade, Franco, Mbelia Bel, Zao, and many, many other women and men is a fait accompli. The corresponding visual dimension to this upsurge is palpably demonstrated in the gathering of works of art surveyed here by Jean Kennedy. Latin blurred into the rise of potent vernacular languages that we now call French, Spanish, Portuguese, and Italian. Similarly, postcolonial Africa has taken on world art history and is "bending" the received forms of paint and easels and pedestals and busts in favor of new, dynamic, vernacular transforming languages, which will take us some time fully to explore and estimate. Meanwhile, operating by analogy with all this creolizing brilliance, there are African-Americans moving in directions similar to those illustrated in this text.

One of the leading dance bands of Haiti now records in Lingala, lingua franca of Kinshasa and Brazzaville, as well as English and Creole. Similarly, American artists, especially those of African descent, will build on *New Currents, Ancient Rivers* and find themselves confirmed.

Ancient constants in creative battle with forces stemming from the so-called modern world form part of the subject matter of this book. But surely the richest meaning has to do with spiritual discernability, extensions of the orisha and the minkisi and other traditional forces, in a vast minting of fresh alphabets of moral visual discourse. Open this book, witness.

Robert Farris Thompson
Professor, History of Art
Timothy Dwight College
Yale University

Introductory Note

When I hear that African art ceased with the production of ancient works, many of which are now housed in museums and private collections, I question the validity of this pronouncement. Most ancient works were made to serve political and religious purposes; in spite of the fact that their contents and the context for which they were created are no longer relevant, contemporary art in Africa is burgeoning.

As I was brought up believing in the sanctity of traditional African art, and served as custodian of traditional African masterpieces for more than two decades, it may appear surprising that I should identify myself with the contemporary art movement in Africa. Although I was involved with ancient artworks it was impossible to ignore the creations of emerging artists. The works of artists without formal art training attracted my attention first because I believed they were purer in form and content in relation to the works with which I was familiar. With time, however, I could not ignore the creations of artists who received art training in art schools in which the teaching methods and aesthetic criteria were based on European models. My initial difficulty in accepting their works lay in the fact that I was always looking for the "Africanness" in their works, and when I failed to find it, I distanced myself from them. But the varied types of contemporary art thrive with incredible success in all parts of Africa. This development is not unexpected in a society that is open to influences and striving to maintain and realize its own identity. The resulting pluralism of styles has enriched the many countries of this continent.

Looking at the activities of African artists as chronicled by Jean Kennedy we see that African art has enjoyed a renaissance; an art of bold, new forms, full of diversity and vitality. That this is not widely known in the West may be partly due to the erroneous belief that African creativity ended with the advent of colonialism. However, the major reason may be that until now, little effort has been made to bring this glorious present to the wider world. This is why Jean Kennedy's work is such a welcome event.

Jean Kennedy has spent much of her life in the service of contemporary African art. She has undertaken special studies and promoted with great success many contemporary artists. I am pleased that she has written this book, which will bring to the fore the creative talents of contemporary Africans and act as a catalyst in generating more interest in the world of contemporary African art.

Ekpo Eyo
Professor, African Art
Department of Art History and Archaeology
University of Maryland at College Park
    and formerly Director General for Museums and
    Monuments, Nigeria

Preface

Most of us are familiar with major works of traditional African art. However, we know little about the work of new artists of that continent. This is our loss, for there is great artistic ferment in Africa: modern artists are creating new images and expressing new ways of life. Their boundless creative energy keeps bursting the seams of preconception—changing the whole artistic character of a continent.

In writing this book, I have chosen artists in Black, or sub-Saharan Africa—those whom I feel are at the forefront of this modern expression and whose art is fresh and imaginative. Thus this book is not all-inclusive; it focuses on fewer than 150 artists. The artists included represent a number of directions and styles. Their paintings, graphics, tapestries, and sculptures are an important part of a growing renaissance. In them I find vitality and originality. Each artist has a distinct direction and a consistent body of work. Collectively, the artists mentioned in this book have created art that combines elements of contemporary life with foreign technology and that, although it does not serve traditional ends, embraces certain basic traditional rhythms.

Some have studied in France, Germany, England, and the United States, returning to reassociate themselves with their own beginnings. Many have attended local art institutions. Others have emerged without any formal academic training. Most are men. African women, albeit active as traders, like women in other parts of the world, were not given the same kind of career opportunities as men; however, their past artistic contributions are now being documented.

My choices have been shaped by working with African artists who were the focus of my life for seven years while I lived in Africa from 1961 to 1968, and by the succeeding eighteen years when I arranged and developed exhibitions for many of them. My own experiences as an artist in Africa and elsewhere have undoubtedly influenced my perceptions too. To suspend judgment would deny art its function as a carrier of values and feelings that cross geographical, ethnological, and philosophical boundaries. This book, therefore, is my effort to share my experience of the excitement and beauty of the continent's creative energy, not to comprehensively chronicle the history of contemporary artists in sub-Saharan Africa.

The exclusion of Egypt and North Africa from this account is not for lack of strong cultural ties to the rest of Africa, but because of space requirements. I have chosen, therefore, to discuss sub-Saharan African artists, and have grouped them by country or area in order to refer to their specific historical influences. Characteristically distinct artists have developed in six countries: Nigeria, Senegal, Sudan, Ethiopia, Zimbabwe, and South Africa. In addition to groups from these major countries, I have included a few exceptional artists in West, East, and Central Africa. Since Nigeria has, by far, the largest number, a greater portion of the book is devoted to artists from that country.

With few exceptions, the artists covered in this volume represent the period of the last forty years. They were selected on the basis of a single criterion: the quality of their work. In some instances, the meager attention accorded reflects a lack of available information. A few exemplary self-trained artists are also included to give the reader an indication of the many whose work goes unremarked outside of their immediate communities. Though the pottery, baskets, fabrics, and myriad artifacts of Africa are an intrinsic part of life and the artistic milieu there, it is not possible to include them as well.

All of the artists mentioned work primarily to please themselves rather than the public; each has produced a consistent body of work that demonstrates a fresh, imaginative vision. I have chosen to quote them whenever possible to convey a feeling for the dimensions of their lives and works.

Because the arts of Africa are still so interrelated, I have included several artists who are not painters and sculptors—for example, two filmmakers—and described briefly their influence. My intent is not to survey other art forms but simply to help in the understanding of the interaction that exists in Africa today among all the creative arts, whatever the medium.

To the many artists of excellence throughout Africa who are not mentioned here due to limits of space, I express my regrets. I hope this book will in some way extend parameters beyond what has already been said and seen. I look forward to other books, especially by African writers and artists who will disclose qualities and histories as yet unrevealed, or still being dreamed, still being shaped. The time is ripe, and such notice is overdue.

Acknowledgments

First of all I must thank each artist for the gift of inspiration, which is the heart and purpose of this book. Without the initial encouragement of James Hinton, I would not have begun. Without the patience of Richard, Miriam, and Rebecca Wolford, I could not have continued. My thanks to Irma and Jack Willis for their unlimited generosity; Georgina and Ulli Beier for their vision and inspiration; Warren Robbins for his direction; the Djerassi Foundation for three months of quiet production, and Leigh Hyams, its supportive director, for her enthusiasm and critical guidance; and Frank McEwen for extended help and information. In addition to David Gamble and Janet Stanley, who were tireless providers of bibliography, Bettie Allen and Letitia Strong, who gave time and dedicated assistance; Robert Barde, who shared files; Acha Debela, who offered encouragement and information; Ronald Warwick, who provided access to records at the Commonwealth Institute; and the Embassy of Senegal, Washington, D.C., all deserve thanks. Dennis Duerden, John Povey, Ted and Traudis Kennedy, David Brokensha, Rhoda Levinsohn, Sondra Hale, Eli Leon, and Peter Mark gave valued advice. And importantly, Yusuf Grillo, Muraina Oyelami, Ibrahim El Salahi, Bruce Onobrakpeya, Gavin Jantjes, Uzo Egonu, Haile Gerima, Elimu Njau, Tesfaye Tessema, Wosene Kosrof, Louis Maqhubela, Amir Nour, and many other African artists each provided insights, information, and responses to my questions. The special support of Sigrid Vollerthun, Marvin Silverman, Joyce Carol Thomas, Claudia Vess, Terry McGlone, Sara Dickerson, Christine Lando, Dan Moldea, Kathleen Kennedy, Deborah Cowan, Tracy Krumm, Carolyn Trujillo, Nancy Westsmith, and Claire Polakoff are appreciated. Assistance from Lenrie Peters, Katherine Van Wick Brown, and Alice McGaughey should also be mentioned. I must also thank Amy Pastan, Ruth Spiegel, Jeanne Sexton, Kathryn Stafford, Kathy Kuhtz, Carole Jacob, Jenifer Blakemore, E. Barbara Phillips, and Alan Carter; their counsel has moved the manuscript to the printed page. For suggesting the book and for encouraging me to pursue it, I thank Felix Lowe. That so many individuals have given time and effort is a measure of that gift of inspiration by Africa's contemporary artists.

I've known rivers:
I've known rivers ancient as the world and older than
  the flow of human blood in human veins.

My soul has grown deep like the rivers.

  (Langston Hughes, "The Negro Speaks of Rivers")

Introduction

New forms appear in every aspect of the African landscape today. Change and surprise are constant. Energy, urgency, and excitement are a nourishing presence. As old ways die, new voices are born in sub-Saharan Africa: an area of the world with the earliest record of human life, the ancient ways of a rural countryside, and modern cities with high-rise office buildings. These juxtapositions shock and strengthen. On one hand, the loss of great traditions creates a vacuum. On the other hand, because boundaries and restraints are few, new possibilities arise. However, the past and its wisdom are often close at hand, and like the rivers of Africa, run deep as time.

In many instances classical traditions provide a background against which to appraise the present expression. For many African artists, a commitment to traditional values is a fundamental element in the alchemy of creative genius. Some synthesize allusions to the past with contemporary content; others create imagery with mythical or ritual references. But the artists, though rooted in tradition, use materials, methods, and images foreign to traditional art, and their art is usually based on a personal aesthetic.

These artists, who have emerged throughout sub-Saharan Africa in the last forty years, and who are working in new ways with new materials, address their art to a wider public. In the past their relationship to a community gave them structures and styles. Now, often separated by thousands of miles, the artists are linked in a network of the literary, performing, and visual arts by conferences, festivals, exhibitions, and literary movements. Despite problems of great magnitude—many of them attributable to colonialism—the artists continue to redefine African art, reflecting the changing social, political, and cultural environment.

There have been a number of beginnings: some artists have had academic art training in art schools, colleges, or universities, others have had alternative or experimental workshop experiences. Many have developed without the help of either. The earliest of the academic efforts took place in the thirties with the founding of two colleges: Achimota College and the School of Fine Arts at Makerere University College. Achimota College, near Accra, Ghana, was established in 1936. The art department was later moved to the University of Science and Technology in Kumasi, Ghana, with a formal arts and crafts program. In Kampala, Uganda, the School of Fine Arts at Makerere University College was founded in 1939. It was a technical college when Margaret Trowell came from England to begin teaching. Trowell advocated the use of African subject matter but practiced conventional European teaching procedures, thus producing easel painters.

In 1943 outside Kinshasa, Zaire (formerly Belgian Congo), Frère Marc-Stanislas, a Catholic priest, created the École St. Luc (later renamed Académie des Beaux-Arts). This school adhered to Belgian educational methods and taught classical European art. In Sudan three years later a school was founded, which eventually became the most important focus for contemporary

African art in northern sub-Saharan Africa: the Department of Arts and Crafts, now the College of Fine and Applied Arts, of the Khartoum Technical Institute. This school is now the center of an impressive movement.

Other activities included the establishing of two institutes in 1951 in both Zaire and Congo (then the Belgian and French Congos). One school, the Académie des Beaux-Arts et de Metiers d'Art in Lumbumbashi, was run by Laurent Moonens, a Belgian artist. It later incorporated a workshop school established in 1944 and headed by Pierre Romain-Desfosses. The Desfosses school took an experimental approach, but work produced was routinely decorative. The other institute, The Centre d'Art Africaine, also known as the Poto-Poto School, was founded in Brazzaville by Pierre Lods. Lods attempted to foster an "African" approach, but much of the resulting art was also highly decorative and repetitious. The style took hold as a fad, spawning tourist art, which sold throughout the markets of West Africa.

The training of some of the finest artists in Africa occurred at the Nigerian College of Arts, Science, and Technology (now the Art Department of Ahmadu Bello University). Founded in 1953 in the northern city of Zaria, by 1960 it had graduated artists who strongly influenced artistic developments in the country, and who became known throughout the continent. Nigeria's other early art school, the Department of Art, Design, and Technology at the Yaba College of Technology, established in the Lagos suburb of Yaba in 1955, also produced prominent painters and sculptors.

Four years later in Ethiopia another important center of contemporary art, the Fine Arts School, was established. Its graduates have produced some of the most original work in Africa. Finally, as late as 1966 the last of the seminal institutions, a school now famous for the production of tapestries, was created: the Manufactures Nationale des Tapisseries at Thiès, Senegal.

Additional significant efforts to encourage expression occurred in unconventional settings. While workshop schools in Zaire and Congo had emphasized the value of indigenous art forms with results that were often romantic, later nonacademic or experimental approaches pioneered in the fifties and sixties generated exciting and imaginative works. The most important of these workshops were in Harare, Zimbabwe (then Salisbury, Rhodesia), under the direction of Frank McEwen; in Maputo (then Lourenço Marques), Mozambique, under Pancho Guedes; in Oshogbo, Nigeria, under Susanne Wenger; in Oshogbo and Ife, Nigeria, under Georgina Beier; and short workshops organized by Julian Beinart in Nigeria, Zambia, Kenya, and South Africa. In these workshops, creativity was encouraged and formal teaching methods were scorned; the artists who developed exhibited originality and consistency of direction.

European missionaries ran workshops too, but often with mediocre results. For example, Father Kevin Carroll's workshop in Ekiti, Nigeria, utilized an apprentice system, and carvers became technically astute. But because they were no longer carving for the original cults, but for Christian purposes, creating madonnas and crucifixes, their work lacked intensity. Modern potteries in Vume, Ghana, and Abuja, Nigeria, established by Michael Cardew became known abroad for the results of the work there. Clerics of the Swedish mission at Rorke's Drift in South Africa had more successful results with the development of artists who created strong black and white graphic prints.

A number of artists sought training in Europe and in the United States. Some found their experience irrelevant. Others produced some of their finest work abroad, adjusting to new situations and reflecting their adjustment to foreign lands in the syntheses they created.

Contemporary African artists have faced difficult struggles, especially when confronting prevailing Western misconceptions and prejudices about Africans and Africa. The use of the word "primitive" and the anonymity accorded indigenous art by foreign institutions have worked in subtle ways to the artists' detriment, denying them respect and recognition. These stereotypes are further fostered by pervasive efforts to categorize African art in conformity with Western aesthetic criteria. Every aspect of African culture is, in some way, stamped by others. While setting traditional art apart in museums and books has value, it can suggest that it is complete and finished. The reverence accorded it is sometimes construed to suggest that change is a travesty.

Such obstacles imply that whatever the direction of the new artists, danger lies ahead. They are criticized both for leaving traditions behind or for embracing traditional elements. Holding up past achievements as the epitome of artistic endeavor is a heavy burden for any creative artist. Africans who study abroad and avoid African subject matter or employ a style that is not recognizably "African" are sometimes considered betrayers of their inheritance. Clearly this attitude is unnecessarily limiting.

Indeed, attributes of some contemporary African art, which critics suggest are influenced by cubism or German expressionism, relate to the traditions of African art that motivated those modern European movements. The older, indigenous arts, as author-critic Ulli Beier points out, contain the seeds of every modern movement.[1]

The variety encountered in indigenous cultures makes the task of creating canons to define either traditional or contemporary African art a difficult one. Although traditional elements—the frequent use of symbolism, metaphors, organic forms, inherent rhythms, and (much of the time) religious contexts—do link cultures on the continent, they also connect the continent to the diaspora.

These traditional elements are often present in the works of contemporary Africans who, like other artists, select qualities appropriate to them; but the variety of approaches, styles, and forms among Africa's artists today demonstrates their openness. Like other artists, they respond in their work to political and social change, and to momentous processes or events, such as the inroads made by Christianity and Islam, the Nigerian Civil War, the altered political system in Ethiopia, and apartheid in South Africa.

In spite of their topical subject matter, they need more local patronage. Government support, in the form of commissions, purchases, or exhibitions, is gaining ground—especially when it recognizes that an artist's work can be used to express the country's identity. Foreign businesses have commissioned works as a way of cementing relationships with host countries. Nevertheless, because much of the work of modern African artists exists outside religious contexts, they are denied the traditional constituency of the community. Now, however, their accomplishments have commanded attention around the world, and more of their compatriots are becoming their clients.

Postscript

The modern renaissance occurring in Africa has set a pace that continues. During the process of this book's publication, a number of artists not included here have begun to receive critical attention; among them is Tapfuma Gutsa of Zimbabwe, who was featured at the Studio Museum in Harlem *Contemporary African Artists: Changing Traditions* exhibition in 1990, and who received an honorable mention at the Venice Biennale in the same year. (Bruce Onobrakpeya of Nigeria; Henry Munyaradzi and Nicholas Mukomberanwa, both of Zimbabwe; and El Anatsui of Ghana and Nsukka, Nigeria, were also included in the exhibition and were similarly honored in the Biennale.)

Others not mentioned or mentioned briefly are Youssouf Bath from Ivory Coast, whose works were also included in the Harlem show and are a sensitive exploration of colors, materials, and subjects; Nigerian artist and critic Olu Oguibe, whose incisive reviews in *West Africa* are read by all interested in African culture; Nigerian Tayo Adenaike, whose poetic watercolors and drawings were displayed at a recent exhibition in Washington, D.C., and who is a member of the new Aka artists' movement in Nigeria; South African Helen Sebidi, whose works reveal her talent as a powerful painter of human struggle; Sudanese Hussein Gunaan, whose works are filled with spirited animal symbols; Nigerian Olumuyiwa Amoda, whose sculpture is of impressive size and artistry; and Zairean Cheri Samba, whose works challenge the viewer with their dynamic images and urgent messages. An account such as this is never finished. Today's African art, like the river that never rests, runs its course with new energy and vision.

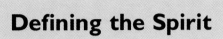

Defining the Spirit

1   Sources for Synthesis

Art, fed by experience, is enriched by inspiration from diverse streams, including the cultures of other societies. Most contemporary art is responsive to injections—cross-cultural and cross-personal. Often similarities in the arts of geographically distant areas can be explained, as Carl Jung would explain them, as the result of a shared subconscious experience, but whatever the connections and similarities, the art forms of traditional cultures—now more accessible to the world at large than ever before—demonstrate their impact on those societies to which they are integral.

For example, many sub-Saharan societies take art so much for granted that there is often no one word to describe it. So although discussion continues among art historians, with their subjective biases, as to whether canons exist that define what is or is not "artistic" in indigenous West African cultures, these questions of aesthetics may be considered irrelevant and esoteric within the societies themselves.

We know that art in Africa has always been interwoven—one form with another and all with life itself. Whether art was created for kings or shrines, was inspired by gods or myths, or was a record of historical events, this interrelationship of art forms, as a given, is a pervasive, abiding presence. Because it acted on behalf of and as the embodiment of religion, art was a communicative structure like language, an ongoing process rather than an object. Individuals became participants and members of the larger group—the keepers of the communal energy; as guardians they retained their potency as individuals.

Through rituals the arts of African societies mark life's major events—birth, puberty, death, and rebirth. Performance of these rituals links the world of the living to that of the dead. Ancestors and their worship are necessarily involved. Such ceremonies create harmony, ensure prosperity, restore balance that has been disturbed, effect judicial processes, unify the community, and establish the "right" relationships between society and the natural and metaphysical worlds. In addition, in times of trouble or difficulty, rituals of purification function to maintain the psychic unity of a community and strengthen the terms of its existence, its sense of reality, order, and propriety.

Often rituals are accomplished by means of masquerade: transformation with mask and costume, music, dance, and poetry. Masquerade is "the public face of the secret society," adding drama, "humor, fear, awe, admiration of skill" to life.[1] It also provides an opportunity to translate myths and to make fun of existing idiosyncrasies and transgressions, thus bringing transgressors into line. It may involve rituals for healing and even serve political purposes.

It is out of such contexts, where the pervasiveness of the arts, of myth and legend still endure—in spite of the enormous changes taking place—that the new artists of Africa, working for different purposes, create works that interpret their humanity and aspirations. As the works articulate inner visions, they express the vitality and identity of a continent.

When investigating indigenous societies and attempting to fathom the ways, some subtle and some dramatic, that change occurs, one comes close to understanding the creative process. Change, operating via the synthesis of two or more elements—such as subject, style, content, rhythm, language, composition, or technique—with some formerly alien element, is producing fascinating mixtures. Together the new and old form a syncretic combination that reconciles differing beliefs and philosophies.

Like the veins in a leaf, this synthesis structures contemporary African art just as it has older forms that also were subject to change. This blending of cultural elements occurs in various ways. It has taken place, for example, through gradual assimilation of foreign influences. It has also occurred when influences were forcibly superimposed by colonial domination. In the latter case, this process has had an overwhelming impact on the original culture. By seducing whole cultures, the resulting shocks have often promoted consumerism rather than creativity, leaving the indigenous cultures little chance for survival.

In some areas of the world there is evidence of resistance to this kind of assimilation. Rather than being overwhelmed by foreign cultural invasions, artists themselves are adopting new elements and selecting new techniques, as well as adapting old forms to suit their contemporary visions. Looking at such artists and their works, one sees a strength of focus and resolution of identity.

Just as syncretism encourages growth, it also provides a framework for seeing. Examining the ingredients, one can approach cultural history from a perspective other than a linear or chronological one and gain a better understanding of how image makers work. Looking at the strong new images and fresh directions of many contemporary African artists, a number of whom are now prominent both at home and abroad, one finds new visions and vital statements, truly part of the process of defining the spirit, the contemporary Zeitgeist of Africa south of the Sahara.

2   Image and Metaphor

Because Africans "see" with language, constantly creating imagery through the liberal use of proverbs and figures of speech, the traditional poetry of Africa is a counterpart to the visual arts. This characteristic persists in the work of African writers today who formed a cultural vanguard and preceded—except for a few early painters and sculptors—the contemporary visual artists. Usually working in colonial languages, that is, in English, French, and Portuguese, they created a new literary genre in each.

Modern African poetry has many forms. It reveals patterns reminiscent of indigenous poetry, suggests influences from Western poetry, and is prophetic, contemplative, or romantic. The various strands have a common element: an emphasis on visual imagery. While this is common to most poetries, it is particularly apparent in African poetry.

In French-speaking West Africa, the Negritude movement, which began in Paris in 1939 with a group of African and Caribbean poets, and the journal *Presence Africaine* (published in Paris) were forerunners of what eventually became a literary renaissance.[1] In English-speaking West Africa the Nigeria-based publication *Black Orpheus*, a journal focusing on the literary and visual arts, gave writers from various parts of Africa and the Caribbean an important platform.[2] Begun in 1957 by author-professor Ulli Beier, the journal continued to find talent and challenge readers with fresh material twenty issues later when new editors took charge. *Black Orpheus* and Beier's activities as founder and editor have been

documented by author Peter Benson in his book, *Black Orpheus, Transition, and Modern Cultural Awakening in Africa* (Berkeley, Los Angeles, London: University of California Press, 1986). Benson credits Beier with having stimulated a cultural renaissance in Africa via the magazine. Originally begun as an effort to encourage writing in English-speaking West Africa by publishing translations of the works of French-speaking authors, the magazine afforded now well-known writers and artists access to an audience. It also inspired other publications. The most vital was *Transition* magazine, founded and edited by Rajat Neogy in 1961 in Kampala, Uganda.

By the middle sixties, after many countries had gained political independence, both *Black Orpheus* and *Transition* were actively publishing African, Caribbean, and African-American writers and including reviews of artists' work. Poets and writers from across the continent became linked by conferences and by publications, which were often illustrated by artists. Small as the groups of writers and artists were at first, they provided inspiration and stimuli that grew as their numbers did.

Many African writers also had certain influences in common, for example, oral traditions that operated in concert with other art forms. Africa's traditional poetry and literary lore were integral to music, as music was integral to drama and masquerade, and as drama was integral to myth and religion. Each art was appropriate, yet each was but a segment of a repertoire that was continually being revitalized. But when outside political systems imposed on African societies brought confrontations with foreign ways of life, changes and disruptions of indigenous life occurred. The work of writers and artists reflected the changes. Significantly, the links formed by writers, artists, and musicians continued traditional connections between the arts.

Artistic creativity in the sixties was usually centered in the cities where contrasts between colonial culture and traditional ways provoked new expression. The relatively small number of painters, writers, actors, and composers throughout the continent were aware of the varied artistic endeavors taking place, and they demonstrated an ability to move from one discipline to another. For instance, an actor might also be a poet. A writer might become a filmmaker. A painter might also be a musician, a dancer, or a poet . . . the traditional flexibility remained viable.

Nevertheless, foreign influences often threatened not just the creative instinct but also the ability to draw from indigenous sources. Those writers and artists who forged new alloys from many sources and did not allow influences from colonial cultures to overwhelm them or seduce them into producing weak imitations of the foreign forms have become a strong creative force in Africa. In syncretizing these elements, the modern imagery of poets and artists in today's Africa extends some aspects of traditional form.

One important constant was the use of myth and symbol. In most African societies, as in many other societies, symbol was an integral cultural component. As examples: Masks embodied deities and spirits as well as humor and whimsical fate. The Fon people from the Republic of Benin, for example, use symbols to designate dynasties and record history on appliquéd banners. Colors too are used symbolically. The Nigerian Mmuo maiden-spirit mask is white, symbolizing spiritual beauty and the incarnate dead. The Nigerian Yoruba use red and white for Shango, the god of thunder and lightning. So, too, many African artists today have retained this use of color as symbol, and animals and other organic forms as metaphor.

Myths also have a visual countenance. As the very foundation of traditional art forms, mythic heroes and gods are frequently present in the work of visual artists, especially those who had a start via an experimental workshop, as did the Shona sculptors of Zimbabwe and the artists of Oshogbo, Nigeria. Such artists refer to old myths, and extrapolate from them. They also personify elements of the natural and spiritual worlds.

Although traditional African poetry and music served history-recording functions, they were also oriented to the moment and responsive to improvisation. In addition, the prophetic nature of much African poetry drew on ancient wisdom for topical purposes. Scholar Daniel Crowley comments that "the importance of skill in

word use is widespread in Africa, and explains the popularity of riddles, proverbs, improvization [sic], even so-called 'drum languages,' and all the double entendre, far-fetched imagery, and allusion that display verbal prowess and quick wit. . . ."[3] This talent for the subtleties of language meant that proverbs became metaphors and were often used parenthetically or only in part because listeners were so familiar with the whole.

As traditional poetry, music, and incantation incorporated personification and metaphor, they worked hand in glove with symbol. For example, the Nigerian Yoruba poem "Incantation to Cause the Rebirth of a Dead Child" personifies death and describes Shonponna, the god of smallpox and infirmity, as a snake:

Death catches the hunter with pain.
Eshu catches the herbalist in a sack.
Shonponna is the snake that dies.
And carries its children away.[4]

From Gabon, the Fang "Hymn to the Sun" describes night as a "black cloak" and the sun as having a "lightning eye" and "a fiery quiver":

The fearful night sinks
Trembling into the depth
before your lightning eye
and the rapid arrows
from your fiery quiver.

The poem continues, "you tear her cloak/the black cloak lined with fire/and studded with gleaming stars. . . ."[5] A Sotho praise song from South Africa describes a victorious chief as a "heifer striped with fire" whose shield "shines like glowing embers, he himself like the half moon."[6] These visual images play with the eye. The same could be said of imagery in poetry elsewhere, but in the many African traditional poetries, such imagery is particularly fundamental and pervasive.

The persistence of visual imagery is especially evident in Yoruba poetry. For example, in the praise song "The Timi of Ede," the chief is addressed: "huge fellow whose body fills an anthill,/You are heavily pregnant with war/All your body except your teeth is black." This is followed by another metaphorical device, the introduction of a parallel idea in the form of a couplet: "No one can prevent the ape/from sitting on the branch of a tree." The next verse relates the couplet to the previous text with the line, "No one can dispute the throne with you."[7]

Other links between the arts occur in a romantic genre. Modern popular literature usually involves a foreign-to-Africa language, French, Portuguese, or English, and is often the result of the marriage of two languages, the indigenous and a foreign one. Such syncretism frequently produces original forms and from these forms, fresh literary expressions develop and grow. Nigerian novelist Amos Tutuola has created some of the most sparkling language in contemporary literature with this kind of juxtaposition. Nigerian popular writing from Onitsha, Enugu, and Port Harcourt is well known for adventures in language. Such chapbook titles as *Public Opinion on Lovers, Mabel the Sweet Honey that Flowed Away, Romance in a Nutshell, Saturday Night Disappointment, Nancy in Blooming Youth,* and *Rosemary and the Taxi Driver* suggest the romantic flights of fancy and original, spontaneous use of English typical of Nigeria's high-life era in the early sixties. It was a time when the collision of cultures and the euphoria of independence inspired imaginative and highly romantic expressions by self-taught writers. Some of these expressions were manifested in popular novels, and others were illustrated on lorries and on signs painted by self-taught artists.

In the large and growing body of work by well-known writers and poets of sub-Saharan Africa, subtlety, complexity, and a merging of intellect and vision are more typical characteristics. The writings of Chinua Achebe, of Wole Soyinka (the 1986 recipient of the Nobel Prize in literature), and of many others are intrinsic to African studies programs and essential to an understanding of African cultures. In addition, African writers' accomplishments, as they touch upon or are tangential to those of the visual artists, offer a frame of reference for the art.

For example, both writers and poets in Africa use language in ways that are sometimes viewed as surrealistic, a description also used in connection with African art. But, unlike European surrealism, in African literature the references are to an organic universe. Modern African imagery displays a unity with the natural world that is antithetical to the Western surrealist inclination to separate imagery from social systems and the organic world. Contemporary African writing, like oral literary lore, is usually connected to society and its vicissitudes.

Often referred to as a surrealist, the late Malagasy poet Rabearivelo wrote poetry that relies on a conscious identification with nature and not an encounter with the subconscious. His images are visual without being pictorial, and his work exemplifies the metaphorical links between the arts. In an untitled poem that begins, "The hide of the black cow is stretched," he projects images such as: "Stretched is the hide on the sounding box of the wind/that is sculptured by the spirits of sleep."[8]

Another of Rabearivelo's poems illustrates the prevalence and powerful use of metaphor:

What invisible rat
comes from the walls of night
gnaws at the milky cake of the moon?

Tomorrow morning
when it has gone,
there will be bleeding marks of teeth.[9]

Likewise, in his poem "The Renegade," the late David Diop of Senegal chose metaphors to describe the African divorced from his roots. But his images are Western and so emphasize the alienation: "You give your master a blue-eyed faithful look/My poor brother in immaculate evening dress/Screaming and whispering and pleading in the parlours of condescension/We pity you. . . ."[10] Similarly, in "The Vultures" Diop uses such images as "When holy water slapped our cringing brows," and "the metallic hell of the roads."[11]

Gambian Lenrie Peters also writes of alienation. His images carry the sharp resonance and economy of proverb. From "He walks alone":

Exile go home
under your bed a bowl of tears
leave back streets
nightmare evenings kneeling in pews
brassy noises of homely fires[12]

Another poet who expresses alienation and anguish is Tchicaya U Tam'si of Congo. With images rooted in antiquity, the poem, "Presence," has both monumental and metaphysical references:

traitor christ
here is my flesh turned to bronze
and my blood clenched
by my innumerable selves copper and zinc
by the two stones of my brain
everlasting by my slow death
coelacanth[13]

Metaphysical and archetypal qualities characterize the poetry of the late Christopher Okigbo of Nigeria. Okigbo created word images that have the aural power of religious incantation. Operating as metaphors, they are also self-propelling, as though inspired by a special legacy from oral tradition. With intricate allusions and insights to be interpreted, the word images also function as visual-auditory entities without reference to meaning. Okigbo created a new fusion for this incantory power, a fusion of African and Western liturgies that assembles—from diverse rhythms and rituals—his own iconography. The effect he achieves is evident in "Siren":

Suddenly becoming talkative
   like weaverbird
Summoned at offside of
   dream remembered

Between sleep and waking,

I hang up my egg-shells
To you of palm grove,

Upon whose bamboo towers hang
Dripping with yesterupwine[14]

It has been said that the "conventional wisdom of Dante is sufficiently concrete to be capable of representation in the visual arts, as in Blake's drawings, and even in music, as in Tschaikowsky's [sic] *Francesca da Rimini.*"[15] The same could be said of the African literary arts. The strong relationship between artists and writers of Africa is such that Wole Soyinka's description of African poetry might also be used to describe the work of visual artists. In his anthology, *Poems of Black Africa,* Soyinka points out that the wide variety of poetic genres in Africa, ranges from "a muscular impact of cumulative images as in much of U Tam'si's poetry, reflective as in Lenrie Peters' . . .," to "visionary as in Rabearivelo's . . ." and includes many that are influenced by or are imitative of foreign poetry.[16] The same diversity exists in other arts, and artists and writers whose work grows from a synthesis of new elements and the "metaphysics" of the African world stretch the meanings of language and symbol and demonstrate the interrelatedness of the various arts.

II

Responding to the Challenge

3   Bridges

Predecessors in Nigeria

The wellspring of today's varied forms and styles among Nigeria's contemporary artists is in large part the diversity of its traditional cultures. A visit to the Nigerian Museum in Lagos highlights their complex and manifold heritage. The vast array of the great treasures it houses suggests the reasons why poet and former president of Senegal Léopold Sédar Senghor called Nigeria, "the Greece of Africa." The dynamics of form in the wood carvings and in the bronze, terra-cotta, and stone sculptures represent a gamut of styles and periods spanning "two millennia or more."[1]

The museum is the result of the efforts of the late Kenneth Murray, originally a schoolteacher who became the museum's first director of antiquities and formed this impressive collection. The breadth of the museum's collection makes it hard to believe that these cultures exist within the geographical boundaries of one country. Having the largest population of any African country, Nigeria presents endless variety with 3 major languages, 250 dialects, and almost as many peoples: Yoruba, Hausa, Fulani, Igbo, Ibibio, Bini, Urhobo, Efik, and Ijaw, to name a few.

With this rich heritage already well represented in the major art museums of the world, an important exhibition of a hundred major sculptures in terra-cotta, stone, ivory, and bronze from the ancient Nok, Igbo-Ukwu, Ife, Owo, Benin, Tsoede, and Esie cultures traveled abroad from Nigeria in 1980. Organized by the then director of Museums and Antiquities, Ekpo Eyo, its importance had to do with the fine quality of the pieces. The exhibition was also noteworthy because of the omission of wood carvings, erroneously considered synonymous with African art, specifically Nigerian art. Accompanying the exhibition was a comparative chronology demonstrating Nigeria's place in the aesthetic annals of the world.

This impressive legacy is background and source for the largest group of contemporary artists in Africa, and it is out of this traditional context that new art is being created. Collectively, these artists are proving to be the most prolific in Africa. Most come from among the Yoruba of southwestern Nigeria, the Bini of midwestern Nigeria, and the Igbo of eastern Nigeria, all peoples and areas with long artistic traditions. The north of Nigeria and its southern delta regions have also produced artists, thus reinforcing its image as a country of artistic diversity.

Contemporary artistic eminence became evident when the Nigerian renaissance, which began in the sixties with political independence, spread like a contagion among writers and artists who combined traditional forms with modern ones. The syncretic results were fascinating: some were romantic, or strongly influenced by Western imagery, or intensely personal, or strikingly original, or mixtures of several of these characteristics. Echoing this marriage of disparate elements, the Nigerian poet Gabriel Okara's "Piano and Drums" expresses the confrontation between old and new, East and West:

Then I hear a wailing piano
solo speaking of complex ways
in tear-furrowed concerto;
of far-away lands
and new horizons with
coaxing diminuendo, counterpoint,
crescendo. . . . And I lost in the morningside mist
of jungle drums, and the concerto.[2]

Although old values have been lost or modified, modern artists in Nigeria are not separated from their predecessors by a gap of several hundred years, as were the Shona sculptors in Zimbabwe (see chapter 12). The colors and forms of indigenous culture are still apparent in many aspects of Nigerian daily life—in dress, theater, dance, and masquerade. The ability of Nigerian artists to strike out on behalf of change might be attributed in part to the sense of security and rich traditional sources (for synthesis).

Nigeria's artistic heritage is enriched by sculptural art from numerous cultures. Of the many fine Yoruba carvers, the three most widely known are Areogun (ca. 1880–1954), Bamgboye (life dates unknown), and Areogun's son, George Bandele (1915–), all from among the Ekiti Yoruba, who have one of the most impressive carving traditions in West Africa. Pieces by these three carvers, which include large, imposing Epa masks as well as doors and house posts, are more carefully documented than other carvers' works, perhaps because they have been sought by museums and collectors.

Following in the wake of such traditions, however, is not easy, and many new artists turned to other media. Although a number of artists who were born in the twenties did become sculptors, the acknowledged predecessors of the modern Nigerian renaissance were Chief Aina Onabolu (1882–1963) and Akinola Lasekan (1916–). Both were competent portrait painters who were strongly influenced by Western expression. Ben Enwonwu (1921–), an Igbo sculptor and painter, is also considered, along with Onabolu and Lasekan, a progenitor of the modern movement. Lamidi Fakeye (1925–), who was trained by Bandele, works in the same traditional style, and now carves pieces mostly for collectors and commissions rather than for religious use. All these early artists were faced with the problems of continuing to work and survive economically in an atmosphere not particularly conducive to, or sympathetic toward, modern artistic expression. Often their dichotomous position—between tradition and modernity, and between Africa and the West—is evident in their work.

The artists born in the thirties, the majority of whom were painters, had some form of academic training based on French or British models. A number became educators as well. In addition, alternative workshop experiments produced important artists, and finally, like the self-trained popular writers, many artists developed on their own.

However, of all the first modern artists, the sculptor Ovia Idah of Benin (1903–1968) alone was an iconoclast working within and for indigenous cultural purposes. He grew up among the centuries-old traditions of Benin, but his sculpture was an expression of his zest for life, not just a vague repetition of past forms. Equally uninterested in replicating conventions of the past or capitulating to the tastes of tourists, he imbued his work with vigor and a sense of himself, bringing a spirited approach to even the more official works commissioned for the Palace of the Oba (king) of Benin.

Idah died in 1968, and a chief in Benin is quoted as saying, "Idah's name will be remembered a thousand years in Benin."[3] The sculpture he created for the Palace in Benin was a mixture of cement and earth, and the color of Benin, its rust/red roofs, brick red laterite soil, and regal coral vestments.

Having been taken when he was seven years old to the oba's court to work—an honor proclaimed by the bronze ankle bracelets he wore—Idah grew up in the midst of Benin's traditional art.[4] Interestingly, the reigning oba, Eweka, was himself a carver who passed along his craft to young Idah.

As a youth, Idah moved to the Lagos capital where he studied carpentry and later taught wood carving at King's College. His originality was already evident when, at the age of fifteen, he carved a large wooden mold of a hippopotamus and cast it in cement for a bas-relief on a public building. His penchant for synthesis surfaced when he carved a wooden bedstead in which the figure of a Benin oba was flanked by a pair of Victorian sconces.[5]

When he returned to Benin after twenty-seven years in Lagos, his skills as a craftsman led to his appointment as a court sculptor by Oba Akenzua, a childhood friend. As director of the Benin Crafts Workshop, Idah encouraged and promoted the work of many young carvers.

One of his most famous statues, that of Oba Ozolua, a late fifteenth-century warrior, stands at the main entrance in the palace courtyard. Idah claimed that he received the order to create this statue in a dream—that the ancient oba himself had demanded it, telling Idah precisely how it should look and ordaining a force that would keep anyone from taking a good picture of it![6]

As court sculptor, Idah produced numerous official works. His wall reliefs (some of Idia, the first queen mother of Benin) and other pieces in ivory, ebony, and bronze adorn the palace. The doors he carved for the Benin Divisional Council are a lively evocation of important events, unlike many such carvings that are often static or rote.

A favorite image was the elephant. Once when Idah became ill, he created a huge elephant for his grave marker, "but when he recovered, he took it apart to use the cement blocks for something else."[7]

Apart from his palace sculptures, Idah's own dwelling, though it no longer survives, might be considered his major work. Built directly into the old Benin wall, it contravened city ordinances until the oba discovered whose house it was and granted a variance. Here his talent as a *bricoleur* asserted itself. Using both things he made and those he found, Idah created a unique house and garden. The porch, a dramatic presentation with its steep entrance stairway, had a cast of sculpted characters that included two lively cement elephants, one assailing a man and the other—ears flapping—defying a seated figure.

The house was originally conceived in the shape of an elephant. The entrance hall took the form of an elephant's head. Inside, the rooms contained a marvelous conglomeration of found items carefully assembled alongside Idah's works and those of other African artists. Using crockery, art nouveau movie seats, and other curious relics that appealed to his unusual sensibility, Idah created a kind of African Bohemia. His house mirrored the personality of a man, who—although steeped in the traditions and history of Benin—possessed a strong individual bent.

In his last works, terra-cotta reliefs done in his seventies and commissioned by Ulli Beier, Idah abandoned past mediums and methods to achieve his greatest freedom of expression. In these panels he molded energetic figures that seem to be moving across the surface and emerging from it.

Demonstrating this versatility as a *bricoleur*—a description first applied to him by Philip Peek—Idah found various means and materials with which to create, transform, and communicate.[8] He worked in materials not used by other Benin carvers: cement, ebony, and terra-cotta. His artistic spirit, amazingly independent of local custom, could not be brought to heel by the authority of tradition.

The late Yemi Bisiri (1910–ca. 1970) also challenged tradition, though he too was as connected to Yoruba tradition as Idah was to Bini tradition. The scion of a family of brass casters (*eledan*) working with the lost wax process, Bisiri worked for the Ogboni cult producing sacred images (Edan Ogboni). Given the title *Akedanwaiye* which means "he who brings the Edan down to earth (from heaven)" by his father, Bisiri was the first such artist to create figures representing the powers of the Ogboni cult tradition. These figures were also valued and purchased as modern pieces by art collectors.[9]

Bisiri lived six miles from the western Nigerian city of Oshogbo in the small village of Ilobu where he was born. He had to travel sixty miles or more to find the beeswax used to make the original core image around which a mold is formed. The lost-wax technique he used was an arduous one that involved melting brass with a fire sustained by bellows. Producing between fifty and a hundred figures a year with the help of one apprentice, he kept his finished pieces hidden from everyone except Ogboni cult members and a few privileged customers.[10]

Bisiri's Edan Ogboni figures were produced for a cult to which the worship of earth is central, with sky and water representing powerful forces. Chthonian creatures such as snakes and crocodiles are venerated because of their closeness to both earth and water. Bisiri's sculptures are symbols of the earth (Ile), with its life-creating power, and of the conquerors of water, characterized by the amphibious nature of snakes. The sky, or "mighty calabash," is represented by an arched structure over the figures.

Some Edan are ritual objects and some are used for magical purposes only. Because traditional Edan images are so different from Yoruba wood carvings, they illustrate the stylistic variety within Yoruba culture.[11] Edan have definite formal components: either a female with children or a male with horse and retainers. Some

Yemi Bisiri, *Figure*, 1967, brass, 7" high. Private collection.

pieces commissioned by the relative of a missing person have a magical function and can be used to help locate a person. However when the person is located, the sculpture must be destroyed "for it would be fatal for him [or her] to encounter his [or her] double. For this reason these pieces can practically never be seen or acquired."[12]

Bisiri worked in a style which, though appropriate to the Ogboni cult, differed dramatically from the traditional conventions of his predecessors; his style was livelier and more energetic and exemplifies the way that change occurs within traditional art forms. Though living in a remote location, he had new experiences: the radio, the automobile, the contemporary political system, and voting.[13] Like Idah, Bisiri considered expressing his own energetic view more important than imitating past conventions.

Bisiri's original wax forms are hand-rolled, much as a potter rolls clay coils. The bodies are column-like and enriched by rings, spheres, and twisting coils. The rough-textured brass catches light on myriad tiny plateaus—unlike most Ogboni statues that are filed smooth, are sharply defined, and usually end in sharply pointed finials. Bisiri's pieces have supporting pedestals, and with their lavish accretion of form, color, and texture are at once armature and embellishment. Bare bones of structure supporting the baroque excrescences have a skeletal aesthetic. Both elements seem to move, to proliferate, and to reach into space. They are startlingly expressive.

The inspired vision of artists like Idah and Bisiri that forms a bridge between past and present does not always prevail. In urban situations where foreign architects have imposed an "international style" seen around the world in the cities of Asia and Latin America as well as in Africa, it is especially difficult for local artists to maintain a relationship to any past values. Current buildings often have no relationship to indigenous architecture, being closer to European concepts and aesthetics. As a result, there is a feeling of sameness in these cities. It is not the willingness to accept change, described by South African writer Es'kia Mphahlele as "African strength and weakness," that one has to regret, but rather the influences that overwhelm, that are not synthesized.[14]

Similarly, those first modern African artists who worked as individuals rather than in response to a religious purpose, were confronted with the preconceptions of their audiences—usually foreign. Furthermore their training often left little room for their own artistic predilections. Those not caught up in efforts to produce commissioned portraits or to express images conditioned by foreign training often accepted a tired European cubist legacy, the inspiration for which originated in Africa. Ironically, it now returns via Europe.

Faced with this situation, Ben Enwonwu, born (1921–) in Onitsha in eastern Nigeria, worked in several styles, encouraged by his teacher Kenneth Murray. At one point Enwonwu painted and sculpted in a pictorial fashion for those with European, American, or Western-influenced Nigerian tastes. At another point Enwonwu experimented with what he calls his "African style," which emphasized pattern and abstract forms. He employed a very competent portrait style for a life-sized bronze of Queen Elizabeth (located in front of Parliament in Lagos) and a bronze of Nnamdi Azikwe, the former president of Nigeria. One Enwonwu sculpture combines both styles (pictorial and abstract). A slender stemlike figure entitled *Anyanwu (The Awakening)*, it is installed on the outside wall of the Nigerian National Museum.[15] The body is a beautifully orchestrated series of highly stylized forms that unfold like a fern, but the head and hands are suddenly and inexplicably naturalistic.

Ben Enwonwu, *Anyanwu (The Awakening)*, 1961, bronze, 82" high. Collection, United Nations, New York City. The figure is also mounted on the front of the Nigerian National Museum, Lagos.

Enwonwu epitomizes the confusingly dichotomous position of the contemporary artist not only in Africa, but in many countries where rich traditional heritages are under siege by the mores, technology, and individualism of the West. Nonetheless, as an art advisor to the federal government, he has influenced younger artists. Perhaps his most important legacy is the insistence that the work of African artists be judged by a set of canons appropriate to their own cultures.

Tayo Aiyegbusi (ca. 1930–) like Enwonwu, was an artistic presence in the late fifties. Of western Yoruba origin, he was the first of his generation to recognize the strength of Nigerian culture, to abjure seduction by the West, and to support a selective synthesis of new and old, foreign and familiar. Though no longer a painter or printmaker, Aiyegbusi (a design graduate of the Slade School of Fine Art in London) is now a successful designer. His insistence on creative quality and technical excellence was an important influence on the modern scene during the first "rush to expression." A founding member of the Society of Nigerian Artists, Aiyegbusi was also a part of the team that produced the famous journal *Black Orpheus.*

Sculptor Lamidi Fakeye (ca. 1925–), unlike Yemi Bisiri, works in wood. Born in the town of Illa Orangun, he is the descendant of two generations of wood-carvers. Although he studied in France for a year and has traveled extensively, Fakeye works in a traditional style, but, unlike his forefathers, he is often commissioned by collectors and by individuals for pieces that have Yoruba religious functions.

Like most carvers born into the wood carving tradition, Fakeye began carving at an early age. A Muslim, in his twenties he attended the workshop in Oye-Ekiti that was established by a Catholic priest, Father Kevin Carroll, to provide new opportunities for carvers as their traditional clientele diminished.

There were a number of skilled carvers at Oye-Ekiti. In particular, Fakeye worked with master carver George Bandele, the son of Areogun, a renowned carver from Osi Ilorin. The carvers at the workshop executed pieces both for Christian churches in Ekiti and for traditional Yoruba cults, but Fakeye did not carve Christian subjects. He is candid about the difficulty of meeting the standards set by his master: "When I got there and saw the work of Bandele, I was a bit ashamed. Father Carroll asked me to become an apprentice under Bandele. I worked under Bandele for three years and suffered much. In the evening times I was working on my own work, and began to become a good carver."[16]

For traditional carvers, working for Christian churches perhaps requires a less drastic adjustment than assuming their new function as modern artists who create for museums, galleries, and collectors. Either situation is difficult. This leads one to ask whether great modern

Lamidi Fakeye, *Epa Mask,* 1962–63, wood, 44½" high. Collection, National Museum of African Art, Washington, D.C.

works will emerge in a relatively short period of time, or whether products of transition such as Fakeye's works will exhibit the same spirit as carvings created to serve in a religious context.

Father Carroll maintained the arguable position that Yoruba carving was not "so essentially religious" and therefore might be easily transposed to Christian purposes.[17] And transposed it was! The style of the new carvings remained the same, but while competently done, they were placid and unexciting, especially in contrast to the vitality of a Gelede mask, an Ibeji figure, or a Shango staff.

However, Fakeye held audiences transfixed when he gave carving demonstrations in U.S. universities in the seventies, for he works with great professional skill, attention to balance, detail, and finish. Some of Fakeye's carvings were commissions for public places including the Palace of the Oni of Ife, the Roman Catholic Chapel at the University of Ibadan, the House of Chiefs at Ibadan, Northwestern and Western Michigan universities, and the John F. Kennedy Center for the Performing Arts in Washington, D.C.

The questions raised by the work of artists like Enwonwu and Fakeye and by others who form a bridge between tradition and modern individual expression inspired friendly ongoing controversies among artists in Nigeria. These debates made the contemporary art scene in the Lagos capitol from the early sixties until today an excitingly alive and changing phenomenon.

A central figure in the arts of Nigeria and in these discussions is novelist Chinua Achebe. Achebe takes a firm position on the role of the African writer. In his collection of essays, *Morning Yet on Creation Day* (Garden City, New York: Anchor Press/Doubleday, 1976), Achebe states his opposition to an "art for art's sake" attitude in Africa. In his chapter entitled "The Novelist as Teacher" he writes, "The writer cannot be excused from the task of re-education and regeneration that must be done. In fact he should march right in front." To emphasize his point, Achebe quotes the Ghanaian philosopher William Abraham: "Just as African scientists undertake to solve some of the scientific problems of Africa, African historians go into the history of Africa; why should African literary creators be exempted from the services that they themselves recognize as genuine?"

Achebe does not exempt himself from such service:

I would be quite satisfied if my novels (especially the ones set in the past) did no more than teach my readers that their past—with all its imperfections—was not one long night of savagery from which the first Europeans acting on God's behalf delivered them. Perhaps what I write is applied art as distinct from pure. But who cares? Art is important, but so is education of the kind I have in mind.

To Achebe art and education need not be "mutually antagonistic."[18]

Similar concerns preoccupied visual artists. Yusuf Grillo, and Solomon Wangboje, both artist-educators, have also frequently expressed their ideas about the role of the artist in Africa. These two symbolize a special era in Nigeria—a time when new directions, some antithetical to traditional concepts—were being explored by artists educated in art schools in Nigeria or abroad.

Grillo (1934–) was for many years the director of the School of Art, Design and Technology of the Yaba College of Technology, one of the first institutions for art training in Nigeria. In addition, he was for sixteen years president of the Society of Nigerian Artists.

Grillo bridges the gulf between artists like Aina Onabolu, Akinola Lasekan, and Ben Enwonwu, whose sculptures were strongly influenced by Western academic styles, and by younger Nigerian artists. Although Enwonwu and Grillo both have academic backgrounds, Grillo does not work in two styles, one that is more African in spirit and another that is Western and academic. Instead, he consistently maintains his own recognizable, expressionist style which is characterized by an angular geometry reminiscent of African sculpture.

However, Grillo's identification with Yoruba culture is not like that of an artist from a place like Oshogbo, a Yoruba town known for its artists. He explains, "If I were to say that as a child I listened to folk stories, saw masquerades, was put to sleep by drumming, I would be lying. I was born and brought up in the city of Lagos away from such things."[19]

His theories about art and artists are very much a part of the contemporary scene in Lagos. His accomplishments and his forthright articulation of his views contribute to his prominence. They continue to motivate students and other artists. Speaking with me in the United States on April 22, 1971, Grillo questioned the interest in African art in the United States.[20]

Grillo: I am somewhat of the opinion that there is an artificial emphasis on African art [in the United States]. Why not Greek art? Why not French art?

Kennedy: But African art has a vitality and energy needed in a world confronted with total mechanization.

Grillo: It works both ways—we have something to gain from Western art. I feel that cultures must go full cycle. We are going through a cycle we must go through.

Concerning aesthetic criteria in traditional African art, Grillo believes that styles were accepted because they developed in slow progression:

Grillo: It is just because people were used to a mask, for example, because the first man who carved—if you can say that—to take a hypothetical case—the first carver carves a thing a certain way because that's the way he knows how to do it and it becomes acceptable. Therefore as the other carvers follow, style changes, but society is conditioned to accept it because it is a slow progression.

Kennedy: But what about standards—perhaps not thought of in terms of beautiful or not beautiful, but acceptable on some terms?

Grillo: No, if you ask a man, he often cannot describe the mask, the eyes, the shape of the head. He may not even look at it—it is only the power he will describe.

Kennedy: But isn't the power an all-inclusive term that may include these other elements—spiritual, symbolic, and aesthetic?

Grillo: No, the average person has no aesthetic evaluation of these objects. He may hide them, he may even bury them. They may only be in use occasionally, maybe he sees them once a year. He does not put them on the wall and admire them.

Many years earlier at "Art Looks at Cities: The Artist as a Social Critic," a conference held in Lagos during the mid-sixties and sponsored by the Society of Nigerian Artists and the American Society of African Culture,

Yusuf Grillo spoke of the artist's role, but not as educator in the manner described by Chinua Achebe. He took issue with those who saw the artist's role as a political one:

> The artist as a part of society normally reacts one way or the other to all goings-on. This is natural. Everyone does. But I don't think he needs to (as far as his art goes) make this his concern. Art is now a very individual, personal matter. The artist is no more the anonymous being he used to be. He decides completely on his own what he wants to say and how he wants to say it. Inspiration for art is got from any subject and today in even no subject. The artist should not necessarily be concerned (as an artist) about the problem of the cities: art is not a very effective propaganda vehicle and should not be primarily.[21]

Grillo considers that "art which makes propaganda its motivation and remains conscious of this is bound to be uninspiring aesthetically."[22]

He also asserted, "For the modern Nigerian artist to express himself sincerely in a style which will read 'Nigerian,' the right type of atmosphere must exist because the artist creates out of his experiences." He commended the effort to revive traditional festivals, but warned against "slavish apeing [sic] of the past" because the resulting art will not be as good as "the authentic things [or] . . . creative adaptations."[23]

Often himself the center of controversies about the role of the African artist at home, Grillo has made contributions beyond Nigeria's borders, executing commissions abroad and frequently taking part in international conferences. Interestingly, there are certain international implications in his work.

Because we are familiar with cubist forms, we see his work as "international" in character. His imagery is architechtonic in structure; the forms he creates can be described as influenced by the West, but are shapes derived from African art as well. "I surround myself with—traditional pieces of art," he said in 1981. "I collect them almost compulsively and I study them, I analyze them. They influence my work. . . . The clear-cut definition of planes . . . this has worked its way into my work."[24]

While his forms may seem familiar, his use of color is not. His palette often consists of blues, greens, and mauves with blue predominating. Using blue as a skin color, Grillo evokes a mood that is solemn but reflective of Yoruba culture, identified as it is frequently with the hand-dyed indigo fabric created and worn by Yoruba women. Grillo is well known for his paintings of women; their blue faces seem to connote meditative power. In works such as *Mendicants* or *Blind Minstrel,* angles and triangular forms are taut and dynamic and intensify the anguish and pathos.

Yusuf Grillo, *Drummers' Fag,* 1971, oil on hardboard, 48″ × 30″. Collection, Mr. and Mrs. Caws, London.

In Grillo's mosaic murals, forms are more subdued and appropriate to an architectural surface. One of the most successful of these murals, at the Lagos City Council Building, conveys a strong sense of motion, a quality often present in his work. As a whole, his art represents a notable modification of the influence of nineteenth-century Western pictorialism pursued by earlier artists Onabolu of Nigeria and Antubam of Ghana.

Both Yusuf Grillo and Solomon Wangboje are among the well-known, early (1959–60) graduates of the Nigerian College of Arts, Science, and Technology (now a part of Ahmadu Bello University at Zaria in northern Nigeria) who formed a kind of network. Having come together at Zaria from the East, Midwest, North, and Southwest, the group reflects the diverse cultures of Nigeria. The group of artists who graduated in 1960 were still working together in the eighties on numerous projects, including the founding of the National Gallery of Modern Art now located in the National Theatre, Lagos.

Wangboje (1930–), a key member of the Zaria group, continued his art education at Cranbrook Academy of Art in Michigan where he received a master of fine arts degree in 1963. In 1968 he earned a doctorate in art education at New York University. Like Grillo and some of his other Zaria colleagues, he has had a dual career as educator and artist. As director of the Ori Olokun Cultural Centre at Obafemi Awolowo University (formerly University of Ife), he headed the art education program there.

While at the University of Ife, Wangboje initiated a grass roots project inspired by the successes of experimental workshops in the Nigerian town of Oshogbo in the mid-sixties. Providing space and materials to would-be artists, and dispensing with an academic approach had interesting results. Although the original workshops in Oshogbo were unhampered by an academic teaching method, Wangboje began by using a live model for a drawing workshop. He was astounded to find that the participants, though observing the model sitting, would draw the model standing, and though observing from one angle, would draw from another. Drawing from a subject was not, for these would-be artists, particularly appropriate. Their visions, it turned out, were already in their heads.[25]

About the Ori Olokun workshops where there was no formal instruction, only a demonstration of techniques, Michael Crowder, then director of the Institute of African Studies at Obafemi Awolowo University, observed, "If there is an underlying philosophy it is to encourage each artist to seek his own personality. . . . The artists themselves come from all walks of life. . . . They share one thing in common: an intense dedication to the life of the artist, preferring its excitement to the security of a regularly paid job."[26]

Returning to his alma mater in Zaria in 1971, Wangboje became a full professor and head of the Department of Fine Arts in 1973. While there he pursued a program which he had earlier described: "Our country—like others, I expect—is rapidly losing the knowledge and skills of its several hundred master craftsmen. I would utilize their talents by setting up a program under which they could be appointed as visiting or resident artists to teach traditional arts to prospective teachers."[27] Because traditional arts were created for certain functions, this approach had its drawbacks. When original purposes are not served, the arts themselves are easily corrupted, potentially subject to tourists' tastes. The teaching of these skills, however, was obviously a worthwhile endeavor.

Wangboje describes himself as "essentially a printmaker with emphasis on technique and what the medium can do."[28] *Male Ego I*, a silkscreen-lithograph, is an original interpretation which uses forms freely to convey mnemonic meanings rather than to represent

Solomon Wangboje, *Male Ego I*, 1966, silkscreen and lithograph, dimensions unknown.

physical reality. The design pattern it contains is delicate, restrained, and subservient to the major forms. In some of his oils, such as *On the Dock,* colors and forms have a more sculptural orientation.

In recent years Solomon Wangboje's career activities as an educator and as president of the Society of Nigerian Artists have taken precedence over his own work. His opinions that have grown from these experiences parallel those of Achebe. They both feel the arts should serve a useful purpose. In both their views, art and education are irrevocably connected elements working in tandem to help rectify the distortions of colonial history. Wangboje states, "All art is propaganda. A work of art may be illustrative, anecdotal or just a recorder of events, yet it is still a means of propaganda and self-glorification at least for the artist who tried to stamp his personality into his work."[29]

Having just completed his tenure as deputy vice-chancellor of the University of Benin in December 1986, Wangboje sees his mission as an educator "because I feel that art education is the only field in which I can help Africans—and especially our children—to discover their rich cultural heritage through the most universal form of communication. . . . [A child] must be offered an aesthetic as well as a practical education. . . ."

Moreover, Wangboje makes a strong case for art as an integral part of African social and philosophical life: "In Africa, art is a basic part of our philosophy and way of life of our forefathers. . . . I believe art education is a social need, a part of the development of each country, stimulating both cultural pride and artistic expression."[30]

Wangboje's views are at the heart of the problem faced by African artists today and addressed by Grillo and Achebe. With a history of art that is integral to society, the dilemma of artists in most African countries is one of African values versus Western values, traditional influences versus modern expression, and community needs versus individual careers.

Achebe feels it is the duty of the artist to use his art for the education of his people. Grillo sees today's artist as an individual who is not necessarily committed to art for propaganda or political purpose. Wangboje views art as central to education. They each express ideas and philosophies that preoccupy their fellow artists.

In spite of the fact that the very first two artists were painters in an academic European style, other pioneers like Idah, Bisiri, and Fakeye came directly from their own specific sculptural traditions. While Idah and Bisiri demonstrated an independence of direction even though working for traditional clientele, Fakeye retained a traditional style and yet was confronted with the waning of that clientele. Enwonwu illustrates the dichotomy of the situation with his two styles.

Together these artists demonstrate that the diversity—the hallmark of Nigeria's traditional forms, and the wellspring of the new expression—continues. New materials, new techniques, and new syntheses of influences and values are the ingredients that describe the work of the many artists who followed them.

4 Creating a Tradition

Vanguard Sculptors, Printmakers, and Painters of Nigeria

A group of artists rightfully considered Nigeria's "vanguard" artists were born in the late twenties, and grew up in the thirties and forties. Most had some academic training and came into their own in the sixties. Some, like Grillo and Wangboje, formed a bridge between the older and younger artists, and belong themselves to both groups. The discussion of these artists approximates the chronology of their development and groups them loosely by stylistic affinities and media. They have as a collective background the great traditions of wood sculpture, carved ivory, and cast bronzes from Benin and Igbo-Ukwu, as well as the arts of adornment, scarification, body painting, wall design, and textile.

The artists from the country's midwestern region reflect the past artistic prominence of Benin and its environs. For instance, Festus Idehen (1928–) was born in Benin and like Idah, was influenced by Benin traditions. Idehen came under the strong artistic influence of his grandfather, Ebomwoyi, the carver for the oba of Benin and head of the artists in the city. Ebomwoyi selected his grandson, then nine, to follow in his footsteps. Idehen's mother, a priestess of Olokun (the god of the sea) also gave him strong direction, teaching him to work with clay as she created the large mud figures dedicated to this diety's cult. Later, in his twenties, Idehen entered the Yaba College of Technology, studying under British sculptor Paul Mount, with whom he later collaborated on a large sculptural wall for the Chase Manhattan Bank in Lagos (now the Standard Bank of West Africa).

Despite all that influenced him, there is nothing eclectic about Idehen's style. By eschewing the decorative influences of the later Benin bronzes, and handling detail with great restraint, he achieves unadorned strength. His style is his own, yet his boldly formed figures have a sense of stability and calm authority reminiscent of the monumental Olokun mud figures he helped his mother create.

Idehen's forms found an admirer in British sculptor Henry Moore. According to Idehen, he met and struck up a friendship with Moore while on a trip to Europe. It is easy to understand why Moore responded to the monumentality of Idehen's sculpture, in which triangles and right angles reinforce a dynamic structural geometry. This structuring is evident in Idehen's early work and became an architectural language that served him for architectural commissions. One monumental commissioned work—a wall of large interlocking figures constructed of pink-tinted cement and heavy gravel grout—shields the entrance to a modern building from noisy traffic on Awolowo Road in Ikoyi, Lagos. His commissions also include works for the presidential palace in Monrovia, Liberia, and for the German Embassy and the City Hall in Lagos, Nigeria.

While Idehen usually relies on the rough texture of cement, sculptor Ben Osawe (1931–), born in Agbor between Benin and the Niger River, works in wood, creating smooth, polished surfaces. Osawe's father had learned carving at the Palace of the Oba of Benin, but discouraged Osawe's interest in carving, preferring that

Festus Idehen, *Sculpture,* date unknown, cement, colored and mixed with a gravel grout. On Awolowo Road, Ikoyi; in front of house by architect Allan Vaughn-Richards.

his son take up some "professional" career. Needing money as a child, Osawe tried to make rubber stamps for sale. He found it difficult, and so gave the work to a school friend. Osawe explains, "This boy did not know that I could not make stamps. He must have thought that I had so much work on hand that I had to give some out to help other boys who were less fortunate."[1] Watching the boy, Osawe learned the process. Later, he taught himself how to letter and became a sign painter, and eventually decorated walls in Nigerian cafes. Encouraged by a sympathetic school principal, Osawe is essentially self-taught. He states, "Nobody taught me wood-carving. The technique I use is wholly mine."[2]

For ten years he studied and worked in England, exhibiting there and in Scotland during the sixties. In a review of the Commonwealth Festival held in Glasgow in 1966, a critic described Osawe as a "stylist of some consequence and conscious deliberation" and said of his works, "They are the most impressive exhibits in the whole exhibition, his sense of scale and mass and profound consciousness of the qualities of the material being highly developed. . . ."[3]

In addition, his delicate sense of proportion is enhanced by superb craftsmanship. Working with closely grained wood such as ebony or iroko, he eliminates detail, concentrating on major forms that he polishes to a high sheen. In this way Osawe transmutes the essence of an African carving. Though reminiscent of masks, his pieces seem designed for contemplation rather than for the lively activity of masquerade. And further, Osawe "explains that every work must have in it some philosophy and poetry, 'and this is what matters.' "[4]

As a student at the Camberwell School of Art and Crafts in London, Osawe was well acquainted with the art of such sculptors as Barbara Hepworth, Henry Moore, and Constantin Brancusi—sculptors whose

works have African references. Osawe does not believe that his British experience made him any less an African artist. Accepting what he felt appropriate, and rejecting other influences, his philosophy parallels that of Nigerian poet Christopher Okigbo who, like Osawe, turned more and more toward his African roots, and once said:

> [A]ll we hear nowadays of men-of-two-worlds is a lot of nonsense. I belong, integrally, to my own society, just as, I believe, I belong also integrally to other societies. . . . the modern African is no longer a product of an entirely indigenous culture. The modern sensibility, which the modern African poet is trying to express, is by its very nature complex; it has complex values, some of which are indigenous, some exotic, some traditional, some modern.[5]

Both Okigbo and Osawe have made allowances for a syncretic process that permits artists to select elements from both inside and outside their own culture.

Ben Osawe thinks that artists who have to explain what their works are about may not have a good idea about what they are doing. An artist should be "able to criticize himself objectively without compromise. This is

Ben Osawe, *Union,* date unknown, wood. Location unknown.

why you will find the artist is more realistic about life." Osawe believes this realism extends to racial attitudes: "The race issue concerns the artist in a different way. He sees everything and every race as being beautiful. People who are not as realistic as the artist think that he is a Bohemian or an outcast because he refuses to conform."[6]

Like Osawe and Idehen, the late muralist, painter, and sculptor Erhabor Ogieva Emokpae (1934–1984) was also a native of Benin. He studied in London and at the Yaba College of Technology with Paul Mount. Emokpae was familiar with the African sculpture that startled the French avant-garde in the first decade of this century, and in his own work he stripped away the unessential to simplify form with a modern, almost reductionist result.

Emokpae executed several major murals in Lagos—at Western House, at the Standard Bank of West Africa, at the Murtala Mohammed Airport, and at the Institute of International Affairs. The mural at the latter is a long, high relief frieze entitled *International Cooperation.* It is composed of roughly textured concrete figures set against a sun-reflecting background of colorful mosaic tiles.

The figures symbolize people of all races moving toward a central circle that represents both a "Common purpose" and "the world and its regular and constant changes." The more static images on either end suggest old Africa, and the movement of figures "away from them [static images] reflect[s] the dynamic mood in Africa today; a movement from the old toward the new."[7]

Emokpae's mural for the Standard Bank of West Africa literally uses money as its medium. A freestanding vertical collage recording the history of Nigerian currency, it presents all the historical mediums of exchange from manillas (brass bracelets) and cowrie shells to modern currency.

Erhabor Emokpae, *International Cooperation,* ca. 1966, mosaic and cement, 244″ × 744″. Institute of International Affairs, Victoria Island, Lagos.

Many of the images depicted in Emokpae's murals have an icon-like presence, and they often merge with a background pattern made of traditional African symbols and masks. Sometimes he used political symbols such as the hammer and sickle, the swastika, and the star and crescent.

From 1959 until 1984, he worked as a graphic designer. In the late seventies and early eighties, Emokpae's paintings showed an abrupt change of style: a shift toward photo-realism. Like the stills from historical films, each painting documents a Nigerian hero set against, for example, a spectacle of the traditional northern Nigerian durbar (horse race) and its charging horsemen.

Upon his death, as an unprecedented gesture of honor, his body lay in state at the National Theatre, also the site of the National Gallery of Modern Art, where his work hangs. Emokpae's art as a whole is an important part of the record of the first fifty years of modern Nigerian art.

Agboola Folarin (1938–), like Emokpae, is a sculptor-muralist who has created large wall sculptures. He studied at the Yaba College of Technology in Lagos; the Regent Street Polytechnic, Hammersmith College of Art in London; the Central School of Art and Design in London; and at Howard University in Washington, D.C. He has graduate degrees in fine arts and architecture.

His works demonstrate a relationship between the two arts. The murals are also an integral part of the structure on which they are located. Folarin uses forms cast in fiberglass or shapes cut from aluminum, steel, or copper and then welded together. The resulting assemblages in four buildings at the Obafemi Awolowo University, at the National Theatre in Lagos, and at the Murtala Mohammed Airport in Ikeja, for which he won a prize in 1978, add glistening metal planes and classical African forms to the modern buildings. The old forms depict modern situations such as a board of directors' meeting, and their angles and curves intensify the rock-hard brilliance of the smooth, polished surfaces.

Folarin says his art career grows from experiences he had in primary school. "One discovers about oneself after awhile. I first thought of being a scientist or a doctor, but 'one's talent is one's destiny.' So I followed my talent and discovered my destiny." He thinks of an artist as "a pathfinder, a prime mover of the society and of its time . . . and a communicator." "Yes, painting needs to have a message. . . . Even the abstract paintings of the past have messages, though the messages are hidden. . . . A type of homogeneous language is what we all look for. . . ." Folarin, like other African artists of his generation, speaks of synthesis: "No culture can exist without taking ideas from the outside, but selectivity is my watchword."[8]

Reinforcing his opinion that art disciplines should be integrated, Folarin is also active as a creator of costumes

Agboola Folarin, *Faces at Conference*, 1977, welded steel, 96″ × 204″. Obafemi Awolowo University Conference Center, Ile-Ife, Nigeria.

and theater sets, especially at Ife where he is a principal art fellow at Obafemi Awolowo University in the Department of Fine Arts. He has designed costumes and sets for film, for Olympic Games performances, for two musical compositions by Nigerian composer Akin Euba, and for productions of plays by authors Wole Soyinka, Wale Ogunyemi, and Ola Rotimi.

Idah, Bisiri, Idehen, Osawe, Emokpae, and Folarin have created original and interesting three-dimensional works in a variety of materials, but there are others who have been carving wood for many years. They include Okpu Eze (1934–), from Umuobialla-Isuikwuator in eastern Nigeria, and Emmanuel Taiwo Jegede (1943–), from Arigidi Ekiti, in the western part of the country. Jegede is also a ceramicist. A newcomer who shows particular promise, Olumuyiwa Amoda (1959–), from Okere-Warri in the Niger delta area, works with metal to create dynamic sculptures.

Endowed with the same legacies as sculptors Idehen, Osawe, Emokpae, and Folarin, Nigeria's printmakers and painters treat compositional areas not as background and foreground but as strongly defined units like the planes of traditional carvings. They also use patterns that recall textiles, body decoration, and wall painting.

Printmaker and painter Uzo Egonu shares this sense of pattern and form with Nigeria's other major printmaker, Bruce Onobrakpeya. However, each artist's style is distinct and recognizable. For example, there is a startling difference in scale between the two. Egonu's forms spread across the surface as though seen through a close-up lens. In *Restaurant at Bad Orb*, for example, he makes use of portions of buildings and figures. Onobrakpeya, in contrast, has a tendency to see even

"large" subjects in great detail and as clusters of small shapes. See, for example, *Forms in a Landscape* (cover).

Egonu's thick black lines, repeat designs, flat color planes, and interstices of starchy white paper work like puzzle forms that construct what seems a tantalizing segment of a larger universe. While Onobrakpeya creates a miniature cosmos, Egonu offers an intimate fragment of the whole.

Egonu's art is rooted in traditions that date from at least as early as the ninth century A.D. At that time the remarkable Igbo-Ukwu culture—with its graceful and delicately ornamented vessels and its objects of leaded bronze—flourished east of the Niger, the same area where he was born. Like many other eastern Nigerian artists, Egonu manifests these influences in allover patterns, shapes, and sinuous lines also associated with "uli," the body and wall-painting culture of Igbo women. Before 1973 he used Igbo folktales as subject matter; after 1974 he focused on traditional African religious themes.

His latest prints are stunningly bold, and they often illustrate contemporary situations. In *A Cup of Coffee in Solitude*, he emphasizes the beauty of the paper by using it as a compositional element. Onobrakpeya, however, usually fills space with color and forms.

Moving back and forth between silk screening and painting, Egonu reinterprets traditions with bold, curved forms and repeat patterns. This is especially true of paintings such as *Restaurant at Bad Orb*, in which planes change as colors change, creating a sense of sculpture. The patterns run parallel like syncopated themes invoking the polyrhythmic beat of traditional music. When the patterns collide, they recall the disjunctive patterns found in West African strip weaving and the poetic enjambment typical of the poetry of Christopher Okigbo. In addition, Egonu adds a dimension by depicting his images from above; a head, an arm, or a foot cut off by the frame again convey the feeling of looking through a camera lens at just a portion of a scene.

Egonu's perspective was altered recently when he suffered deterioration of his eyesight. He worked without interruption through the period of impairment (a condition now improved by surgery); seeing in new ways, he explains, his deficient sight enhanced his perceptions. For instance, the stark branches of trees in winter were a revelation to him, suggesting human forms and how to delineate them, not just by enlarging dimensions but by expanding interpretive visions. In retrospect he says, "While painting now, I feel like a mountaineer, who climbs a mountain and rests at different points, leaving footprints."[9]

Egonu (1931–) was born in Onitsha and was encouraged to develop his talent by his father, who arranged for studies with an art teacher. Eventually he went to

Uzo Egonu, *A Cup of Coffee in Solitude*, 1981, screenprint, 19⅞″ × 27⅞″.

Uzo Egonu, *Stateless People*, 1982, oil on canvas, 56″ × 79″.

Uzo Egonu, *Mending*, 1980, screenprint, 25⅝″ × 33½″.

London to study at the Camberwell School of Art and Crafts. Like other African artists who have lived in London, he discovered an anomaly: the availability of African art in British museums for study.

Still living in London, Egonu has had fourteen one-person shows, and has participated in more than ninety major international exhibitions. His awards include a first prize from the British Broadcasting Corporation (1970), a bronze medal for a Brussels exhibit, The Arts in Europe (1971), and a prize from *African Arts* magazine (1972).

Bruce Onobrakpeya has also exhibited widely. A 1960 graduate of the Nigerian College of Arts, Science, and Technology at Zaria, his first major show took place in 1964 when the Nigerian Museum, primarily devoted to the traditional arts of Nigeria, opened its doors to a contemporary artist for the first time.

Two striking works in this exhibition, *Man with Two Wives* and *Leopard in a Cornfield,* suggested the brilliance that was to follow in later years. The seated figures in the first painting, regal with colors and garment folds, are reminiscent of the dignity and authority of images in old Benin plaques. They recall an ancient hierarchy as well as social and family structures. A strong feeling for Benin art and its configurations is an important element in much of Onobrakpeya's work.

The second painting, *Leopard in a Cornfield,* described by Onobrakpeya as mystical, is very different. The juxtaposition of incongruous elements—a fierce leopard, surrounded by birds and cornstalks—communicates an ineffable sense of nature's unity. Onobrakpeya recalls that the painting was inspired by a work by Rufino

Tamayo.[10] Onobrakpeya has written a poem about this leopard:

I don't know how old I was then
But for a child there is no difference
Between a living leopard and
Leopard on a wall, guiding shrine entrance.
I feared the beast may attack.
And I cried.
Tugging at my mother's feet for protection.

Many years have now passed
And still that memory strongly abides.
This same leopard
Like an imprisoned genie
Exploded full-bloom out of my mind.

Now I know him,
He's a beast, but I tame him,
And let him roam freely in the grassy wild
With tantalizing birds flying above.
I call him "Leopard in a Cornfield."[11]

Many of Onobrakpeya's subjects are based on traditional themes such as a priest with divination implements, an elephant masquerade, or Urhobo festivals, and his prodigious body of work is firmly grounded in a sure sense of design and craft.

Such attributes have contributed to his teaching, which he began in 1956. Upon receiving a teaching certificate after a year's postgraduate study, he resumed teaching at St. Gregory's College in Lagos, a post he held for seventeen years. During this period he illustrated a number of books and executed several murals. As a whole his work demonstrates the same interesting sculptural component as that of many other African artists who may not be working as sculptors, but whose works are never far removed from the sense of sculpture.

For example, Onobrakpeya is best known for his "deep etchings," which are sculptural entities in themselves, produced as they are from plates built up with other materials and then carved into. He has also pursued this "depth dimension" by arranging old blocks (from which prints had been made) in collage-like formats to create bas-relief assemblages. He learned carving from his sculptor father at an early age in Agbarha-Otor, the town in midwestern Nigeria where he was born in 1932.

Onobrakpeya's art also demonstrates the way stories and symbols still inform the arts of Africa. He says, "Nigerian legends, myths and religious philosophies are powerfully imaginative and inspiring."[12] Moving easily from culture to culture within Nigeria, he integrates a variety of design patterns and symbols. For example, in the print, *Have You Heard?,* he incorporates traces of

Bruce Onobrakpeya, *Man with Two Wives,* 1960s, deep etching, 19¾" × 26¾".

Bruce Onobrakpeya, *Have You Heard?*, 1970, deep etching, 27⅛″ × 19¾″.

Bruce Onobrakpeya, *Ekpen Gha Mue Wue Vbudezi*, 1973, deep etching, 26¾″ × 19¾″.

imagery from Yoruba adire (starch-resist) fabric with symbols from Hausa embroidery.

As a student in northern Nigeria, he was impressed and influenced by Hausa patterns: "In Kano the walls of the Emir's palace were decorated with pebbles stuck into the mud, producing [the] impression of rich earth colors with endless rhythm."[13] He employs pattern very much as do traditional artists in textiles, pottery, or basketry—not just to delineate form but as an integral compositional element. Like Egonu, he also demonstrates the facility for "break-patterning," Robert Farris Thompson's definition of the juxtaposition of forms in traditional African textiles, by sculpting the surface of his etchings with block motifs.[14] Indeed syncopated pattern permeates his work.

A book illustrator himself, Onobrakpeya has some definite opinions on the subject of illustration: "The task for the illustrator . . . is to create illustrations which are very alive, suitable for any age . . . that invite children to read and develop their critical sense and love for beauty."[15] In 1979 he created a set of illustrations for a German prayer book, including seven vertical pictures inspired by the format of the book itself. The new

compositions had an unusual shape "in which all the forms were held together like a piece of sculpture."[16] The first of these long, narrow prints, *Awana*, was inspired by an object of the same name, a kind of rattle for invoking the gods. The image demonstrates Onobrakpeya's talent for free exploratory form and line as well as for decorative but organic pattern. *Awana* includes references to traditional Yoruba and Bini ritual objects, but the spirit of *Awana* is original and lyrical. In the same group of prints, *Afieki I* and *Afieki II* convey the "mystical atmosphere" of the alleys near the market where magical and medicinal items are sold.[17]

Onobrakpeya's illustrations stimulated his interest in printmaking methods. He describes his approach: "I do not produce prints just for the joy of getting many copies of an idea. Sometimes I never go beyond three successful pulls. Concepts are sometimes enriched by accidental results. Printmaking should not be dull routine. I like to improvise, to leave room for discoveries. This is why I run experimental series."[18] This proclivity for improvisation finds a counterpart in the work of African-American quilters. Sherry Byrd describes her approach to quilts and to patterns by saying, "You know, I don't like to do the same things over and over, and so I just kind of build my own quilts as I sit at the machine."[19]

One of the major motivations for Onobrakpeya's printmaking occurred in August of 1963 when Ru Van Rossem, a Dutch printmaker, went to the city of Ibadan to give a graphics workshop organized by Ulli Beier. Onobrakpeya was invited to attend, and he made a beautiful print of an old tree trunk, embossing the forms by applying extra pieces of metal to the plate. This was the beginning of his many embossed prints, or deep etchings, for which he invented several different techniques. For example, in 1968 he created prints by pressing paper into a carved block and then rolling the ink on the exposed surface of the paper—a technique often used to transfer stone inscriptions or carvings to paper.

When Van Rossem went to Ife for another workshop organized by Beier in 1973, Onobrakpeya served as assistant director. Here many techniques were explored: monoprints, collographs, deep etchings, linoleum cuts, silk screens, and various methods of intaglio etching. Some fifty individual prints were created by seven participants. Onobrakpeya completed a series of twenty etchings that year, described in a booklet he issued as dealing "with life as it is shown through mythology, beauty of nature, human ideals and people."[20] Onobrakpeya periodically assembles and issues these small, handmade booklets with detailed descriptions of the series of prints he is publishing. For each print he explains his imagery, believing that there should be meanings and morals to be gained. His book, *Symbols of Ancestral Groves* (1985), is a survey of his accomplishments from 1978 to 1985 and is probably the most comprehensive account of the work of any African artist.[21]

Onobrakpeya speaks of "making meaning out of landscape" as an important purpose for him. Of the print called *Landscape with Trees,* he says, "This print is based on some sketches I made while still at the Art School in Zaria. I roamed the bushes . . . studying. . . . Forms like trees, stunted and deformed yet very sculptural and interesting; rocks showing different shapes and colors, and the prickly bushes changing from greens to golden browns."[22] Elsewhere he writes, "Ant hills have interesting sculptural forms, especially when they become old or slightly eroded by the rain. If an ant hill is still active, that is if the ants still live in it, you can always find new layers of earth growing around the old one thereby forming contrast in colour, texture, and form."[23] He is always alert to the power of natural forces: "Sometimes I stand and look at a tree. Ants have changed it, and I discover unusual aspects. They assume a larger importance, so that the tree is deformed and extraordinary. Then I use it as an image in my work."[24]

In his etching *Forms in a Landscape* Onobrakpeya uses "forms like mushroom[s], leaf motifs, a tangle of plants and ropes behind a rock. The form across the top is like a mummy and in the central position are shapes like those of people asleep."[25]

This connection to nature is not new, and some of today's artists put it to use. For example, Nigerian poets also "make meaning" of landscape or use nature metaphorically. The poem "Emergency Commission," by J. P. Clark, from midwestern Nigeria like Onobrakpeya, speaks of political turmoil as a howling storm:

Self-tossed out of heart
No outside hand could touch
Still the storm howls on,
Heads, rock and root adrift.
And before cock crows a third
Time, yet another tree that
Seemed beyond reach of wind
And bolt, topples down,
    Or shows the blast.

Good God! What great grove
Is this under whose spell
We have these several
Seasons dug up old secrets

Of the soil, though aboard
Stars, when mahoganies
Show a centre too rotten
For rings, and twigs and grass,
Already denied room and sun,
    Carry the crush and shock?[26]

And Onobrakpeya, describing influences from nature, relates: "In this Savannah climate, a great number of trees manage to grow to great heights and among them is the fan palm, patterned and grey. In the distance there was always a sound from the grain pounding. . . . Look up and you will find huts shaded underneath a cluster of trees. The echo from the poundings have some magic about them, they lure you here and there in the open landscape to explore. . . ."[27]

Although subjects inspired by nature and indigenous cultures are enduring elements in his work, Onobrakpeya always explores new media. He explains a new medium he has developed: "I use wood panels and I build up the surface with a plastic glue compound. Then I carve into the surface. Over it I pour plaster of Paris, creating a negative image. From the negative I can make limited editions of positive, low relief sculptured panels by pouring plastic resin into the negative mold."

Now devoting his time to both printmaking and such sculptured works, Onobrakpeya has a studio in a two-story building that would be the envy of any printmaker. It also contains a library, an office, and a gallery. He says, "My studio space contains six tables, each 48 inches by 96 inches where twelve people can work at one time. I have two people working for me, and in the summer there are always several art students there all the time. Saturdays I leave free for visitors. I abandoned my teaching. It was hard at first because I didn't know if we would eat, but now I am happy doing the thing I really want to do."[28]

Like Chinua Achebe, Onobrakpeya sees traditional forms and philosophies as necessary didactic tools for Africans living today and for future generations, and he translates them into contemporary language. Steeped in both Urhobo and Christian traditions, he works by integrating disparate elements: "I try to speak to the present about the future and in the process choose what I want from the past."[29] He synthesizes elements from an array of religions, traditions, philosophies, myths, and peoples. The world he creates allows for these differences, but it is not just a temporal world; it is also the "Leopard in the Cornfield"—the world of nature mystically united with the world of the spirit.

A colleague of Onobrakpeya's at The Nigerian College of Art, Science, and Technology in Zaria, Simon Okeke was a sculpture major. After graduation in 1961 he worked in the research laboratory of the British Museum in London, and traveled to a number of European countries preparing for a career in museology. He followed this career until the outbreak of the Nigerian Civil War in 1967. In 1971, just as the war came to an end, he was killed in a plane crash. His death was a loss to the group of Nigerian artists who worked closely together to achieve common national and continental goals, one of which was a movement to keep some contemporary works at home during the fifties and sixties when a large portion of those being sold left the country.

In addition to these endeavors, he worked as a sculptor. However, Okeke is to be remembered for his monochromatic drawings. Rendered mostly in browns and siennas, the shapes seem to be derived from sculptural forms and are carefully rendered in three dimensions. The resulting compositions, self-contained, cameo-like enclosures, usually depict women and children. Their bodies, which look soft and malleable like clay, appear to merge as though anatomically related.

One is tempted to see in his work influences from the famous bronzes at Igbo-Ukwu, east of the Niger River, where Okeke was born in 1937. He had become familiar with them in the Nigerian Museum when he worked there as a member of the antiquities department staff.

After his death, one of the projects on which he worked was realized in the building of the Nigerian National Arts Theatre for FESTAC, the 1977 festival of African culture that brought 17,000 artists from 56 countries to Nigeria. The building houses the National Gallery of Modern Art and its collection of contemporary art.

C. Uche Okeke, a distant relative of Simon Okeke, was born at Nimo near Awka in the eastern part of Nigeria in 1933. After graduation from the Nigerian College of Arts, Science, and Technology at Zaria, he became involved with the visual and literary traditions of his Igbo people. In one early painting entitled *Christ*, which has the formality of a traditional Igbo carving, the figure is described by Ulli Beier as "detached and withdrawn and dressed like a Muslim mallam."[30]

A fascination for Igbo literary lore led him to collect hundreds of stories, which began to show up in his visual imagery. His book, *Tales of Life and Death*, describes people "who grew roots where they should have had legs; some had no heads at all while others had as many as ten heads!"[31] "The tortoise, or Mbe," he explains, "is the folk hero of the Igbos. It is widely acknowledged that there is no tale or life drama without its Mbe. . . . [it] must exist in order to generate the desired bitter-sweet situation." Okeke also notes, "The notion that spirits have fantastic forms is evident from the masks and the symbols of the nature spirits, or Alusi."[32]

Okeke's drawings reflect this world of spirits. His lines also echo the lines of Igbo uli wall or body decoration, traditional art forms that his mother practiced and that he began to research in 1958. His incorporation of uli symbols—each of which embodies some meaning—has recently been re-initiated by other artists. A group of prominent Igbo artists including Chike Aniakor and Obiora Udechukwu also employ uli elements in paintings, drawings, and sculptures.

These symbols and linear configurations, which are an integral part of the supernatural beings created by Okeke, delineate wings and webbed feet. Patterns derived from organic forms of feathers, shells, and scales of supernatural beings give these images substance. They offer tantalizing suggestions of the mythic realm over which they are guardian.

Okeke's recognition of such forces in traditional life gave him his own direction as an artist. He sees traditional art as philosophy: "a complex system based on unity or oneness of human and natural elements and the acceptance of supernatural law. It is a religion, a way of worship; it is a social system, a way of protecting or strengthening the moral code of a dynamic human group with common ancestry and destiny."

But Okeke is also well aware of the futility of trying to recreate or rehearse the past. Speaking of the tourist-art collector who expects the artists to do just this, he says, "revival is certainly not the word for a society going through the throes of sweeping changes." Though

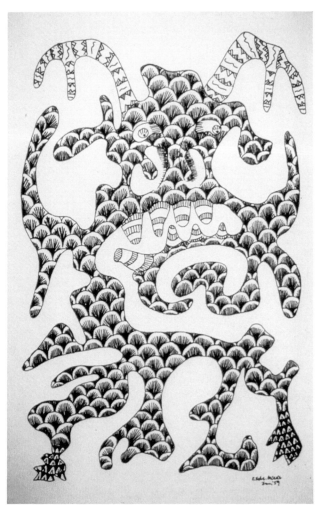

C. Uche Okeke, *The Unknown Brute,* 1959, silkscreen, 8″ × 12″.

he further explains, "The world of the new artist is the great wide world, not the narrow world of his ancestors, peopled as it were by mysterious beings, living and dead," and points out that the contemporary African artist must "go back to his own [world] for re-education, to disabuse his mind of stories of the glories of Europe."[33]

With such an outlook Uche Okeke, like Bruce Onobrakpeya, accepts synthesis as his direction, and describes that direction as necessity: "In order to come to terms with his roots the new artist now digs deep into his folk tales and legends."[34] In 1965 when his works that combined an African design sensibility with Igbo mythological sources were shown at the Goethe Institute in Lagos, some viewers complained that the drawings exhibited references to modern European art such as that by members of the Blaue Reiter.

The charge is not new: the contemporary artists of Africa are branded as being influenced by modern Europeans like Picasso and others—who themselves were

influenced by African art—rather than by their own forefathers. Okeke speaks to the question with, "In his quest for truth, he [the artist] has accepted the synthesis as the means of resolving the crisis—he must know his past, he must live in the present and face the future with confidence. . . . He employs new materials and techniques to express or interpret his African soul."[35]

Okeke has also pursued his concepts with other projects, among them a cultural center and library established in 1959 in the northern Nigeria town of Kafanchan (where he grew up). He moved this center to Enugu in 1964. It became affiliated with the Mbari Centre there the same year and became known as the Mbari Art Center (see chapter 6). After the war, as a successor to the center at Kafanchan, he founded Asele Institute in Nimo to promote aspects of Igbo culture.

Okeke's works in Nigeria include the murals painted in the early sixties at the original Mbari Club in Ibadan and the more recent large woven tapestry in the V.I.P. Lounge at the Murtala Mohammed Airport. As head of the Department of Fine and Applied Arts at the University of Nigeria, Nsukka, until 1990, he encouraged students and artists to relate to their own traditions, especially in the use of such cultural emblems as uli.[36]

In 1986 a display of such influences occurred with an exhibition of works in a variety of media by a group of thirteen artists living in the Nsukka area. This group, which calls itself Aka Circle of Exhibiting Artists, has a yearly exhibition. In coming together these artists say: "Aka is not an art movement or a school but a circle of exhibiting artists. A forum for the interaction of kindred spirits, professional artists, Nigerians and expatriates—working in the Anambra State."[37]

Aka means "hand" in Igbo, and Chike Aniakor tells us in the introduction to the catalog that "The hand . . . becomes in this context, the means of manipulating artistic tools in order to transform icon (in this case creative experience) into act (the work of art)."[38] The catalog also asserts, "The hand is also made of individual members, the fingers, whose collective enterprise gives direction to the whole. . . . [Thus] each artist retains his individuality. After all, the fingers of a hand are not identical."[39]

The major artists in this group who work in the Nsukka area are Obiora Udechukwu, Chike Aniakor, and Tayo Adenaike. They use line as a compositional entity, paralleling the use of calligraphy by some Sudanese artists (see chapter 9). Udechukwu (1946–) grew up in Onitsha. After studying in Zaria and at the University of Nigeria, Nsukka (where he now teaches), he, like Okeke, put his academic learning aside in order to reassociate himself with his own artistic heritage.

In an interview with Ulli Beier in *Okike* magazine, Udechukwu described the way uli murals are painted by women: "The mural painting employs four colours: white, red, yellow and black." Some of the uli symbols used on walls can be identified with human figures. However, the body decoration itself is always abstract and ". . . the uli proper is drawing on the human body with indigo pigment." For the ceremony of Ududonka in Agulu, his father's village, the "walls of the shrine are divided among the villages around . . . the women from the various villages come . . . it is like a public exhibition: the people go around and comment . . . : ah, this one is better than that and so on."[40]

The aesthetics of traditional wall painting are religiously based, with each motif having a distinct meaning. In rendering a symbol the painters "use another colour to go around it with a line. The hemming of the motif is a means of accentuating it . . . [the wall] is reddish latterite [*sic*]. Then, if they have a yellow motif on that, they might emphasize it by 'hemming' it with a white line. If they want to texture their motif, they may use their finger, dip it into yet another colour and stipple the inside. . . ." To give a certain elegance to their designs, the artists elongate the motifs. This is called "sharpening the mouth. . . . [T]his kind of thing increases the lyrical aspect of the design."[41]

Udechukwu began to combine uli designs with symbols he created from other traditional sources in 1970, incorporating them in drawings with political and social relevance. Although social/political commentary was traditionally performed by satirical songs rather than by the visual arts, it became a pressing necessity for Udechukwu during the Nigerian Civil War. He reiterates his belief that social commentary is a vital function of the modern artist by quoting Robert Motherwell: "[W]ithout an ethical consciousness, a painter is only a decorator." Expressing social protest with a line that divides space with grace and bravado, drawings such as *Tycoon, Longshoreman,* and *Nightsoilmen* clearly demonstrate the conjunction of an ethical and artistic sensibility.[42]

These drawings contain a lyrical dimension that contrasts dramatically with the more geometrically structured work of Yoruba artists such as Grillo. Udechukwu's flowing line turns back on itself and transforms space into mass. Teasing gravity and stretching line, the backbone of his composition, to a delicate thread, he tests integrity by pulling in one direction and then returning to establish balance with an ending flourish.

Udechukwu's drawings capture the "directness" and "cleanness" of uli painting. Sometimes he starts with a concept and sometimes he lets the drawing happen, usually without preliminary sketches. He sees a parallel in Chinese art—a subject he researched while at Nsukka where he obtained his master's degree—and its process of drawing directly. He notes the "correspondence be-

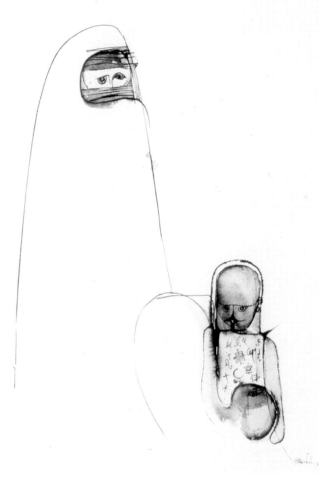

Obiora Udechukwu, *The Poet and the Muse,* 1982, ink, dimensions unknown. Collection, Iwalewa Haus, Universität Bayreuth, Germany.

tween Igbo and Chinese traditions. . . ." such as "spontaneity . . . prominence of line and this equal importance of positive and negative areas, . . . the brevity of statement, the economy of means and the relationship between calligraphy and painting. . . ." In both traditions "sometimes the painter is also a poet."[43]

A playwright and poet himself, Udechukwu has had poetry as well as paintings and drawings published in numerous publications. After reading Christopher Okigbo's poetry, which has been compared to uli painting, Udechukwu began to write poetry, stating ". . . I believe like the Chinese that the painter should also be a poet and that all the arts are somehow interlinked . . . giving each intuition the most appropriate vehicle."

Other African artists reflect such theories by working in several disciplines feeling, no doubt as Udechukwu does, that "There are certain experiences which can be best communicated through a particular medium, say, words, in which the appeal is auditory and verbal, intellectual. On the other hand there are other ideas and

Obiora Udechukwu, *Alhaja,* 1978, ink drawing, 20½″ × 12⅝″. Collection, Iwalewa Haus, Universität Bayreuth, Germany.

Obiora Udechukwu, *Stevedores,* 1979?, ink drawing, 15″ × 10¾″. Collection, Iwalewa Haus, Universität Bayreuth, Germany.

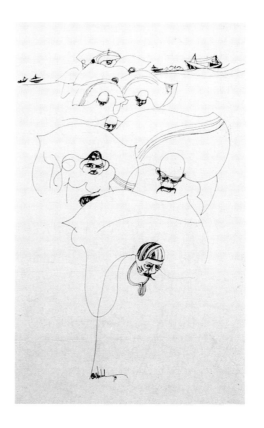

experiences that call for something with a visual appeal. The finest artists, and they are very rare, will continue to be those who are able to express themselves in almost every medium available to the creative person. They can reach every one, the blind, the deaf, the old, the young."[44]

Chike Aniakor was born in 1940 in Abatete. Like Udechukwu and Okeke, he is on the faculty of the University of Nigeria, Nsukka, and like Udechukwu, has developed the concept of uli as a modern ingredient. Uli lines in his paintings and drawings are sweeping asymmetric curves in eloquent apposition to human forms.

In his drawings *Rites de Passage* and *Okwe Players,* Aniakor has grouped figurative elements into single vignetted shapes with central axes. Each of these works features a mass of clustered figures in a thickly patterned area and lines that feather outward, giving the images an aura like the sense of water rippling or fire flickering.

Chike Aniakor, *Okwe Players,* ink drawing, dimensions unknown.

Omogbai applies paint in bold, free strokes. Her compositions have a raw, arresting quality; their painted surfaces are thickly encrusted in much the way that a shrine wall or a sculpture might be with paint or the substance of ritual. She says, "I started to work in the academic manner, but later found this boring, monotonous and uninteresting, and slowly developed a new way to interpret nature in a pure, personal language in which mood, tension and feeling could be represented."

"The resulting paintings . . . are abstract interpretations and a personification of themes like 'misery', 'grief' and 'courage'."[47] There is nothing romantic or pretty about *Woman at the Mirror.* Its angular forms create jarring tensions. In contrast to the organic sculptural wholeness that characterizes much of African sculpture, Omogbai's arrangement of forms is new and unexpected, unencumbered by tradition. Forms are pulled asunder, pierced, and severed. They startle and

Thus unified, diverse figures work together as a compositional whole but mythical and psychological allusions suggest struggle and conflict. He describes how concepts for such works develop: "My painting ideas are carried over months in the antipodes of the mind, undergoing creative mutation, occasionally surfacing to be synthesized. . . . These ideas mature with time like the sprouts of yam seedlings."[45]

A poet and a leading Igbo scholar, Aniakor's visual and verbal expressions are inextricably linked—one the extension of the other. Collaborating with Herbert Cole, he is co-author of *Igbo Art: Community and Cosmos,* the catalog for a pioneer exhibition documenting the historical art forms of the Igbo people.[46]

All of these men artists had the opportunity for art education at a time when most women artists were, like the mothers of Festus Idehen or Uche Okeke, filling traditional roles by creating shrine figures or uli designs, or like many Nigerian women, traditional potters, weavers, and dyers. However, a few women, such as Afi Ekong and Clara Ugbodaga-Ngu who sought careers in the arts, are considered pioneers. Although they are far outnumbered by men, the number of women artists is increasing. Colette Omogbai and Sokari Douglas Camp have appeared, and they too are exploring their personal and community identities as artists.

Colette Omogbai grew up in the town of Uzebba near Benin where she was born in 1942. She attended Ahmadu Bello University in Zaria, and she graduated in 1964. Attracted by the Ibadan Mbari Club, she exhibited there, and in 1965 helped to organize a similar venture, the Olokun Club, with Idah in his Benin compound. Later she went to New York and Chicago to study.

Colette Omogbai, *Woman at the Mirror,* mid-1960s, oil on hardboard, dimensions unknown. Location unknown.

disturb the viewer. Like totems, the part-bird, part-animal images take on the attributes of a community and depict its sorrows. The feeling of sacrifice as a physical and psychological presence is projected by these torn parts, harsh angles, and clawlike shapes, and is reinforced by her titles: *Accident, Sacrifice, Agony, Anguish,* and *Grief.*

Colette Omogbai rearranges the syntax of composition in the same way that some Nigerian poets rearrange the elements of verse, juxtaposing words in unexpected ways. Compare, for example, the words and ideas of Okogbule Wonodi, a poet from the Niger delta, when he runs them headlong into each other: "birthcry," "playgrounds that jump and chatter," "Your eyes toe-set" and "our mouths taleful."[48] J. P. Clark, also from the delta area of the Niger, does the same thing with images such as "I have bobbed up bellywise/from stream of sleep."[49] Or think of such a phrase as the "arm-pit dazzle of a lioness" by the late Christopher Okigbo, from eastern Nigeria.[50]

Omogbai rips human and animal forms from their original context, infusing them with a sense of violation, and then fixes them in another context, one informed by drama that is inherently psychological and poetic. Her forms become carriers that share the stigma and passion of a community. Her work is visual poetry of a searing sort.

Sokari Douglas Camp (1958–), with dramatic new successes in London, is the recipient of the Henry Moore and Princess of Wales awards.[51] She participated in more than ten exhibitions in the last three years while still a student at the Royal College of Art in London. Her work evokes her Kalabari origins and incorporates other influences in ways that have stimulated critical notice. For instance, writer Dennis Duerden says, "Sokari is plundering Europe. She has taken the cubist idioms of 20th-century art, derived principally from the works of African art seen in museums, and literally turned them inside out. . . . Sokari has developed a recognizable and unforgettable style without appearing in anyway to be consciously creating it." He explains further, "Sokari gives her work the appearance of living and breathing skeletons, forms in which we can see a skeletal framework, but which also appear to have skin and flesh. They are like the pre-Colombian gods of Central America, always acquiring blood from the life and work of human beings, but constantly losing it in order to have it replaced."[52]

Douglas Camp's recognizable style has firm connections to the Nigeria delta area where she was born in Buguma. Her sculpture has the fibrous texture of the boats, nets, thatched roofs, and house walls typical of the Kalabari culture. She glues wood, sawdust, and fabric together in a web of forms to create sculptures that recall the indigenous mask traditions of the delta area. The look of these reedlike images also suggests antecedents in the duen fobara, or "faces of the dead," memorial screens. They are Ijo shrine assemblages made of wood, split palm rib, and raffia and have powerful connections to Kalabari spirits.

However, while her sculpture may have textural and mystical connections, it is not meant to be viewed frontally as the screens are. The freestanding pieces invite the viewer to walk around and to participate, and—in the case of *Audience*—to become one of the spectators in the piece by sitting in the chairs it incorporates. Although both art forms are schematic in form, the traditional screens are static and symmetrical, while Douglas Camp's works are spatial and kinetic. It is evident that Kalabari culture nurtures her work, for it has the energy of a delta festival.

Although schooling away from Nigeria does not seem to have affected these indigenous influences, Douglas Camp describes her sojourn at the California College of Arts and Crafts, Oakland, as a formative period. "I think in an indirect way the Bay Area did have an influence on my work, but I was younger and very social and I had my friends from all over the world at CCAC. It was this that really pushed my work."[53]

In fact, having lived and studied abroad from early childhood and now living in London, Douglas Camp is fascinated with the experiences of visiting home and making video records there. About a trip to Buguma in Christmas of 1984 she said, "I am going home to make a film—Buguma is having a hundred year celebration and lots of traditional things will be done that I have never seen before. . . . There will be two-storey canoes manned by forty men from each compound. Women will shave their hair and dress according to where they originated in the Delta. Women have different patterns of dress which identifies their heritage. This is the sort of thing I find interesting."[54]

The lavish use of fabric by women and the importance of dance in Kalabari culture are also intrinsic to her work. She assembles cloth fragments with various elements in ways that reinforce one of her primary aims—creating a sense of motion. It is as though scraps of cloth and wood were glued together in an accidental meeting. Her forms have an inherent sense of impermanence, as though caught up in wind or cast ashore by waves, and still moving.

Some of her loosely constructed pieces are motorized to suggest the sound of wind rustling and dancers shaking. It is a case of "physical objects [which] can only be seen by being heard," seeing because you also sense and hear.[55] In addition, some of the limbs are partially formed or modeled as if flesh were peeled away to expose bone, a fragility that might simply evoke a vivacious spirit. Hearing such pieces, one asks, Is this a spirit or a rattle of bones, a spectacle of death as dancer?

Sokari Douglas Camp, *Church Ede (Decorated Bed for Christian Wake)*, 1984, steel, cloth, 96" high. Location unknown.

Lively and macabre, such compositions define a horizon that barely divides the living and the dead, and convey the feeling of nets at sea, the dizzy shudderings of trance, and the will-o'-the-wisp contact between the spirit and human worlds—contact that must be constantly reinforced. Reiterating this contact in her unusual way, Douglas Camp pays tribute to her Kalabari lineage.

A piece that emphasizes this contact and has broad human connotations is a tribute to her father. Entitled *Church Ede (Decorated Bed for Christian Wake)*, she created it after his death. It is a shrine that commemorates beginning, dreaming, and dying. With its metaphorical references, this landmark piece evokes the sense of a lifetime and an entire culture.

Unlike Omogbai and Douglas Camp, painter Jimo Akolo (1935–) from Kabba, conveys the texture of wood and the feeling of wood sculpture without referring overtly to either. An early student of Dennis Duerden, Akolo is also one of the sixties graduates at Zaria. It is interesting to note that he wrote his dissertation on arts and crafts in Nigerian teachers' colleges and was granted his doctorate for this effort by Indiana University. The Nigerian University Press published in 1982 his *Handbook for Art Teachers in Nigeria*. Working with similar art education efforts at Ahmadu Bello University, he

Sokari Douglas Camp, *Iriabo (Woman) and Child, Part of Audience Ensemble,* 1987, steel, paint, woman: 72″ high; child: 46″ high. Collection, the British Arts Council, London.

offering them as elements from an inner psychological space and as encounters with the ineffable or the spiritual side of human nature. The forms become viable metaphors for the conflicts of contemporary life.

The best known artist in the northern part of the country, Akolo was commissioned to paint murals in the building that houses the legislature of what was then the regional government. He won an honorable mention at the Sixth Biennale in Sao Paulo, and in 1982 his works were acquired by the Nigerian consulate general in New York City.

Unlike most Nigerian painters and sculptors, and perhaps closer to a writer like Wole Soyinka, painter, ceramicist, and architect Demas Nwoko has demonstrated a talent for satire. He uses form and design to dramatize aspects of the human condition such as irony, bitterness, loneliness, cruelty, and—sometimes—humor and dignity, but rarely does he express ebullience, euphoria, or whimsy.

Jimo Akolo, *Man Hanging from a Tree,* date unknown, oil on canvas, 64″ × 39½″. Collection of the artist.

divides his time between designing art teaching programs and his own painting.

In Akolo's painting, the kinship to sculptural forms is heightened by a rich textural approach, which includes the sensation of fiber and other assembled materials typical of some African sculpture. His subtle abstract forms incorporate qualities that project the feeling and weight of Yoruba history.

Some of Akolo's early figurative paintings seem related to those of Yusuf Grillo. But in his later paintings, such as *Man Hanging from a Tree,* form is less angular and imagery is not obviously figurative. In addition, this painting and others such as *King of Kings* are powerful evocations of a past that has survived to confront the present. While Uche Okeke imagines such beings as tree spirits that inhabit a supernatural space, Akolo incorporates the forms of Egungun or Gelede traditions (complex cults with sculptural forms in dance and mask),

Demas Nwoko, *Ogboni Chief in Abeokuta,* date unknown, oil.
Location unknown.

Born in the Asaba area in 1935, and another of the
sixties graduates from the Nigerian College of Arts,
Science, and Technology, Nwoko has lived most of his
adult life in Ibadan, where he was head of the original
Mbari Club. However, using a scholarship awarded after
graduation, he went to study in Paris at the Académie
des Beaux-Arts; he later pursued theater design in
Japan. He demonstrates this varied experience in several
ways. His pioneering effort in 1967 to revive a northern
Nigerian tradition of terra-cotta sculpture from a culture
that reached a zenith some three thousand years ago in
the Nok period, produced figures that reflect the moving
and enigmatic quality typical of their ancient predecessors.

Nwoko's paintings contain elements that seem derived
from the masks and figures of his own Igbo culture. The
images are statue-like, and their faces have firm, geometric features. In fact, all the forms seem to have
evolved subtly from sculptural sources; some hug the

flat canvas as though cut out and pasted on, and others
appear as bulky three-dimensional volumes.

Nwoko combines this sense of sculpture with themes
that focus on the human condition. *Street Scene* makes
sardonic comments on European life. From his *Adam
and Eve Series,* executed between 1963 and 1965, this
work depicts a kissing couple surrounded by drab,
careworn commuters on a London tram. Their harsh,
indelible features are carefully rendered. The man and
woman look like two sleepwalking paper dolls with
noses and mouths merged. They and the others are
strangely expressive: a commuter with black stockings
and legs that look like columns reinforces the sense of
sculpture, as does another figure with blunt, clasped
hands and fingers that look like knobs. A child standing
by looks desolate and vulnerable. All the inhabitants of
this environment are disturbingly passive and static. The
painting describes a cold, passionless society.

By contrast, Nwoko's painting *Ogboni Chief in Abeokuta*
is monumental. It communicates the strength and
power of one of the most important cults in Yorubaland:
the Ogboni, once the judiciary authority in every Yoruba
town. The bare-boned face, severe and gaunt with tiny
piercing eyes, evokes power, longevity, and perhaps
death. The mantle, a symbol of office, is split down the
center suggesting two worlds: the earthly and the supernatural. The simple elements of this composition—face,
hand, broad hat, staff, sky, and landscape are combined
in an archetypal portrait of invincibility. The feather
cloak and hat belong both to farmer and aristocrat. The
whole figure, especially the skeletal head, has the iconic
quality and spiritual authority of a traditional Ogboni
bronze.

In other paintings of this period, Nwoko assails the
hypocrisies and brutalities of colonialism in Africa with
scenes suggestive of a kangaroo court. For instance,
three implacable white officials—images of decadence—
sit like judges in front of a row of Nigerians. Ignorant of
life around them, the officials appear imperturbably
mad.

Nwoko's incisive and stinging portrayals might be the
visual counterpart to Wole Soyinka's poem "Telephone
Conversation," which describes an attempt to rent a
room from a racist landlady in England: "rancid breath
of public hide-and-speak,"[56] but they lack the sharp
Soyinka wit. Another painting, *Beggars,* is reminiscent of
the beggars in Senegalese Ousmane Sembene's *Xala,* a
film in which the beggars keep turning up to confront
the country's rapacious business profiteers.

Such versatile interpretations by Nwoko also extend
to theater with the creation of striking costume and
stage design. In one highly acclaimed effort, he captured
the eerie fantasy of Amos Tutuola's *The Palm-Wine Drinkard* with his costumes. (He also directed the production,
which was a high point in African theater.) One critic

Demas Nwoko, *Figure*, 1967–68, terra-cotta, 18½" high. Private collection.

called the costuming "lavish, alive, original," and said that " 'god and wife' are Nwoko at his laughing best," dressed as they are in "battered and tattered western evening wear. . . . But perhaps the most inventive idea is Nwoko's costume for the inhabitants of *Dead's Town*, jet black tubular figures of varying heights. The general impression is that of a thing you hear and look at, but neither see nor understand. It sent a cold shiver across the packed auditorium."[57]

In addition, Nwoko has produced designs for Wole Soyinka's *Dance of the Forests*, and an Ibadan production of Bertolt Brecht's *Caucasian Chalk Circle*. He, like many other Nigerian artists, moves from one medium to another, and in 1978 began an educational arts journal, *New Culture: A Review of Contemporary African Arts*. In recent years he has been involved with architecture, creating a striking design for the Dominican church complex in Ibadan.

Having also designed and built studios, one for paint-

ing and another for sculpture, he now has the facility for pursuing painting, carving, and casting, and making terra-cotta sculptures. With this kind of flexibility, Nwoko and others of his generation have helped to challenge many younger artists who are already showing signs of the same energy and vitality.

In contrast to Demas Nwoko, many Nigerian artists are relatively unknown. They have broken away from traditional forms and functions, and retain only the merest suggestion of historical precedents. Largely self-taught and inspired by the modern currents that touch their lives, they are responsible for some of the most vibrant expression in the country today.

One such artist from Yola, a town in northern Nigeria, is Musa Yola (1939–). Of Kanuri-Fulani parentage, he has been described by David Heathcote as having decorated walls in "twenty to thirty" northern villages. After seeing a wall painting in 1967, he was inspired to try

Musa Yola, *Cyclist*, 1971, medium unknown, 36" × 24". Location unknown.

Akan Edet Anamukot, *Untitled*, date unknown, fabricated metal. Ibibio area of Nigeria.

one himself. Like Middle Art (August Okoye) a Nigerian sign painter, Yola paints images of chiefs and local people. His murals reflect the lively bustle of village life, and make dramatic changes in the physical look of a town—at the same time they "can be visually explosive among the greys, white and subdued earth colours of a Hausa village."[58]

Heathcote comments that because Yola's work is not "transportable" it is not subject to the seductions of tourists. In fact his history is singular in that he produces only on commission for local clients, not for foreigners. He is, therefore, closer to the traditional artist. Because he paints on cement-faced mud walls, which must be refaced in time, he is like the traditional wood carver who, when a piece is eaten by white ants, is called on to create a new work, thus perpetuating the tradition.[59]

Artists with the lively spirit of Middle Art and Musa Yola have counterparts all over Africa—Ibanehe Djilatendo (see chapter 11) from Zaire, and Mario Massinguitana and Jose Mazoio from Mozambique, for example. Two others, Akan Edet Anamukot and Sunday Jack Akpan, are imaginative and talented artists who work apart from the academically trained, or otherwise encouraged.

The Keeper of the Horniman Museum in London, Keith Nicklin, and Jill Salmons have written in detail about Anamukot and Akpan.[60] Although very different, each draws from the rich, innovative cultural complexes in the Cross Rivers area of southeastern Nigeria.

The work of these artists reflects the diversity of Ibibio culture. Anamukot, working with corrugated metal, hammers it flat, then welds, rivets, and paints it, creating light, airy mobile sculptures of airplanes, birds, and weather vanes with sharply defined outlines. His animals have the graphic grace of the uli symbols adopted by the Nsukka artists.

His white birds stand like specters or quizzical witnesses. With elegant profiles, long slender necks, and pointed beaks, they are ethereal; as wind-borne creatures, they are curiously mated to his airplanes. His propellors and weather vanes exhibit some of the linear schema evident in the aerial conformations of the large Ijele masquerade headdresses.

While Anamukot's pieces are aerial, Akpan's cement figures are stolid, earth-bound portraits of community members and Nigerian notables, usually commissioned posthumously. His compound and his "Natural Authentic Sculptor" studio is the backdrop for this cast of characters. Nicklin calls the effect a "veritable Disneyland beneath the palm trees."[61] The figures have a startling presence—sitting, standing, facing the passerby who is in a strange way the focus of the group. They might have been subjects for Middle Art (see chapter 6), but

Sunday Jack Akpan, *Untitled*, date unknown, cement. Ibibio area of Nigeria.

they also recall the funerary figures in the Anyi and Brong areas of Ivory Coast, and the figures on military "castles" built by the Fante in Ghana. Like the barbershop signs, paintings on trucks, and popular writing in chapbooks, Anamukot's cement figures constitute an indigenous art form.

These artists, who have broken with the past, prove the point that Jacqueline DeLange and Philip Fry make in the Introduction of *Contemporary African Art*, the catalog for a 1969 exhibition at the Camden Art Centre in London. They caution that attributing traditional African characteristics to the works of modern artists always presents a danger. It extends European cultural imperialism that has for so long defined African art, not only to the rest of the world, but also to Africans themselves. They charge that "we still stagnate in the same ideological atmosphere as our parents—Africa is a conservatory, a continent-wide museum, and is refused the right to take a living, creative part in the construction of a new world."[62]

Nigerian artists, like other artists in and outside Africa, define their culture by selecting what is appropriate to their individual imagery and expression, not only from classical traditions, but also from the world at large. This opens the door to innumerable combinations of form, content, design, and composition. From the past comes their view of various art forms as interrelated, and from

the West come new mediums and the concept of art as secular.

Onobrakpeya, Grillo, Egonu, and Uche Okeke are artists who have found that synthesizing diverse elements offers viability without dislocating purpose or content. Some see art as an educational imperative, but differ as to whether its aims should be political as well as aesthetic. Christopher Okigbo, before he was killed in the war, began to draw closer to indigenous sources, saying that if you are ready, what is there will reveal itself.

All I did was to create the drums, and
the drums said what they liked. Personally
I don't believe that I am capable of saying
what the drums have said. It's only the long
funeral drums that are capable of saying it,
and they are capable of saying it only at that
moment. So I don't think I can claim to have
written the poem; all I did was to cover the
drums, and to create the situation in which
the drums spoke what they spoke.[63]

Creative attitudes such as these have helped foster talent and confidence. The results are evident in the Nigerian renaissance to which all of these artists have made important contributions.

5   Artists of the Shrines

Oshogbo

The story of the artists of Oshogbo is a story about the emergence in the early sixties of a whole cultural complex involving artists, actors, musicians, and the sacred shrines of a community. Located near the city of Ile-Ife, the ancient religious home of the Yoruba people, Oshogbo is rich in the traditions of the major Yoruba cults as expressed in masquerade, dance, music and myriad other ritual forms. Although a lively trading town of about 120,000 where merchants from north, south, east, and west buy and sell, for fifty years no Yoruba carver has practiced his art here.

A number of "Brazilian" or "San Salvador" "upstairs houses" with elaborate balustrades and baroque embellishments give the town special character. Houses like these were first built along the coast by slaves returning from Brazil in the second half of the nineteenth century; the influence moved inland later. The town is also known for its large festival held each year on the banks of the Oshun River where, according to legend, the city's first king met the goddess Oshun. The festival pays homage to her as caretaker and patron saint of the town, and commemorates its founding. Out of this milieu the new artists began to create with spontaneity and urgency, and as they worked, a new image of the town emerged.

Although there were originally two groups of artists—one working on the reconstruction of the sacred shrines and related stone or wood sculpture and the other working for secular purposes in a variety of media—

their roles were never rigidly defined. Theatrical talent existed in the persons of Kola Ogunmola and Duro Ladipo, brilliant men who set standards and attracted talent. Some painters were also actors and musicians, and some artists working on the shrines undertook secular projects as well. The excitement generated was infectious, as shrine-building progressed, performances took place, and artists created mosaics, repouśse metalwork, cast bronze sculptures, paintings, etchings, graphic prints, appliqued and embroidered wall hangings, and batiks—drawing on modern as well as legendary, indigenous religious, Christian and Islamic sources. All of this activity turned the town into one of the major centers of modern African art.

Four individuals were catalysts in this transformation: Susanne Wenger, the late Duro Ladipo, Ulli Beier, and Georgina Beier. Arriving in Nigeria in 1950, Wenger initiated the reconstruction of the shrines in and around the town and she has maintained an unprecedented involvement in this effort for thirty years. Born in 1915 in Graz, Austria, she left a career as an artist in Paris and went to Nigeria. Frustrated for a year by illness that threatened her life, she was advised to return to Europe but she refused. While recovering, she studied Yoruba poetry, philosophy, and language as the protégé of Ajagemo, a wise and revered priest. Before his death, he requested that she build dwellings for the Orisha, the Yoruba pantheon of gods. At the time it didn't seem a possibility.

Susanne Wenger, *Shrine* (detail), 1970s, cement-covered clay. Oshogbo environs.

Susanne Wenger, *Shrine for Iya Mapo*, 1970s, cement-coated (adobe-like) clay. Ebu Iya Mapo, Oshogbo environs.

Susanne Wenger, *Iledi Ogboni House*, completed in 1975, clay (probably covered with tinted cement). Oshogbo environs.

Susanne Wenger, *Untitled*, 1970s, batik, dimensions unknown. Private collection.

Believing that art is an expression of a religious philosophy, she inaugurated an ongoing revitalization of the sacred shrines. Wenger sees the continuity of religion as more important than the maintenance of style, and believes that a religion is alive in direct proportion to the inspiration and interpretation it generates. The shrines, in disrepair and suffering from neglect as a result of psychological inroads made by Muslim, Christian, and other foreign influences, now reinforce the links between art and religion. In many instances no relic of the original structure remained, but worshipers still came to pray. Now the shrines help sustain traditional values and impart contemporary relevance.

In 1968 Wenger described the conflict between traditional values and Christian influences: "Early Christian missionaries imposed their colourless synthetic god who resembled a hypocritical school master on a world where God lived virtually in its bones, its heart, its head as well as . . . in man's actions and dreams."[1] On the other hand, she explains, "I am not against Christianity but I am against all types of pseudo-religiosity. I always was and I still am aware of the beauty and strength of Christianity . . . the people who most deeply understand what I try to do are monks and nuns. I am distressed by the effects of religious degenerations generally . . . on mankind and so on art."[2]

She sees art as an archaic language that has a natural affiliation with religious principles. "Love could be also in another sense a second name for Orisha [the Yoruba pantheon] if one considers that love changes its face and character with the kind of heart it originates in." For her own work, Wenger says she is "using the language of the local flora and fauna as well as the local religion and philosophy." She declares, "I am no missionary and no prophet."[3]

In addition to Islamic and Christian missionary zeal, business and agriculture enterprises threatened the areas in which the shrines were located. Although funds for materials and labor were scarce, efforts to protect sites and create structures progressed steadily, subsidized largely by the sale of Wenger's own works. A few private donations were obtained, but the task remained formidable. Eventually the Department of Antiquities declared the Oshun shrines a national cultural property and provided two caretakers; the University of Ibadan also made a contribution supporting an auxiliary Museum of New Sacred Art.

The shrine structures are hand-built, like pottery, from earth with the consistency of clay. Figures and buildings take shape and change with the moods of those who work on them. Like those of traditional buildings, the earthen walls are thick and sculptural. At first only two bricklayers, Raifu and Lani, and later carpenter Buraimoh Gbadamosi helped. Eventually other individuals joined, working much like builders of Gothic churches.

From the outset, the spirit of the sacred Oshun grove, a sanctuary of giant trees, asserted itself, inspiring workers to imagine and create images simultaneously. Susanne Wenger says that meditation and the forms of leaves and trees in the holy groves guide her. Many of the forms, especially the extraordinary soaring images of the Ogboni house shrine, defy comparison. Wenger's figures of Obatala and Alajere (gods in the Yoruba pantheon), increase the magic aura of the place. They grow from the landscape, intensifying the natural beauty of the sacred sites and creating a mystical fusion of art and nature. These images, described in a film about the renaissance in Oshogbo, *New Images: Art in a Changing Society,* are "art in the midst of life" rather than for museum walls.[4]

". . . [B]ecause we are very much alive ourselves, we do not argue or assume that humanity is in suicidal condition, nor that we are all lost because humanity has contracted spiritual consumption," Susanne Wenger explains. "We give ourselves up to that creative life, allow ourselves to be part of what we love: life for life's sake, creation for creation's sake. We seek the encounter with human hearts in revealing ours to them."[5]

Wenger's grasp of the nature and complexity of Yoruba belief and philosophy was recognized when she was ordained a priestess by religious leaders in Oshogbo. Her Yoruba name, Iwin Funmike Adunni, means "by the grace of Iwin, the spirit, a gift which is to be treasured and which we really have." By contrast she is often criticized by foreigners who have little understanding of her commitment. This lack of understanding was demonstrated when foreign cinematographers came to make a film about the shrines and did not want to mention her in the production. But, Wenger remarks in Richard Attenborough's television series "Tribal Eye," "Europeans do not step out very far from their cars and reservations. And if one steps out, it is an anthropologist. I am not an anthropologist. I am living that life."[6]

In addition to her work on the shrines, she continues to design and execute large batiks. Of her graphic prints, a critic writing in the Lagos *Morning Post* noted, "In Susanne Wenger's interpretation there is nothing feeble about Yoruba religion: everything is clear, hard and intense. The forms as well as the ideas are severe and pure at the same time."[7] As an artist whose philosophic perceptions place her in a distinct category, her position is similar to that of religious artists.

Many artists have evolved through association with Wenger. The most prominent of these are Asiru Olatunde, the first contemporary artist in Oshogbo; Adebisi Akanji, Buraimoh Gbadamosi, and Saka, shrine builders; and Sangodare Gbadegesin and Isaac Ojo Fajana, batik artists (see chapter 6).

Adebisi Akanji, Wenger's primary colleague, worked

closely with her, translating her concepts into actual structures. Originally a bricklayer and cement mason, his life as an artist began when he entered a competition initiated by Beier to encourage the revival of the heraldic sculpture that decorates the balustrades of the town's "San Salvador" houses. The art had died out, but Akanji has become its inventive and prolific exponent.

After his initial success in the competition, he expanded his efforts to create large openwork screens of cement that serve as walls or balustrades, allowing for both breeze and shade. Akanji designed screens for the shrine of Eshu in the Oshogbo market, the Palace at Otan, for the Esso station in Oshogbo, and for the University of Ibadan, Oshogbo. He is also responsible for figures decorating the main entrance to the Ojubo Oshun shrine. In response to a commission from abroad, he built large cement screens at the home of Waldemar Nielsen, the past president of the African-American Institute. Nine of the screens were installed at 91st Street and Madison Avenue in New York City, where they enclose a courtyard. Another is located at the Nigerian embassy in Washington, D.C.

These screens have perforated walls and provide an extraordinary panorama of Yoruba life with startlingly expressive animals, masqueraders, drummers and dancers, as well as whimsical figures of convivial palm wine drinkers and Ulli Beier driving his car. Beier describes the walls of the Esso station: "Lions smile innocently. Strange creatures, from a medieval bestiary perhaps, stretch their decorative limbs. It all adds up to a dream in cement, a crazy petrol station, a work of art that is typically Yoruba and characteristic of the essential Oshogbo. Everyday life and fantasy form one and the same world. The old and the new, motor cars and masqueraders, live side by side without tension. Adebisi's art is powerful and playful at the same time, a typical Yoruba synthesis, one in which the serious and comic aspects of life present themselves as an inseparable whole."[8]

Also an accomplished batik artist, Akanji creates wall hangings of intricate imagery with delicate polychrome colors and contrasting dark indigo areas. The images exploit the transparency of the medium, and their forms seem suspended. His batiks contrast dramatically with the crisp, angular vocabulary of his cement sculptures. In both mediums he invents vigorous shapes that cluster like tree limbs weighted with foliage and move far beyond references to the sculpture on older San Salvador upstairs houses. His work on the shrines is his reinterpretation of Yoruba religion in contemporary terms.

Akanji, a Muslim, is committed to his religion, but he is also a member of the Egungun cult. This is not unusual because Yoruba religious thought is not dogmatic or exclusive, and it allows for the incorporation of

Adebisi Akanji, *Untitled*, 1960s, cement. Esso station opposite Mbari Mbayo club, Oshogbo.

Adebisi Akanji, *Untitled*, ca. 1974, batik, cotton cloth, 68" × 68½". Private collection.

Adebisi Akanji, *Untitled*, 1969, adire (starch-resist) cloth, 35½″ × 54″. Private collection.

other philosophies. His work seldom fails to combine humor and vitality and he is an avid documentarian of Yoruba life. In fact his business card reads: "To build a person or anything with cement consult Salau Adebisi."

Buraimoh Gbadamosi, also a drummer, is a practicing Muslim and an Egun like Akanji. Once a carpenter, he has also sculpted stone, cement, and wood figures that stand in the sacred groves where devotees come with small offerings to ask for the protection of children. In contrast to Akanji's animated figures, Gbadamosi's are stolid and staring with hypnotic eyes. Sitting or squatting like ancient androgynous gods, they seem immobilized by trance. In groups they have an uncanny presence with archetypal references that recall other cultures but which in sum are original.

In Susanne Wenger's house shrine, Gbadamosi's figures look like stamens growing from the curved forms of the architecture around them. Many of his shrine carvings, some as high as twenty feet, are totem-like structures that support, for example, the thick thatched roofs of the house for Ogboni cult members and the Busanyin shrine where the Ataojo, the king of Oshogbo, worships.

Saka is the other important shrine artist who has carved many roof posts. Using the traditional medium of

wood, in a non-traditional style he produces contemporary religious art. A bricklayer, hunter, and farmer, Saka was reluctant to become an artist, working for three years primarily as a cement mason and assistant to Adebisi Akanji, his long-time friend. Encouraged by Susanne Wenger, he created his first works in the forest amphitheatre at Oja Orunmole. Beier compares Saka's work to that of Henry Moore. There an elephant, hunters, and other spirited creatures are placed as though transfixed in various theatrical roles. Some provide surfaces for sitting, thus involving the viewer. They restate visually the intensity of a religious philosophy in which even "thought is creation."[9]

Wenger has encouraged artists who are not closely involved in shrine-building. Asiru Olatunde (1922–), one of these and the first contemporary artist in Oshogbo, where he was born, lived near Susanne Wenger. However, it wasn't until she found a small ornament on the ground and traced it to him that she had a sense of his talent. Olatunde was also an accomplished drummer who had been forced to give up drumming because it was frowned upon by adherents of his father's Muslim faith. Originally a blacksmith, he gave up that profession after tuberculosis had weakened him physically.

He had been making and selling bangles in the mar-

Buraimoh Gbadamosi and Saka, *Untitled,* ca. 1977–78, wood. Iledi Ogboni House, Oshogbo.

Buraimoh Gbadamosi, *Shrine Figure,* 1968, stone, 29″ high. Location unknown.

ket, but the importation of cheap trinkets put him out of business. Wenger encouraged him to work in a larger scale by melting down scraps of brass and copper. The hammered repoussé figures of animals he initially created were as expressive as Akanji's, and often incorporated other creatures within them. Eventually he used large sheets of aluminum and copper to make numerous panels in which texture and line respond to reflection, thus giving the aluminum a soft, silvery glow.

Reflected light is intrinsic to his work, and he exploits it in his depictions of trees. A tree by Asiru Olatunde is an archetypal vision of the tree of life with sprays of branches and hundreds of leaves, each reflecting light. He transforms the aluminum into elegantly textured images and episodes from life and legend. Even battle scenes in his panels of the Fulani wars have a formal grace, which the sheen of the metal enhances.

Over the years Olatunde has documented hundreds of scenes from the history, religion, and daily life of Oshog-bo. As a visual storyteller who creates parables, he uses the archaic power of myth to convey his vision. Al-

though his depictions of stories from the Bible have local settings, they often combine symbols from disparate cultures. In panels for church doors, a great fish represents God, the woman with four breasts is the Oshun River; a snake is both the tempter of Eve and the great boa of Yoruba culture; a trinity with three heads (one of which is Eshu, the god of chance), represents Olodumare, the god on high.

The importance of a figure often determines its size, but all of his images have an indelible presence. This gives them stature and links them to archetypes. As he works, the sound of his hammering, like his drumming, creates intricate rhythms.

Asiru Olatunde, Adebisi Akanji, Buraimoh Gbada-mosi, and Saka are examples of a new thrust in African art. Although Olatunde's commissioned works have been installed all over the world—in banks in Europe, at the University of Bristol, and in palaces in Nigeria, including the Palace at Otan, the Palace of the Ataujo of Oshogbo, and the Iddo Oshun—these artists are a part of an artistic nucleus that nurtures and is nurtured by

Asiru Olatunde, *Oshun River Legend,* date unknown, hammered aluminum, dimensions unknown. Private collection.

Asiru Olatunde, *Olodumare,* 1967, hammered copper, 76″ × 38¼″. Private collection.

Asiru Olatunde, *The Story of Osun,* 1960s, hammered aluminum, 54¼″ × 34¼″. Private collection.

the community. Rather than defying with modern accoutrements the ways of the past, they dignify past principles by giving them new vitality.

Artistically the shrines are among the most organic forms in contemporary African art, and like the indigenous art of the past, they are an organic part of the community. The work on them began at a time when Yoruba religion was attacked by foreign intrusions; the rebuilding helped reinforce the pride and identity of many artists who worked on them as well as others working in other ways, all of whom have now become known by the town's name.

6   The Spontaneous Spirit

Oshogbo and Ife

Another major catalyst in the Oshogbo renaissance, author and professor Ulli Beier went to Nigeria in 1950 to teach English literature at the University of Ibadan. By the end of the first year he realized that the people among whom he lived and the students he taught had a rich literary lore about which he knew very little. His study of the culture around him expanded. In a sense an ethnologist, a historian, and an advocate for change in the arts as well as for the preservation of indigenous values, Beier sponsored cross-cultural projects that introduced the work of many artists to the rest of the world.

Beier's research resulted in his writing articles for numerous journals including *Nigeria Magazine;* in his launching the now famous *Black Orpheus,* a distinguished art and literary journal, and *Odu: Journal of Yoruba and Related Studies* with S. O. Biobaku;[1] and in his authoring several books and anthologies. An extensive bibliography of his writings, which are in several languages, has an introduction by Ugandan poet Taban lo Liong, and documents his works: anthologies, plays, translations, essays, and books on arts and artists around the world.[2]

As an extramural professor at the University of Ibadan, he organized a variety of activities, including art workshops and festivals. He promoted visual, theatrical and literary artists, often while they were still unknown at home, by circulating exhibitions and arranging for theater performances within Africa and throughout Europe. After a performance or exhibition he frequently wrote a review for a newspaper, or an article for a magazine. In his photography, as in his direct literary style, he conveyed the life and energy of his subjects.

Beier was born in 1922 in Gleiwitz, Germany, now a part of Poland. He lived in Palestine during World War II, and eventually became a British citizen. In 1950 he left Paris for Africa. His observations about Yoruba culture, especially in places like Ede and Oshogbo, have formed the basis for much successive scholarship by historians and anthropologists. Africa is for Beier a vital source of creativity.

During the more than twenty years he lived in Nigeria, Beier looked for originality and sincerity, the thrust of which was spontaneous and intuitive rather than directed by Western training. In Yoruba towns like Oshogbo, he found that kind of strength untainted by western stereotypes. He and his wife, Georgina Beier, made their home in Oshogbo, a center of artistic activity. Inspiration spread like contagion with artists coming and going, pulling etchings, printing blocks, and appliquéing tapestries. Children living in the house began to paint, inspired by the others. Outside, the sounds of drums and praise-singing, to say nothing of the chattering of pet monkeys, contributed to the excitement.

Beier's professional history documents the breadth of his interests and the quality of his energy. Leaving Nigeria in 1966, he and Georgina Beier went to Papua New Guinea where they continued as advocates of the arts. There Ulli Beier founded several journals, organized exhibitions, generated research, made films and wrote numerous monographs. His belief in cross-cultural injections led him to invite Africans to participate, and encouraged the use of their novels, plays and poetry in the educational system.

Returning to Nigeria in 1971 he served for four years as director of the Institute of African Studies at Obafemi Awolowo University (then the University of Ife) where he encouraged scholarship and originated and extended cultural activities until 1974. Back again as director of the Institute of Papua New Guinea Studies from 1974 to 1978, he developed archival materials and encouraged writers and artists. Then in Australia from 1978 to 1981, he wrote for radio and print media, and produced publications promoting the arts.

In 1981 the Beiers moved to Bayreuth, Germany, where Ulli Beier founded and directed Iwalewa Haus, a museum of contemporary African art (with a comparative focus on the arts of other "third world" peoples) at the University of Bayreuth. As director of Iwalewa Haus, a position he still holds, he has arranged artist-in-residenceships for Africans, and organized scores of exhibitions and concerts. Traveling to India in 1980 and 1984, he interviewed artists, and documented the modern movement there, one with parallels in the Nigerian renaissance.[3]

During the first part of that Nigerian renaissance, Beier, then an extramural professor, lived in the compound of Duro Ladipo, a primary-school teacher in the town of Oshogbo. He and Ladipo had frequent discussions in Ladipo's, "Popular Bar." The liaison these two men formed was a long and productive one. When they met, Ladipo was a "mission-educated young man, . . . brilliant . . . with an open mind."[4]

Ladipo (1933–1978) was also a talented musician and a member of the Anglican congregation for which his father was a catechist, and for which Ladipo created songs and hymns. When he created and performed in the church an imposing piece entitled *Easter Cantata*, the church fathers—not least of all his own father—were shocked to hear drums in the church. (Later the Anglican church ardently supported cultural activities that developed.) Beier suggested that Ladipo perform the piece on television, in schools and in Ibadan at the Mbari Club, a cultural center formed by writers Wole Soyinka, J. P. Clark, D. O. Fagunwa, and Ulli Beier as a meeting, performance, and exhibition space. The response in Ibadan to the *Easter Cantata* was so enthusiastic that Ladipo returned to Oshogbo determined to form an opera troupe, and to convert his compound into a club for theatrical performances and art exhibitions.

The new club, like the original club in Ibadan, was also named Mbari. The club's name, Mbari, connotes creativity in a cyclical sense. Because it is an Igbo word originally taken from the Mbari cult found around the area of Owerri—a town located across the Niger River—

its namesake in Ibadan and Oshogbo emphasizes "the intertribal and indeed international character of the Ibadan club." However, in the Yoruba town of Oshogbo, "the illiterate market women were puzzled by the strange word and in typical Yoruba fashion they reinterpreted it by pronouncing it with Yoruba tones"[5] and adding the Yoruba word Mbayo. With this, the meaning became: "When I see I shall be happy."

The founding of Mbari Mbayo with a gallery in the former Popular Bar was a critical step in the emergence of the Oshogbo artists who began their careers through an extraordinary experiment. Sets and backdrops were needed for the theater, so an art workshop was started as a way to discover talented individuals who could make them. Thereafter, the house was packed night after night, and the club became a lively stopping place. Beier organized exhibits of the work of Valente Malangatana of Mozambique, of Ibrahim el Salahi of Sudan, and of Vincent Akwete Kofi of Ghana, and of the new Oshogbo artists as they developed. While foreigners found their way to the club, townspeople, priests, chiefs, kings, hunters, and children were the regulars and the Oshogbo Mbari was clearly a center rooted in the community.[6]

Outdoors behind the gallery on a wooden stage, Ladipo created theater comprising mime, dance, music, and the spoken word. His talents were evidenced in his early productions, which proceeded in brilliant and flawless synchronicity despite the absence of a conductor. Ladipo's first opera was *Eda*, Beier's Yoruba version of *Everyman*.

Ladipo began to study traditional dance, drumming, and poetry after Beier introduced him to Johnson's *History of the Yoruba*, and suggested three successive productions: *Oba Moro*, *Oba Koso*, and *Oba Waja*.[7] *Oba Koso*, Ladipo's most famous opera, related the story of Shango, the ancestral god of thunder and lightning. "We have made our real historic heroes into gods," Ladipo told Washington, D.C., drama critic Alan Kriegsman. "So, if George Washington had lived in Nigeria among the Yoruba people, we would have made him a god too, and worshipped him."[8]

A Ladipo production was unlike any in the Western world. Here was drama that defied all Western conventions and took theater into the realm referred to by Wole Soyinka when he said, "The umbilical cord between experience and form has never been severed, no matter how tautly stretched. But the reflection of experience is only one of the functions. . . . there is also its extension," explaining that "ritual understanding is essential to a profound participation in the cathartic processes of the great tragedies" and that in Africa, the "mystical and visionary are merely areas of reality like any other. . . ."[9] This is the realm sought by Peter Brook on his famous African trek. The Brook performance in

Oshogbo, in contrast to the productions of Ladipo, lacked the elements that tie drama to life and transform it to ritual. Ladipo achieved an electric fusion of actor, viewer, ritual, and community.

In 1975 Alan Kriegsman of *The Washington Post* described this fusion:

> One could rhapsodize over the spell-binding drumming by the native Yoruba tribesmen, the thrilling dancing, the haunting declamation and song, the stunning designs and colors of the costuming and sets. But this would put the cart before the horse. . . . For what this magical company is showing us . . . is theater in that pristine state of vibrancy and integrity to which all theater throughout history has aspired. . . . What *Oba Koso* discloses is that perfect unit of means and purpose for which we Westerners have so long revered the classical drama of the Greeks, and which the literati of the Renaissance tried so hard to recapture; which Monteverdi and Gluck and Wagner and others attempted to instill into our world of opera; and which our most radical thespians, from Grotowski to Peter Brook, have striven so diligently to emulate. It is that fusion of the art that our partisans of "multi-media" have been shouting about. Only they are obliged to approach it from the outside in, trying to synthesize disparate pieces, trying to restore a wholeness to a conglomeration of separate identities.[10]

This kind of integration permeated the more than thirty operas Ladipo wrote and produced. Many of his operas were performed in Europe, in the United States, and in Latin America as well as at nine major international festivals, always to critical acclaim. He also created television series, as well as individual television programs, and he collaborated in the production of a number of films, including the documentary, *Duro Ladipo,* by Henry Doré. He died at the age of forty-five in 1978. At the time artist Muraina Oyelami, one of the early members of his troupe, wrote, "nobody was ever so honoured in the history of this nation."[11]

Working with Ladipo was the first involvement with the arts for artists, including Oyelami, who were then encouraged by Georgina Beier. A London-born artist who first went to Nigeria in 1959, Beier also worked with Ladipo. She designed sets for *Eda* and developed roll-up backdrops that could travel in Ladipo's truck with the troupe when they toured the country. With Rufus Ogundele, and Jacob Afolabi, Georgina Beier painted sets for *Oba Koso* and *Oba Moro.* She also designed large appliquéd backdrops for *Moremi,* another Ladipo opera.

Georgina Beier (1938–) encouraged a second group of visual artists. She made a commitment to others' artistic potential as well as to her own. This second

Georgina Beier, *Untitled,* 1960s, linoleum cut print, dimensions unknown.

group of artists differed from those working on the shrines because their primary schooling and mastery of English had exposed them to influences from outside the traditional Yoruba world. Independence in 1960 and the high-life era gave life more immediacy, and this they brought to their art.

Beier saw and felt this immediacy in Oshogbo, and became dedicated to its expression. Beier's accomplishments are wide-ranging: she has produced paintings, lithographs, serigraphs, hand-screened textiles, and sculptures; has designed furniture and jewelry; has created mosaics and painted murals for the palaces of Otan, and Iddo Oshun, and for Idah's house in Benin; has illustrated books and has authored a number of publications.

Her large-scale works in metal include a thirty-foot-tall sculpture commissioned by the vice chancellor of Obafemi Awolowo University. She is also remembered for founding at this university the Pottery and Textile museums whose initial holdings she collected and donated. Other large metal works are the gates at the University of Papua New Guinea. In Papua New Guinea she worked with the Village Task Force conducting workshops in sewing, dyeing, carpentry, painting, and printing. A sizable number of artists there owe their success to her encouragement and guidance.

Beier says her role as a catalyst for other artists has been one that includes learning: "Watching others I learned to watch myself, to become more aware of my own potential. . . . Working with Nigerians helped me to free myself of my own cultural restrictions. Moving close to Yoruba culture also enabled me to gain a new perspective on my culture."[12] However, one of her most important contributions to Nigeria is her work with artists in workshops in Ibadan, and later, in Oshogbo and Ife.

Prior to the workshops in Oshogbo, Ulli Beier organized one in the university town of Ibadan. The purpose of the workshop was to break down inhibitions among art teachers and artists. He was inspired by the activities he had observed in Mozambique at the 1960 workshop run by Pancho Guedes. The Ibadan workshop was run by Julian Beinart, a South African architect, and was held at the Ibadan Mbari Club in 1961. Beier organized another in Ibadan the following year, again run by Beinart, this time with the assistance of artist-writer Denis Williams from Guyana. Guedes participated in this workshop and was a moving force and inspiration for participants. Beinart used "Blitzkrieg techniques." He "is not interested in getting his students to produce pretty pictures. . . . Their picture-making is conceived as a series of exercises, a kind of mental limbering up process that will enable them to create more freely later."[13]

A variety of tactics and materials were used to help participants break out of old molds, to work spontaneously, and to aim for authenticity of expression rather than "beauty." In the process participants forgot their self-conscious attitudes and conditioning. Working with great enthusiasm, they produced paintings that were a revolt against banality—an exciting ferment of ideas, colors, and images. A few illiterate participants suggested further possibilities. They did not understand much English and therefore did not pay attention to methods or suggestions and created some of the most original work.

Denis Williams was invited to conduct an August 1962 summer school, or workshop, in Oshogbo aimed at illiterate townspeople, not the sophisticated teachers and would-be artists involved in the Ibadan experiments. In this workshop there were no stereotypes or inhibitions to overcome. Actors from Ladipo's troupe, teenagers, and the jobless came, and it was immediately apparent that talent was abundant.

Jacob Afolabi was an exponent of this workshop, and Rufus Ogundele emerged from the next one organized by Williams in March 1963. Again the workshops revealed an overwhelming presence of talent, but money to keep artists going was in short supply. Afolabi and Ogundele were helped by whatever funds the Beiers could garner, and the Beiers maintained a workspace for them in their house.

In 1963 and 1964 Ulli Beier organized printmaking workshops at Ibadan and Oshogbo under the direction of a well-known Dutch printmaker, Ru Van Rossem. Van Rossem worked with trained artists such as Bruce Onobrakpeya in one workshop, and Oshogbo artists in the other. The prints were exhibited in a number of European and American cities with positive critical notice. (A third printmaking workshop was arranged in 1973 at Ife by Beier. Van Rossem and Onobrakpeya

were leaders and of the eight artists who participated, Muraina Oyelami figured prominently.)

However, one of the most seminal efforts came in the summer of 1964 with a one-week workshop conducted by Georgina Beier with modest funding from the Farfield Foundation. It was attended by actors from Duro Ladipo's theater troupe who participated as much out of curiosity as any notion of future careers. They were joined by passers-by and the result was a kind of festival of activity. During this workshop, the talents of four more artists—Adebisi Fabunmi, Muraina Oyelami, Jimoh Buraimoh, and Twins Seven-Seven—emerged.

Images and brilliant compositions materialized in a flurry of creativity. The blank paper was a vacuum to be filled, and the extraordinary way that lines and forms exploded into being and filled space seemed directed by powerfully intuitive impulses. The spirit that began in these workshops has spread, sending reverberations not only through Nigeria, but through countries around the world.

Each artist had distinct characteristics from the beginning, Georgina Beier explained. "Everybody put down confident images with sure strokes. It was difficult to sift the richer from the rich, the stronger from the strong. At first I was worried a style might develop, and that everybody might turn out the same stuff in the end. But there was too much individuality from the start."[14] Elsewhere she said of the experience:

[S]ome eighty people participated in the workshop, their ages varying from five to sixty. Many people just drifted in for entertainment. It was like a big party. None was over serious: it was a painting party, not a self-conscious exercise in "creativity." People came and went. Some painted the first and last picture in their lives. It was like a mad orgy of colour and making and laughter. Every night fifty luminous paintings were hanging on our walls. One had to be quick to see! The spontaneous artists had to be confirmed in their individual ideas, before their personal vision was destroyed by other influences.[15]

It was hoped that by hanging the strongest paintings on the walls at the end of each workshop day, the artists would acquire a discerning audience, instead of seduction by tourists.

Georgina Beier's approach was to inspire rather than to teach. Working alongside would-be artists, she instilled confidence and explained techniques. From 1964 to 1967 the Beiers' house was a place where artists could work. The success of her method was made obvious by the astonishing art that resulted. Nigerian artist-designer Tayo Aiyegbusi states, "In Nigeria and Papua New Guinea she has become a legend."[16]

Watching carefully for indications of interest and direction, Beier encouraged each artist in a way particularly suited to the individual's bent. Conversant with a wide range of techniques, she helped each artist select a medium appropriate to his or her individual direction. Rather than introduce an array of techniques from which to choose, she supported concentration in a medium suggested by early artistic inclinations before moving on to another medium. Invariably those who continued to work began discovering their identities as artists in a direct and uncomplicated way, gaining satisfaction from the very start, and learning other techniques in accordance with their own timing and interests.

The first of these artists, Jacob Afolabi (1945–), of Ikirin, was a bartender in the Popular Bar and then became an important member of Ladipo's troupe. Eventually he took over supervision of the Mbari Mbayo Club gallery. His style is defined by wriggling, nervous lines of great flexibility. These lines move across the surface and end in staccatto patterns or electric swirls in his prints. In his painting *The Flesh-eating Witch Bird*, the lines enclose amorphous masses of color. Forms are often organ-like with tentacle projections.

In *Acrobats*, his lines are "fluid like plasma: joints can appear in the most unlikely places, . . . arms and hands can spout anywhere. . . . Looking at these fluid, oozing forms, one feels that these figures have no permanent shape, they seem to change in front of our eyes, to congeal or dissolve. Body masses gather together, then split off again into smaller masses like mercury."[17]

One of Afolabi's most important works was the long mural (no longer extant) that encircled the Esso station across from the Mbari Mbayo in Oshogbo. It was an

Rufus Ogundele, *A Village Life Compound*, 1973, etching, sheet: 21" × 21"; image: 15½" × 19½".

aggregation of roving forms that seemed to grow out of the busy, lively atmosphere of the town. The mural's illusion of movement endowed the wall with a sense of motion. It was not a static structure but a series of flowing images, an extension of the townspeople, their colorful lifestyle, and their dress.

The second artist inspired by Georgina Beier was Rufus Ogundele (1948–) of Oshogbo. He too was an actor in Duro Ladipo's troupe. He began by creating paintings that were somewhat similar to Afolabi's, but after being introduced to linoleum cuts, his individuality emerged. His work became more structured; right angles, triangles, and crenelated shapes suggest fragments of Yoruba sculpture. Ogundele's works were abstract, an abstraction of organic origin tantalizingly close to some reality, one that is haunting and undefinable, but distinctly Yoruba in essence.

One of Ogundele's prints, *A Village Life Compound*, has this same geometric control. Carefully orchestrated shapes are reinforced by other forms that surround and connect them, unifying the overall design and conveying a sense of motion. Like the other workshop artists, he has a sophisticated sense of composition, always resolving the total space in a balanced way. He draws on legend, the Bible and episodes from the operas of Duro Ladipo for themes and inspiration.

In 1968 Ogundele was asked to paint a mural at the Ori Olokun Cultural Centre in Ile-Ife, and from that time has spent a lot of time in Ife. Both Afolabi and Ogundele have exhibited in many European countries, including England, Sweden, Germany, Holland, and Czechoslovakia, and in many cities in the United States.

Ogundele and Afolabi illustrate a concept of space

Rufus Ogundele, *Curious Creatures*, date unknown, linoleum cut, 15½" × 18".

Rufus Ogundele, *Man and Pet*, 1973, deep etching, sheet: 25″ × 21¼″; image 15″ × 18½″.

that is resolved by form and pattern rather than by means of the vanishing point. Oshogbo artists seldom depict space as distance. Areas of interacting elements allow no portion of the surface to imitate the illusionist expanse of western landscape painting. Afolabi and Ogundele were followed by others from the 1964 experimental workshop.

One of these, Adebisi Fabunmi—perhaps influenced by the way Yoruba sculpture effects a total involvement with space, or perhaps by the cohesive character of Yoruba towns—divides and subdivides space, filling every inch of composition with pattern. This treatment, especially apparent in his "city prints," is also true of his "yarn paintings." In both media he has used the city as a theme, a logical subject in a part of Africa where city-states were once major political units. The towns of his family's origin, Okemisi and Imesi-Ile, are the inspiration for much of his city imagery.

Benin City, The City of Dead Ghosts, The Empty City of Otan, and many other prints "are a maze of stepping stones, paths, rivers, houses, windows and brooding animals." There is often a tense confrontation between black and white design elements in these graphics, and ". . . forms pile up like building blocks. In *The Empty City of Otan,* for example, they totter at angles to rein-

force the atmosphere of disaster, conveyed as well by a fire-swept sky. . . . a comment on a catastrophe in a near-by town. . . . [H]e juggles the black and white forms like pieces in a jigsaw puzzle."[18]

The configuration of Fabunmi's city prints gradually evolved from the overall city design to a large central figure incorporating symbols of the city within it. Now moving easily from one theme to another, he continues to divide space into careful subdivisions that function as pure pattern and always contain stories and related symbols. Like pictographs, the symbols suggest or underline his themes. Yet even with these signposts—and they are many and interesting—his work retains an element of mystery. He leads the viewer, as does the Nigerian novelist Amos Tutuola with his odysseys, through labrynthian by-ways that coalesce into a compositional whole.

After watching his wife embroider a handkerchief one day, Fabunmi decided it was a technique he could pursue. He created a number of embroidered wall hangings, but found the work slow-going and therefore not economically feasible. He began to search for a new medium, experimenting with yarn after studying a Huichole Indian work. Unaware that the Huichole use beeswax as a binder, he couldn't figure out how they adhered the yarn to a surface, but finally he developed a method of glueing it to a backing of heavy muslin or plywood.

The intricate designs in his earlier works found natural expression in the winding patterns, which evolved from his use of yarn as a medium. Coiling the strands to reinforce outer forms, he enriched the designs. Though his early paintings have dark, moody colors, his works in yarn extend his palette to include various bright colors.

Adebisi Fabunmi, *Benin City,* 1965, linoleum cut, 18¾″ × 24½×.

The diversity of his subjects is reflected in his titles: *Missionary Activity in West Africa, Obatala,* and *Horse on a Mountain.* Some of his largest works relate to the Nigerian Civil War. One eight-foot-high work depicts falling bombs, planes, and parachutes. *Zoo-Keeper, Flying City, Lizard City, City on the Moon,* and *Afro-Apollo II* include uncanny references to modern technology and suggest underlying themes of alienation. *The City of Dead Ghosts* is a print which, like the work of his colleague Twins Seven-Seven, confirms connections to Amos Tutuola's journey of the pilgrim.

Born at Takoradi, Ghana, to Nigerian parents, Adebisi Fabunmi (1945–) attended primary school in Nigeria. Having lived in three of the four former regions of the country, he went to Oshogbo and joined Duro Ladipo's theater group in 1960. He supervised the Museum of Popular Art in the Palace in Oshogbo, created a mural at the Palace in Otan at the Ori Olokun Cultural Centre in Ile-Ife, and served as curator of the Ulli Beier Collection at the Oshogbo branch museum of Obafemi Awolowo University. He explains his purpose, "I am not one of those people who sees something and then copies it. I'm an artist who envisages something in my mind and then must express it publicly."[19]

The same could be said of Muraina Oyelami, another participant of the 1964 workshop. His inclination as an artist, musician, and dramatist and his subsequent successes affirm the viability of the experimental workshop process. Early in his career he found the style that best suited him. Some of his first paintings demonstrate a simplicity of form and subtlety of color, characteristics of his style today.

Perhaps because his initial approach to painting was abstract, it imbued the body of his work with an introspective vision, allowing him to think in terms of composition and meaning rather than representation. "For me mood and action are the same. All my work, whether moral or immoral, comes from my imagination, but [it is] also inspired by recent happenings," he said.[20] Compared to the work of his colleagues, his style and content are remarkably independent.

Oyelami's ability to simplify, and to say what he wants about his subjects with bold strokes, gives his work strength and an artless quality. Like the Sudanese painters Ahmed Mohammed Shibrain and Musa Khalifa (see chapter 9), he paints and draws simultaneously, leaving strokes as texture.

This approach requires sure draughtsmanship. Rather than contain form, his brief but expressive lines are never just outlines, but crisp details that serve to emphasize. Using a palette knife and a roller, he has developed his own technique for applying paint. With muted colors, he probes the subtlety and complexity of the human condition. A face painted solid red has the intensity of a Gelede mask. *Victims* is a painting in

Muraina Oyelami, *Untitled,* 1984, oil on paper, dimensions unknown. Location unknown.

which figures with ascetic faces are white, and therefore bloodless.

There are ironies in Oyelami's work. Because his themes are often introspective, they reveal the vulnerability and fragility of the individual. One of the reasons his work is referred to as poetic is that he paints generic rather than naturalistic portraits. However, he defines character with uncanny precision, escaping the limitations posed by outer resemblance. *East African Hunter,* a figure with henna-dyed hair, a long face and nose, and an elegance reminiscent of works by Amedeo Modigliani (an artist unknown to Oyelami), is an image of traditional authority like Demas Nwoko's *Ogboni Chief in Abeokuta* (see chapter 4). It was inspired by Kenyan artist Hezbon Owiti, who spent some time in Oshogbo and told stories about the Masai. Other paintings of authoritative figures, *Philosopher* and *Self-Portrait at Fifty,* have been compared to pieces by Georges Rouault (also

Muraina Oyelami, *Victims,* date unknown, oil on paper, 18½"
× 23½". Private collection.

Muraina Oyelami, *Untitled,* 1984, oil on paper, dimensions
unknown. Location unknown.

unknown to Oyelami). There is a similar religious power
in the work of both artists.

Oyelami sees humanity in crisis. Innocence, evil,
stoicism, and humor as well as dramatic, ethical issues
are his subjects. Paintings like *Suicide Is No Joke, Prodigal
Son,* and *Acrobats* all have tragicomic aspects. He also
displays a streak of the macabre in *Man's Ghost, Dead
Man's Brain,* and *Uncompleted Creation.* The closely interlocking forms of two heads and a bird in *Newly Weds,*
of black and white figures in *Inter-marriage* and of heads,
eyes, noses, and shoulders in *Three Friends,* convey a
feeling of the profound complexity of human relationships. These subjects and issues have prompted
Sidney Goodsir Smith, writing about Oyelami in *The
Scotsman,* to refer to the "subtlety of his ferocity."[21]

Muraina Oyelami was born in Iragbiji in 1940; his
father, a farmer, planted cocoa, kola nuts, and yams. By

the time he attended the workshop in 1964, Oyelami
had worked as a gas station attendant, a vendor of
medicine, and a seller of records. His experience as a
featured player in the Ladipo troupe from 1963 until
1966 is recounted in his monograph, *My Life in the Duro
Ladipo Theatre.*[22]

Oyelami's experience reveals how surprisingly varied
his talents are. In 1978 he received a diploma in
dramatic arts from Obafemi Awolowo University at Ife
where he directed and produced a number of operas by
others, composing music for many of them; wrote and
produced his own musical dramas; and continued to
teach traditional Yoruba music. He now has his own
workshop center and his own opera troupe.

In recent years Oyelami has spent a lot of time with
his music. "It uses the old and makes it new," he
explains, "The result is abstract and yet it has myth." He
compares it to his painting, "Both are abstract, both
have elements of tradition, yet both are essentially
modern. My work is purely from my imagination or
from a combination of imagination and recent happenings."[23] A sensitive painter and musician, Oyelami also
knows that art is not a problem to be solved, but a
search for another metaphysical reality.

Another member of the 1964 workshop, Jimoh Buraimoh, was the electrician for the Duro Ladipo National
Theatre. Having completed three years of training in
West Germany, he accompanied the troupe when it
toured Austria, Belgium, the Netherlands, and West
Germany in 1964. He also occasionally acted in Yoruba
plays produced for Lagos television.

A year after the workshop, Jimoh Buraimoh was
exhibiting small mosaic plaques and tables inlaid with
tiles and chains of tiny beads. The first show of his
"bead paintings" at the Goethe Institute in Lagos in
October 1967 produced many sales. The material and its
inventive use attracted customers. Quick to take up new
ideas, he enjoyed experimenting with and exploring
new media. However, he was first known for his mosaic
tables made entirely of beads embedded in cement.

Buraimoh's greatest progress came after 1966. Working with linoleum cuts, he began each work with a
sketch, often on a scrap of paper. Sometimes he completed three or four different block prints in a single
week. He said then, "I like to keep the block right
beside me when I am sleeping. Then I can think about
it all the time."[24] He gradually expanded his media and
his artistic output included bead paintings and murals.
In the bead paintings, rather than embedding the beads
in cement as in the tables, he developed a technique of
glueing the already-strung beads onto cloth or wood
thus creating pieces to hang on the wall. As commissions for larger tables and murals occurred, he broad-
ened his list of materials to include bits of glass, cowrie
shells, and even pebbles.

Muraina Oyelami, *Behind My Window,* 1971, oil on paper, 30″ × 19¾″. Collection of Sigrid Vollerthun.

Born in 1943 into a Muslim family, Buraimoh was first influenced by his mother, originally from an area called Waterside near Epe, east of Lagos. She wove the mats that were used for praying, sleeping, eating, and were a traditional Yoruba gift from a bridegroom to the house of his bride. Watching and helping her, Buraimoh developed a sense of color as he chose and dyed raffia for her designs.

Bead painting, the medium for which Buraimoh became known, has as its closest antecedent traditional Yoruba beaded cloaks and crowns. The raised surface, which the use of beads affords, emphasizes form and, in the case of close color changes, creates the illusion of depth; areas seem to rise in steps to plateaus and fall to valleys. Improvising from circles, squares, and triangles, he creates a vocabulary of shapes.

The compactly organized compositions of his early works have given way to free, uncluttered space, but often his imagery is repetitious and decorative. His later work relies on technique and uses the medium to

celebrate color and rhythm. By winding and unwinding the beads in swooping arcs and wheels of color, the beads intimate rhythm. In this way he creates rich brocade-like patterns and a texture of Byzantine brilliance.

Like the other artists of Oshogbo, his subjects have varied sources of inspiration: Yoruba mythology, Christianity, Islam, and Nigerian daily life. He has an attachment to Yoruba stories and proverbs; his strongest work responds to these stories, crafted as he knows them.

Expanding his bead paintings to mural size in 1968, Buraimoh completed a large work for the India Handloom House in Lagos. Eight feet by four feet, it was executed directly in wet cement. Descriptive of cotton being loomed in a fanciful way, he depicted the scene with coils of cowrie shells, glass, and beads. Also in 1968 he completed a commission for a hundred-square-foot mosaic mural on the portico wall of the Ikoyi Hotel in suburban Lagos. Thereafter he completed murals for the Institute of African Studies at the University of Ibadan, the Ori Olokun Cultural Centre in Ile-Ife, and several commercial establishments.

The best-known artist from the 1964 workshop is Twins Seven-Seven (ca. 1945–). Born in his mother's home as Taiwo Olaniyi Salau in the northern Nigerian province of Kabba, he attributes his name to the fact that he was the last surviving twin from seven sets of twins, explaining that he chose Twins Seven-Seven instead of Twins Seven because "'Ibeji Meje' does not sound right. It has to be 'Ibeji Meje Meje.' I needed an unusual name to mark myself."[25]

When Seven-Seven was seven days old, his mother went to a priest named Ifadaron for performance of an Ifa oracle. The priest instructed her to travel with her twins for a few weeks, performing dances and begging

Jimoh Buraimoh, *Untitled,* 1974, bead painting, 24″ × 40½″. Private collection.

for money according to tradition. His mother was not in need of money, being a cloth seller and a weaver, and his father did not like the idea, so they did not heed the advice of the priest. In the seventh week the other twin, Kehinde, died. Saying, "All right, destination is providence," his worried mother found a woman from Akure to take the surviving twin dancing and begging.[26]

At school Seven-Seven joined the Okoro Youngsters Orchestra, but his father, a leather worker and occasional trader from a chief's family in Ibadan, disapproved. The Ibadan compound was Seven-Seven's home until 1952 when his father died and his mother moved back to Ogidi, in Kabba. In 1960 Seven-Seven left school and went to Lagos where he became a driver-apprentice for two years. However, music was still his main interest; after forming several musical groups, he traveled around the country with a juju band.

In June of 1964 Seven-Seven went to Oshogbo as a dancer for a herbalist who went from town to town selling in the markets. Discovering a lively party at the Mbari Mbayo Club, Seven-Seven dashed the man at the gate a pack of cigarettes to let him in. Soon he was the center of attention on the stage in a costume he had designed that was as bizarre as the stories he later depicted in his paintings and etchings. Ulli Beier asked him to stay, paying him the three pounds he had earned with the herbalist. Seven-Seven did take part in a play directed by Kola Ogunmola who, like Duro Ladipo, was a major dramatic talent in Oshogbo.

But Seven-Seven was an independent who had to shape his own course. His love of music led Ulli Beier to buy him a guitar. Soon thereafter he organized his Seven-Seven Wizards Rocket Theatre and the Young Stars Rocky Band; a sign so inscribed identified his house, which he calls the Dramatists' Camp and Hostel. He advertised: Come and Watch Twins Seven-Seven and his seven styles of dancing.

When the 1964 workshop took place, Seven-Seven participated. His first works on large sheets of brown wrapping paper were as distinctive as his later works, and completely unrelated to the work of the others. By doodling, not planning, he produced a line that was delicate and serpentine, or aimless and wandering, or erratic and capricious, but never dull and ordinary as it moved from one edge of the surface to the other.

Seven-Seven's method was one of drawing rather than painting. He worked patiently with great intensity, not stopping for food or drink. Of his ink drawings, he says, "My word for it is 'Pensdream.'"[27] Georgina Beier quickly recognized his way of working as ideal for etchings.

Seven-Seven started on etchings almost immediately, taking them through three or four stages. Beier says that "he does not invent, he depicts as he sees," and adds "A naive artist? Perhaps, but not an unconscious one."[28]

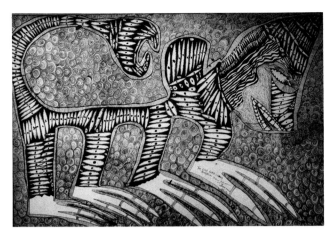

Twins Seven-Seven, *The Eyed Bodied Leopard — Pensdream*, 1960s, ink drawing, dimensions unknown.

Working to please himself, and proceeding in unorthodox ways, he became highly skilled.

He began to paint on large sheets of plywood, allowing the grain of the wood to suggest shapes, often obtaining with flat pattern a curious sense of perspective and dimension. Organic and seemingly anachronistically placed with no realistic relationship to the forms that enclose them, his patterns suggest the texture of bird feathers, snake skins, veined leaves, and fish scales; some areas contain stripes, mosaic-like squares, dots, maze patterns, concentric circles, and even designs reminiscent of medieval armor. Frequently teeth, nails, claws, and eyes define his images. All these patterns join in a kind of horror vacui (a characteristic evident in the work of other Oshogbo artists including Fabunmi's city prints) to cover the surface. No sterile precision prevails, but rather his titles describe a "cat-elephant" with beautiful pink eyes, a "three-horned hunter in the forest of the killed," a "long-nosed monkey," "bodiless elephants," and "endless palm trees."

A relationship to Amos Tutuola's writings is frequently suggested, but the nexus is a cultural one, and not a literal interpretation of narrative. In his paintings, a concept springing from a past having mythological characteristics easily embraces the present and leaps into the future with surprising science fiction traits. For Twins Seven-Seven all of these worlds are congruent. The affinity with Tutuola's writings arises from the fact that they both draw from the same source: Yoruba story telling. They have both created Yoruba odysseys. When Georgina Beier saw the similarity, she gave Seven-Seven a copy of Tutuola's *My Life in the Bush of Ghosts*. Many of Twins Seven-Seven's paintings suggest brilliant passages such as this one:

Immediately the whole Skull family heard the whistle when blew to them, they were rushing out to the place and before they could reach there, I had left

Twins Seven-Seven, *The King of Birds — Pensdream,* 1968, ink drawing, 28″ × 24″.

their hole for the forest, but before I could travel about one hundred yards they had rushed out from their hole to inside the forest and I was still running away with the lady. As these skulls were chasing me about in the forest, they were rolling on the ground like large stones and also humming with terrible noise, but when I saw that they had nearly caught me or if I continued to run away like that, no doubt, they would catch me sooner, then I changed the lady to a kitten and put her inside my pocket and changed myself to a very small bird which I could describe as a "sparrow," in English language.[29]

Supernatural personalities such as "superlady," "complete gentleman," "television-handed ghostess," and numerous others from Tutuola's tales people Seven-Seven's painted odysseys. His works have the same haunting spirits and ghosts and the same strange, fearful aura as Tutuola's books. But Seven-Seven tells his own visual tales, and characterizing his work as fearful or ominous is an error of omission. The witchery that Dylan Thomas

mentioned as "grizzly" in Tutuola's *The Palm-Wine Drinkard* is also wonderful in the way that Hieronymus Bosch is wonderful.[30] It is true, however, that critics were baffled by Seven-Seven's imagery.

Sidney Goodsir Smith writing in *The Scotsman* asserted that Tutuola depicts "a society enslaved by their priests and witch doctors . . . there is no joy here at all."[31] Such analysis is laughable. Yoruba story telling is gripping and bizarre, but it is also rich, humorous, and labyrinthian. Similarly, Seven-Seven's creatures are both fantastic and amazingly alive. A natural storyteller, he deals in legend rather than symbol. Ideas multiply when he paints and talks. Verbally describing a picture, he develops the story beyond the frame of the picture and one painting becomes the basis for the next.

Given his productivity, he was soon exhibiting—within the first year his paintings and etchings were being shown in Oshogbo, Lagos, and London. Eventually there were one-person shows at the Institute of Contemporary Art in London, the Merton Simpson Gallery in New York, and the Carnegie Institute in Pittsburgh. Most recently he has created and exhibited a set of etchings in Australia.

Returning from the London show, Seven-Seven described his feelings exuberantly: "I am a bit very happy. When I traveled abroad, I could see myself that I'm doing a very great thing. Even my mother doesn't see it. I have brought myself up. . . . I believe I have a special thing guarding me." His wonderfully eccentric attire is, he explains, "To differentiate me! Well, you see, I am an artist and can't wear a tie and shirt, so this is more suiting to me."[32]

What some critics have missed is the ebullience of this man whose contagious, outrageous, and often whimsical enthusiasm for life has also motivated him to become a sometime politician. His enthusiasm and energy are embodied in every aspect of his being: his language, clothing, dancing, music, and painting. They permeate his work. Because fantasy and the supernatural are real to him and inherent in his paintings, so too is the side of life which, like Tutuola, Dante describes: "In the middle of the journey of our life I came to myself within a dark wood where the straight way was lost. Ah, how hard a thing it is to tell of that wood, savage and harsh and dense, the thought of which renews my fear! So bitter it is that death is hardly more."[33]

Twins Seven-Seven has encouraged other artists. In his household a sophisticated batik industry thrives. There the prominent designers Nike Davies and Bisi Olaniyi got their start, creating wall hangings and other fabric designs. Prolific artists, they have each created hundreds of pieces, many of which have found their way around the world. Their work suggests influence from Seven-Seven, but their flexibility as designers keeps them artistically independent.

Nike Davies, *Untitled*, batik on cloth, 91″ × 78″. Collection of Roy Ortopan.

Another artist, Samuel Ojo Omonaiye (?–1977), was encouraged by Seven-Seven. While still in his early twenties, Omonaiye contracted tuberculosis, and died, but his spirited imagery still represents a part of the modern expression of Oshogbo. First a tailor and also a trained house painter, he was introduced to Georgina Beier by Seven-Seven. After painting some walls for her, he began painting on glass and then stitching appliquéd tapestries after she suggested the mediums to him.

In the appliquéd tapestries, he composed each image by juxtaposing brightly colored and patterned pieces of cotton in a patchwork assemblage. He affixed them, totem-fashion, on a vertical strip of handwoven cloth with embroidery of the sort used on national dress. The large triangular shapes in his glass paintings were transformed when he began to create whimsical creatures for wall hangings. Jagged forms, outlined by tiny triangles, vibrate and animate the compositions.

From the beginning his works had a kinetic energy, not surprising considering his musical talents as the lead musician and bass guitarist in Seven-Seven's band, the Golden Cabretas. As an actor and musician, he also took part in several Ladipo productions. Often his tapestries—especially his later, more complex compositions—had major figures playing drums or horns. He transposed the contrapuntal rhythms to jazzy patterned cloth.

A precedent for his wall hangings exists in Nigerian leather work and the appliquéd heraldry in the Republic of Benin, but his designs are completely different. Omonaiye had a seemingly limitless store of half-animal, half-spirit creatures. Some winged, some with claw feet, his was an African menagerie of gargoyle-like beasts and dragons, bright and lively rather than fearsome. His large pieces have been exhibited extensively, and *Beast Tamer Dancers* hangs in the office of the British Broadcasting Corporation.

After the 1964 workshop, the number of artists in

Ademola Onibonkuta, *Wall Hanging*, 1971, adire (starch-resist) cloth, 86″ × 38″. Private collection.

Oshogbo continued to grow, with individuals emerging from both in and outside workshop experiments. Ademola Onibonkuta (1943–) had taken part in the 1964 workshop, but became more seriously involved in painting, making mosaic murals, and working with textiles sometime later. Extremely versatile, he was one of the first members of the Duro Ladipo National Theatre, joining in 1962 and traveling with Ladipo's troupe to perform in the Berlin Theatre Festival in 1964. Now as head of the performing arts section of the Oyo State Council for Arts and Culture in Ibadan, he can influence state policy on the arts.

In 1970 Onibonkuta performed in Wole Soyinka's production of *Madmen and Specialists* at the Eugene O'Neill Theater Center in Waterford, Connecticut. He now has his own theater company and his own orchestra, The Orisha. As a composer, he has invented instruments, including a fascinating xylophone he called the odu gongs; inspired by Yoruba agogo bells, Onibonkuta's instrument was constructed after months of research and development. He also includes an ancient lithophone in his band. The story of the discovery of this instrument is described in an arresting account entitled *A Gift from the Gods*.[34]

As artist- and composer-in-residence in 1983 at Iwalewa Haus at the University of Bayreuth, Germany, Onibonkuta performed seventeen concerts, and held a major exhibition of his work. A percussion group he formed with Rufus Ogundele and Tunji Akanmu Beier (Georgina and Ulli Beier's son), created an African-East Indian fusion with: "Dundun drums, Bata drums, Sekere, [Onibonkuta's] . . . Odu iron gongs, a very rare Lithophone, a Mirimba from Mali, Pot drums from Morocco, a Tone Box, The Indian Mrindingam and a Jazz Kit Drum."[35]

In 1986 in Sydney, Australia, Onibonkuta "formed the Okuta percussion group with Tunji Beier and Greg Sheehan—here again fusion with Yoruba, Indian drums and drum kit. . . . The cassette they issued (with brilliant singing from Ademola) shows Ademola's extraordinary versatility and his genius for cross-cultural communication."[36]

Like Muraina Oyelami, Onibonkuta manages to devote time to both the performing and the visual arts. In addition to batik, he creates both adire (starch-resist) cloth and wax-resist dyed wall hangings. As an adire artist, he retains the traditional low contrast of the dyed cloth, but transforms the look of the medium by using it for large, striking images. Quite unlike the amorphous imagery of another Oshogbo artist, Isaac Ojo Fajana (also discussed in this chapter), his designs are decisive statements with each element sharply defined. *Life in Nigeria in the Nineteenth Century* is considered his masterpiece.

Tijani Mayakiri (1937–) was another participant in

Tijani Mayakiri, *Untitled,* mid-1970s, monoprint, 15″ × 20″. Private collection.

the 1964 Oshogbo workshop; he too began his work as a visual artist much later. Joining Duro Ladipo's troupe in 1962, he took the part of Mammon in the play *Eda*—a Yoruba adaptation of *Everyman*—and the major role of Timi in *Oba Koso*. After leaving the troupe in 1966, he formed a troupe of his own and gave performances in institutions and schools in the area.

After participating in a workshop organized in 1967 by Susanne Wenger, he found more time to paint, creating unusual monoprints—dark forms delineated by fine white lines. Like Yinka Adeyemi and Sangodare (also discussed in this chapter), Mayakiri is familiar with the rituals and philosophy of Yoruba culture and they are his major themes.

Moving to Ife in 1968, he became a founding member of another art workshop, Ogun Timehin, made up of the Oshogbo artists living in Ife. He has exhibited in various countries, and Mbari Mbayo has published his book, *Ifa*. In Ife he continued his acting career by joining the Ori Olokun Players of Obafemi Awolowo University, where he was "a star performer in many dance dramas."[37]

With this kind of creative activity in both towns, other visual artists began to develop: Yinka Adeyemi; his brother Adeniji Adeyemi, who attended an early Oshogbo workshop; Yekini Atanda, who lived at Susanne Wenger's house; Wale Olajide, who stayed with

Senabu Oloyede, *Untitled*, 1969, adire (starch-resist) cloth, 68″ × 36¼″. Private collection.

Kikelomo Oladepo, *Untitled*, 1969–70, adire (starch-resist) cloth, 68″ × 34″. Private collection.

Rufus Ogundele and Yinka Adeyemi at Ife; Labayo Ogundele, who was Rufus Ogundele's younger brother; Ademola Oyelami, who was Muraina Oyelami's cousin; Segun Adeku, an expert printmaker who makes beautiful embossed etchings; Funso Adeniji, and Ankobra. Thus a second generation emerged to contribute to the spirit of the Oshogbo-Ife renaissance, and to the reputation, which is now world-wide.

Of those who attended the summer school workshop

held by Susanne Wenger in 1967, Isaac Ojo Fajana, Yinka Adeyemi, and Sangodare became accomplished batik artists. Yekini Atanda did not participate in the sessions, but when he was living in Wenger's house, he began to make batiks as well. In contrast to the traditional adire cloths, which are opaque indigo and usually monochromatic, the new cloths are multi-colored pieces that have a luminosity, and they are especially beautiful when hung against the light. Whereas the older adire cloths, created as women's wrappers, are characterized by repeat patterns, these artists' wall hangings feature images more freely composed. They have taken batik into an investigatory realm and have created a unique movement in Nigeria. Their large pieces are modern statements expressed in the context of an old starch-resist medium.

The starch-resist medium, adire, is also practiced by two modern women artists, Senabu Oloyede and Kikelomo Oladepo. They began as aladire, the title for women who create traditional indigo-dyed cloth. Instead of following the formal repeat patterns of the older cloths, their designs have central images and are meant to be hung on the wall. Daughters of Asiru Olatunde and of Jinadu Oladepo respectively, they have inherited their fathers' talents, but use different media and several colors in addition to the indigo.

Senabu Oloyede reflects her father's imagery by following a similar compositional structure and dividing a narrative story into segments. However, her father's imagery is sedate and dignified and hers is lively and energetic. Kikelomo Oladepo's images have the same iconic quality typical of her father's brass figures, but her larger scale enforces their power. With only a background in traditional dyeing techniques, both of these women have taken unique directions.

Isaac Ojo Fajana (1944–), also accomplished in the use of both adire and batik mediums, is from Omuo-Ekiti in the Western State. His parents were farmers, and he attended school a hundred miles away from his home, finally finishing sixth grade. After 1962 when his father died, his efforts to further his education were frustrated by lack of money, but with the help of older brothers he eventually completed three more years of school. Unable to continue, he traveled to Oshogbo to find work. After considerable hardship, he went to Susanne Wenger.

Fajana says that when Wenger discovered his talent, "She bought hardboard and brush colors for me and encouraged me to paint. . . . I feel very happy with my work and it gives me joy and happiness more than anything. I love making others happy with my work, not because of money alone. As you know, I must live as an artist." Of his current life, he says, "Since I became an artist in Oshogbo with the other artists, we are all friends, no discrimination among us. We love each other, we visit each other and some of them try all they can to help me up."[38]

Fajana paints, makes woodcuts, creates embroidered wall hangings, and dyes starch-resist adire cloths and batiks. In both his paintings and his batiks, figures bordering picture areas are only partially incorporated and serve to frame the major images. He creates the batiks in a painterly fashion, letting the wax flow and puddle on the surface.

Isaac Ojo Fajana, *Osun Festival at Oshogbo,* late 1960s, batik, dimensions unknown. Location unknown.

The style of his starch-resist works is crisp and more defined, but even the smallest stroke moves and twists with vitality. In both media his images, which are reminiscent of those by Jean Dubuffet, seem to totter on a delicate edge between graceful and the monstrous. His forms grow like leaves on a luxuriant plant, often ending in mud-fish feet. Iridescent colors against an indigo ground, and veins caused by the crackling of the wax, create the look of stained glass. Like the other artists of Oshogbo, he has a sense of his own abilities and origins. "Art is in my blood from heaven," Fajana says. "None of my family know anything about art. Even in my hometown there are no artists. Yet, I can not say about tomorrow. People do recognize me and they know the value of my talent."[39]

Yinka Adeyemi (1941–) also produces large, multi-colored batiks. Like Muraina Oyelami, he went to Oshogbo from the nearby town of Iragbiji. His family had artistic talents and interests: his father made beaded crowns, a unique Yoruba art form, and his uncle painted barbershop signs that advertised hair styles. The fact that his mother was a storyteller influenced the content of his work. Adeyemi joined the Ladipo troupe in 1962 as an actor and musician. After traveling with the troupe to Berlin and London in 1964 and 1965 to participate in festivals there, he acted in *Kongi's Harvest,* a film based on a play of the same name by Wole Soyinka.

Then, leaving Oshogbo, he went to work marking farm boundaries for the Ministry of Agriculture. During this time his experiences of various indigenous customs

Yinka Adeyemi, *Untitled*, 1973, subtractive print, sheet: 17½″ × 23″; image: 15½″ × 19½″.

Yinka Adeyemi, *Mural*, late 1960s, clay, cement, and pebbles. Ori Olokun, Ile-Ife.

formed the basis of much of his later work. His batiks, which often featured musicians, were dyed in strong red, yellow, and magenta, rather than in the delicate colors associated with the batiks of Sangodare. Eyes are a dynamic focus in his work, and the texture of pattern and shape crowd the space to create a compact unity. Adeyemi also paints, carves, and creates mosaic murals using cowrie shells and pottery shards.

Another batik artist is one of the youngest and best known. Sangodare's name was Gbadegesin before he became a priest of Shango, the Yoruba god of thunder and lightning. Sangodare was the son of the senior Oshun priest of Oshogbo, and lived in Susanne Wenger's household from the age of eight.

Now grown, he creates brilliant batiks, overlapping five or more subtle colors to intensify the appearance of transparency. In place of color that defines shapes or fills

them, each shape is composed of several colors and forms. The exciting way that these colors merge to form designs within designs gives his compositions a visionary quality. The orchestration of many colors and their hues, of precise, delicate, linear systems, and of many figures into an intense unified composition surely relates to his own spiritual role in Yoruba culture.

Continuing the utilization of diverse materials is Jinadu Oladepo (ca. 1923–), an artist working with metal in Oshogbo. Originally a Muslim and a blacksmith like his younger brother, Asiru Olatunde, he was creating imitation Ogboni sculpture to sell to Europeans. Ulli Beier relates that "Georgina made a number of pendants and bracelets in wax and asked him to cast them for her . . ." thus suggesting indirectly other functions for a brass caster. "Jinadu now began to copy Georgina's work for a while. We found Georgina's pendants and bracelets in a market in Lomé. But very soon he began to produce his own work; then went back to figures—but now moved away from Ogboni conventions. He now has a son named Kasali who produces very fine work indeed."[40]

Since that time Oladepo has made hundreds of cast brass figures, pendants, rings, and bracelets. Because the mold is broken to release the piece, each is unique. Though the pendants are essentially circular in shape, he constantly improvises compositions, using animals, fish, or human figures in new configurations. Oladepo's pendants and belt buckles have become signs of belonging, worn by artists and citizens of Oshogbo as well as by many domestic and foreign patrons.

His small figures, which began as two dimensional works, gradually became a foot in height and are encrusted with a lively surface decoration on all sides. In 1970 a photograph of these figures was featured in a *New York Times* article by veteran critic John Canaday. This was the first major review in the United States of work by the Oshogbo artists. Canaday praised Oladepo's innovative combination of sophistication and humor "mated compatibly with a traditional African spirit."[41]

Though his work is sometimes referred to as Ogboni, it is not made for the Ogboni cult, which is traditionally associated with another juxtaposition of forms. The intricate pieces Oladepo casts might be related to the gold weights from neighboring countries, and might reflect the same technical facility, but they are essentially new images and a part of Oshogbo's renaissance.

In addition, there are two artists from outside the area who did not attend workshops but did become involved in the Oshogbo-Ife renaissance. Both were strongly affected by the Nigerian Civil War. Gift Orakpo, who went to Ife from northern Nigeria, did his most important work in Ife. Augustin Okoye, alias Middle Art, went from Onitsha to Ife where he painted his bitter response to the war.

Jinadu Oladepo, *Pendant,* 1968, brass, 3″ diameter. Private collection.

Subjected to several environmental influences, Gift Orakpo (1953–?) finally achieved his brilliance as an artist by responding to inner visions. Ironically and tragically, it was an inner conflict that eclipsed that brilliance. Recoiling from outside influences with a sense of alienation and driven by the need to communicate, he created work without precedent or relationship to the cultures around him.

Orakpo was born in Otukutu and grew up in northern Nigeria. Unable to speak either the Urhobo tongue of his father or the Igbo tongue of his mother, he felt alienated from indigenous roots. As a speaker of Hausa and as one conversant with Catholicism, which he came to know at school, as well as with the Protestantism, which he learned from his parents, he felt "separate" as a child. Ulli Beier has written that "feeling ill at ease with the society he grew up in, his lone searching led him to the Bororo Fulani, the proud cattle people of

northern Nigeria."[42] Orakpo learned a great deal from the Fulani, especially about their religion, its rites, and their supernatural powers, but he could never really become one of them.

The Nigerian Civil War was a time of chaos for him. At thirteen, he witnessed the slaughter of Igbos. Fleeing with his mother from the north, he tried to help maintain the family of ten children. These experiences at such an early age made an indelible impression. Returning to Jos in northern Nigeria after the war, he completed school. He was interested in becoming an artist and began to paint in the style of the old European masters, though he had been encouraged to look at African art. Still searching for ways to communicate, he eventually created surrealist visions. It was as though he must always search elsewhere.

Jinadu Oladepo, *Cast Figures,* brass, 12″ and 10″. Private collection.

Gift Orakpo, *The Goddess of Water,* mid-1970s, ink drawing, dimensions unknown.

At the urging of Brian Stafford, a British district officer who had sent photos of his work to Georgina Beier, then in Ife, Orakpo moved to Ife. There he had difficulty adjusting to this new situation. Ulli Beier explained, "If Ife welcomed Gift, Gift did not find the new environment easy to take. The Yoruba seemed noisy and aggressive; too expansive and too culture bound, for Gift to communicate easily with them. He withdrew more and more into himself and after a few months became seriously ill and returned to Jos." Beier goes on to say that he did find a direction as an artist at this time.[43]

Leaving Ife and returning three times, he then embraced Buddhism, which exerted a strengthening influence. Orakpo's imagery finally developed from a cryptic alphabet that he created for a diary. At the suggestion of Georgina Beier, he began to develop from this alphabet a calligraphy on which he could draw for imagery. Pursuing this idea, he produced works for his first one-person show at the Lagos Museum in 1972. "This exercise imposed the discipline on him which he needed. It gave him an awareness of form, which had been totally absent from his earlier drawings. . . . Now he acquired a discipline without stifling his surrealist imagery."[44]

His vision had many moods, but surrealist elements are pervasive and set it apart from the work of the other artists. In fact there seems no immediate cultural reference. The rhythmic linear patterns in his ink drawings spread like Rorschach blossoms and form an eerie amorphous structure to support morphous anatomical shapes. They are like mandalas, but always have some unsettling details such as all-seeing eyes, feelers, or tentacles. It was obvious that Orakpo had discovered a way of working that was fecund, such that each work was but part of a rich, ongoing sequence, inventive and self-perpetuating. Driven by recurring disquietude and feelings of separateness, his searching was cut short by suicide.

August Okoye, also suffering from the effects of the war, was brought to Ife by Ulli Beier. Although he has received international attention, he would probably still continue to work without fame as a sign painter who gave himself the name Middle Art, saying "no good for a person to exalting himself. So I don't want to make so much proud. . . . Let the people to exam, and exalt me up. Because if they raise me now, I will not fall again.[45]

Middle Art's chosen name seemed appropriate when he worked anonymously in Onitsha supplying clients' signs and occasionally painting to please himself. His romantic depictions of the ideal family, woman, or leader were arresting because they were so forthright. One of the most famous of these, *The Story of Chukwuma and Rose,* portrays a love triangle. Chukwuma is climbing a tree preparing for suicide, his shoes at the bottom of the tree. Below, Rose is talking happily with her new swain. However, it is Middle Art's works depicting war that are so powerful as to make his name misleading. This impressive body of work has been exhibited and reproduced in catalogs and journals around the world.

Born in Nri in 1936, a village in the eastern part of Nigeria, Middle Art had three years of schooling before he traveled north as the houseboy of a trader. When he was six years old, he was involved in an auto accident that resulted in a year-long hospital stay until a bone surgeon operated and enabled him to walk again. After four years in another town, an accidental fire burned all the houses, and Middle Art returned again to Nri.

Finally settling in Onitsha, the large market city on the Niger, he apprenticed himself to a sign painter. It was there that Ulli Beier noticed his originality and not only became a patron, but arranged for the exhibition of his work and wrote a number of articles about him. An interview in one of these articles includes a dramatic narrative describing his vicissitudes during the war— running from encroaching troops, and changing professions from fisherman to barber to basketmaker. Finally becoming a soldier for eleven months, he shot at attacking planes and helped guide friendly ones dropping bundles of food on the airport runway.[46]

Middle Art (August Okoye), *Painting of the War — Ambush,* 1972, oil on hardboard, dimensions unknown. Collection of Georgina and Ulli Beier.

Middle Art (August Okoye), *Painting of the War — Food Airlift,* 1972, oil on hardboard, dimensions unknown. Collection of Georgina and Ulli Beier.

He documented these experiences in a series of paintings done while he was artist-in-residence at Obafemi Awolowo University. Explicit images—the fiery interception of an armoured motorcade, dismembered bodies, burning boats attempting to cross the Niger—make Middle Art's war pictures particularly menacing. His picture of a family and its bombed house is a harrowing indictment of war, suggesting comparisons with Pablo Picasso's *Guernica* or Henri Rousseau's *War,* but his urgent strokes define the senseless helter-skelter of attack and place it close in feeling to the work of Tanzanian artist Kiure Msangi (see chapter 11). The house, a symbol of rational existence, becomes a house of cards, its walls spread outward like a splayed carcass. His brusque strokes delineate holocaust and its ghastly gray-white victims.

Beier describes his relationship with Middle Art:

He was to my mind an outstanding signwriter. Other than buy a few paintings, I did nothing to promote him until after the civil war. When I came to Ife I learned from Chinua Achebe that Middle Art was very sick, as a result of being wounded during the war. I brought him to Ife primarily to have him cured and to enable him to eat properly and get thoroughly rested and relieve him of his worries for his daily bread.

As his health was improving, I suggested to him that he could perhaps start to paint again—but as he didn't need to earn his living at the time, there was no need to paint barbers' signs etc; I suggested he should paint whatever was closest to his mind . . . he painted the Biafran war and some intensely religious paintings. The war pictures were undoubtedly his greatest paintings. At present he is struggling again in Onitsha with his daily bread, though the Goethe Institute has held a second exhibition of his work. (I organized the first in 1972).[47]

Middle Art's history as a sign painter, who later gained some recognition as a pop artist, parallels in many ways the experiences of the Onitsha chapbook authors who wrote romantic stories for a wide audience, which includes scholars. The interest now accorded him by an appreciative public is not just sociological, but is based on the gripping evocations of his own traumatic experiences of the civil war. One wonders how many other artists who describe life with such precision are working in Africa today as sign painters. How many individuals like Gift Orakpo are alienated and in need of encouragement? Their accomplishment and those of the workshop artists who startled viewers with their originality and talent suggest there is much untapped talent.

In addition to artists who began to work seriously immediately after the workshops there were those who had prolific spurts of brilliance within two years. Others like Ademola Onibonkuta, Tijani Mayakiri, and Adeniji Adeyemi who attended the first workshops but were too busy in Ladipo's troupe to paint, came into their own only years later.

"Rimbaud," Georgina Beier explains, "wrote poetry for only four years—but we don't reproach him with that. Instead we honour him as one of the greatest poets of all times. Seven-Seven painted magnificent pictures for ten years; at times he worked as if in a trance. In the whole of Africa there is nothing comparable to his work. But now he lives himself out in music and bizarre politics."[48] Ulli Beier asks rhetorically, "How many artists have blazed briefly? How many really great paintings does even the most important artist create in a lifetime?"[49]

The whole phenomenon of the short-term experimental workshop and the artistic energy it can unleash has profound implications for Africa and other areas of the world. The workshop is a way of reaching talent; although some see it as a threat to conventional art education. It is also often cited as the cause of a rash of mediocre activity by imitators who have not had the initial experience or some follow-up encouragement and guidance. But pressures exerted by economic needs also encourage imitation. The new artist who is just finding an identity is—without the protective effect of an occasional workshop or visiting artist who offers participatory, rather than teaching, support—prey to the tourist. Academic education in the arts is not a very old tradition even in the West; rooted as it is in a very different cultural matrix, it represents a major concern for the new artists of Africa who deserve the autonomy to do their own selecting undiminished by corrupting influences or impositions of any sort.

7 New Dynamics

The West African Coast

Autonomy is often slow to come. When independent expression set the scene for further experimentation in Nigeria, contemporary Nigerian artists gathered momentum and created numerous examples of independent success. While major movements have developed in Senegal, Sudan, Ethiopia, Zimbabwe, South Africa, and Nigeria, many individual artists and smaller movements have emerged elsewhere on the continent. These movements, large and small, are the result of historical, geographical, cultural and, no doubt, accidental factors. For better or worse, foreign mentors also exerted influences. In addition, demographics played a part. Nigeria, for example, has a population equal to the total population of several East African countries.

In contrast, countries such as Togo, Ghana, Ivory Coast, Liberia, and Gambia have smaller populations and fewer artists of accomplishment. However, an increase in the number of artists is already apparent, and with this as encouragement, the rich traditional forms in their cultures will begin to augment new creativity.

In choosing several artists from West African countries (other than Nigeria and Senegal, described in chapter 8) to illustrate the quality of work, it should be explained that they suggest current artistic directions in their countries, rather than represent their colleagues as a whole. The cultural antecedents of artists in Togo, Ghana, Ivory Coast, Liberia, and Gambia are very different from those of Nigeria, but are equally esteemed by scholars and connoisseurs. Along with the traditions of

dance, music, and poetry, the visual arts are subjects of continuing research, study, and appreciation. The fiber arts are particularly impressive, exhibiting a dynamic gamut of techniques, colors, and patterns. Ghana's royal regalia of woven silks and hand-printed cottons are examples of textile as a fine art form.

Ivory Coast, Liberia, and Ghana, like Nigeria, have formidable sculptural traditions. Ghana is known for its heraldic, religious, and popular arts, including cast gold and brass ritual and utilitarian sculptures and jewelry. The country's cultural history is long and prestigious. Around the eleventh century iron was smelted; by the fourteenth century, there were thousands of smelting sites. Probably during the last half of the fourteenth century, gold, silver, brass, copper, and lead were worked, and the art of lost-wax casting began.[1] The making of terra-cotta figures was also thriving.

Ivory Coast and Liberia, with numerous groups and sub-groups of peoples, such as the Senufo, Baule, Guro, and Dan, are known for their spectacular masquerades and rituals, which offer a wealth of inspiration for modern artists. The arts of smithing, casting, carving, jewelry-making, basketry, leather work, and pottery have all permeated day-to-day life as well as reinforced religious structures. Change within traditional form does occur, illustrating a certain flexibility. For example, traditional masquerades integrate modern elements of dress and other western accoutrements such as gas masks and neck ties.

This flexibility is most clearly seen in endeavors that

are ongoing at a community level. In Ghana the highly ornamented Asafo command post complexes built by the Fante have decks and balustrades and are festooned with "pilasters, structural and ornamental corbels, segmented arches, columns, including salmonic columns, and architectural masks," and "guarded by sculptural animals such as lions, tigers, and deer, and effigies of policemen, troopers, and escort guards."[2] The whole effect, with tiered verandas and the assortment of gaily painted cement figures, even Adam and Eve, is a dazzling pageant.

In Ivory Coast, too, there is a strong sense of an artistic consciousness that is changing and adapting to new elements. The builder-sculptors in the Anyi and Brong areas are creators of ingenious pavilion-shaped grave monuments that present brightly painted cement figures in life-size diorama.[3] As in Nigeria, sign painting is also a brilliant, lively art form, a roadway index of current artistic energy, and an indication of the attitudes toward change.

Throughout the centuries these various arts seem to have had one thing in common: a close alliance to symbol. Their symbolic references give them additional meanings. In addition, symbols often convey rank, parables, or proverbs. In Ghana's Akan society, for example, pulling down the eye means "have seen death" or "don't forget me when I am in the other world."[4] In fact, symbolism in the form of proverbs is "the foundation of the culture," according to Peggy Appiah. "The crab's claw mean[s] persistence; the lion, king, and Anansi, the spider, describe[s] the wise, greedy or foolish."[5] In Ivory Coast, too, the prevalence of riddles, legends, and proverbs enriches language and permeates cultures. So strong is this predilection toward symbolism that it is also intrinsic to such West African–connected religions as Haitian Vodun and Brazilian Candomble.

Sensitivity to myth and symbol on the part of modern artists in these areas is just one aspect of heritage that in its entirety could easily become an expansive study. It should be mentioned again, however, that even with an important heritage it seems fairly obvious that an artist benefits from the evidence of others who have set a precedent of contemporary accomplishment, especially when past excellence seems difficult to live up to and change suggests heresy.

With work that demonstrates the successful integration of traditional influences, El Loko (1950–) is also a model of accomplishment. Born in the small village of Pedakondji, Togo, he went to school in Ghana and was trained as a textile designer. Now a painter and printmaker, he has exhibited many times in Germany, where he has spent years studying and working. Many erroneously assume that the work of an African artist who has lived abroad for a long period will be less

"African." El Loko's subject matter and style are distinctly African despite his German schooling and experience.

El Loko describes his training: "You can study any place on this earth. No place on earth will make a man a king. It is each person's duty to turn his environment into a kingdom." Germany helped him a lot, he says. "I listened to [the professors]. I took something from what they were saying and added something of myself. I worked hard, which Germans admire. I studied with three different professors in what amounted to three stages. The first didn't tell me what to do. I had to find something and then do it. The second told me what to do. The third was in between, he said what he felt, but he didn't expect you to do it his way. I could do whatever I felt."

El Loko speaks of art as transformation: ". . . see, look, take something and transform it into something of your own. This is like the philosophy of Montaigne, the French philosopher: steal [ideas] and make them your own. As a bee goes to a flower and transforms it to honey."[6]

This is what El Loko has done with the image of the bird. In his prints *Liebespaar (The Lovers)*, *La Danseuse*, and *Femme avec Oiseaux* he uses wings, claws, and beaks with other elements such as city buildings, faces, and masks to construct formal compositions in which images are so interlocked that their joint boundaries give each an additional identity, as well as the kind of continuity inherent in sculpture.

El Loko, *Liebespaar (The Lovers)*, date unknown, linoleum cut, 27" × 21".

El Loko, *Tan 2 Festival (Les Acrobats),* probably 1970s, linoleum cut, sheet: 39½" × 13¾"; image: 37" × 9¾".

El Loko, *Femme Avec Oiseaux,* date unknown, linoleum cut, sheet: 27¾" × 19¾"; image: 19¾" × 14½".

This treatment of forms, which has some parallels in the prints of Nigerian artists Uzo Egonu and Adebisi Fabunmi (see chapters 4 and 6), is typical of the work of all three artists: they use pattern in ways analogous to a jazz progression, that is, pattern evolves through improvisation rather than repetition. Black-white or positive-negative images are often given equal importance. They also have similar ways of uniting adjacent forms, using the edge of one shape to define the edge of another.

These three artists came to their imagery quite independently, and their individual styles are distinctive, but each creates a formidable grid of black and white forms that grow and change to provide the forward-backward locomotion and lacunae of syncopative rhythm.

In a further exploration of the bird theme, El Loko

created a brilliant series of birds. Like demons with large eyes, and in strikingly fierce poses, they seem a part of a wary, but dramatic ballet. While there is a suggestion of three-dimensional form in the treatment of the birds themselves, the landscape they dominate is subsidiary and flat. Rather than function as a background over which they are superimposed, the landscape simply fills space around them. The birds thus reign supreme over interstitial elements that appear as alien landscape.

This landscape, with its implications of confrontation, finds a parallel in El Loko's poetry, which co-exists in a delicate cooperative balance with his visual images. The poetry expresses the same feelings of an encounter with new, alien ways of life, as well as a sense of loss and fear engendered by this confrontation. His poem "Abritt" is a particularly passionate cry:

El Loko, *La Danseuse*, date unknown, linoleum cut, sheet: 27½″ × 19¾″; image: 25¼″ × 16½″.

I want to return to humankind
Return to nature
To live in the misery of the day
To experience the misery in its spectacular cavalcade

I want to return
Return from the dead-end street
I want to turn my back
On the wall which cuts off my way

I want to return
Return to the place
Where my journey had its beginning

I want to return
Where the first sun rays received
The birth of humanity[7]

The poem continues, describing a yearning for source and for the purity of anguish. Other of El Loko's poems speak of the traveler who wanders as an outcast. Both his writing and his painting respond to the challenge of synthesis, rather than bitterness or cynicism. His paintings, prints, and poetry reflect the reality of Africa that is a touchstone for a poet-artist visionary.

As was sometimes the case with early artists who studied abroad, synthesis did not come easily. Two of the first modern sculptors in Ghana, Oku Ampofo (1908–), born in Mampong, and Kofi Antubam (1922–1964), born in Opon Valley, were like Nigeria's Ben Enwonwu, in that their work was often constrained by either foreign or African traditions. Like Enwonwu's work, their sculpture is a part of the environment of their capital city. The counterparts of Enwonwu's piece on the exterior of the Nigerian Museum in Lagos, are Ampofo's piece in front of the Accra Museum and Antubam's carved doors of the Parliament building. However, the late Kobina Bucknor (1924–1975), another Ghanaian artist, took positive strides in the direction of claiming his African identity, and synthesizing elements from past and present, to set a positive example for artists to come.

Ampofo, a physician, "discovered" African art in museums during his medical training in Scotland, then undertook art studies as well. On return to Ghana after six years, he influenced and promoted younger artists, eventually founding the Akwapim 6, a group that has sponsored numerous exhibitions. Antubam started the Ghana Society of Artists and was instrumental in encouraging younger artists.

Both these Ghanaian artists were graduates of the art department of Achimota College (now the University of Ghana at Legon). The art department at Achimota College, begun in 1936, was headed by H. V. Meyerowitz, an artist himself. The department later became a part of the University of Science and Technology in Kumasi.

In 1950 after returning from London where he spent two years studying at Goldsmith College of Art, Antubam became the director of art at Achimota School (a distinguished secondary school), a post he held for fourteen years until his death. Antubam actively promoted the idea that African art was "primitive" and a stage in the development of the truly evolved artist, that is, one who has "progressed" to a realist style of expression. He painted portraits of important Ghanaians and executed commissions such as two murals for the United Nations in Geneva and works in mosaic and wood for the state and for industry.

Ampofo, on the other hand, incorporated with didactic intention elements of classical African origin. Working in both wood and cement, the flowing forms of his cement figures are a successful synthesis of old and new and therefore are more convincing than his woodcarvings, which are stilted with less integrated borrowings. However his turning toward forms of the past surely stimulated many artists who followed.

One of those was Ghana's most important sculptor, Vincent Akwete Kofi (1923–1974). His work, which captured the past and present in a powerful synthesis, conveys a sense of the monumental. The great bulk and the largeness of his works reflect an idea or philosophy; rather than sheer monumentality, the feeling is revelatory and heroic rather than dedicatory.

Born in Odumasi, Kofi was a large and powerful man, who had visions that were larger than life. His pieces conform to the original shape of the wood from which they were carved; like the tree in a clearing, they relate to both earth and sky. Large hands and feet add stability and a sense of volume. Although the figures are expressive in the Western sense, the attitudes are stoic and contained, and in that containment there is power. As Ulli Beier points out, Kofi's *Christ* contrasts dramatically with the usual image of Christ. Instead of "the gentle suffering saviour," this is "the all-powerful God, the rock supporting the world."[8]

Kofi's sculpture of Christ is a valid metaphor for other interpretations, and the preoccupation with symbols that permeate the culture and poetry of Ghana makes it easy to draw a parallel with Awoonor's depiction of Christopher Okigbo's death—also a sacrifice. The words of Kofi Awoonor, written as an elegy to Christopher Okigbo, who was killed in the Nigerian Civil War, came to mind: "He stood there rustling in the wind/The desire to go was written large upon his forehead. . . . He marched into the wind howling through door posts. . . . He was erect like the totem pole of his household. He burned and blazed for an ending."[9] It is an image of strength that Vincent Kofi epitomized and that he hewed from his giant logs.

Kofi studied at the College of Technology in Kumasi, the Royal College of Art in London, and Columbia University in New York. He directed the art department at the Prempeh College in Kumasi, headed the art department at Winneba College, Ghana, and finally taught at the University of Science and Technology in Kumasi. His work was exhibited at the Mbari Club in Oshogbo, Nigeria, and in many exhibitions abroad.

He had very distinct views about art and artists. In his book *Sculpture in Ghana,* he wrote "If we accept outside influence as inevitable . . . no virile artistic tradition will commit cultural suicide by 'brainwashing' itself and rejecting its past completely."[10] Describing the danger of these influences, he says, "Western art is often developed to coldly scientific limits that seem to dominate the poetry," and defines art in Ghana as "an obsession with poetic and spiritual themes. . . . Form will look after itself."[11] Many details in Kofi's sculpture recall traditional forms—the head of the Akua-ba fertility figure, for example—but his achievement is a modern one, a synthesis, and to paraphrase Christopher Okigbo, he was a giant among the poplars.[12]

A younger Ghanaian artist, Nii Ahene-La Mettle-Nunoo, has also lived abroad, spending a number of years in New York, studying at the Printmaking Workshop, and also working at the Weusi Nyumba Ya Sanaa Gallery. His works have been exhibited at the Studio Museum in Harlem, in New York, the National Museum of African Art in Washington, D.C., and at the Africa Centre in London.

Encouraged by the late Kofi Antubam, Mettle-Nunoo became a member of the Ghanaian Pioneers. In this group he was inspired to work with his hands, making leather goods. He describes his beginnings: "My grand-

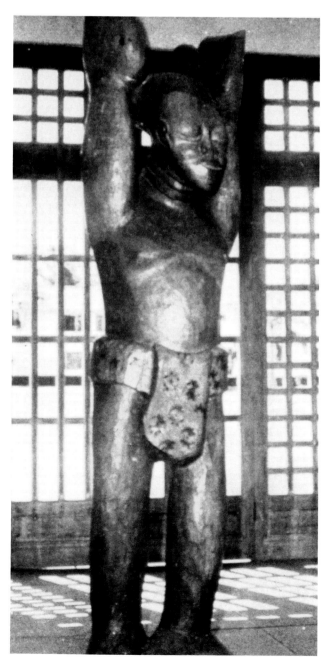

Vincent Kofi, *Christ,* early 1960s, wood. Legon University.

Nii Ahene-La Mettle-Nunoo, *Arrow of God*, 1973, viscosity etching, 13" × 9¾".

mother also influenced me. She didn't understand anything about it, but she was interested and used to ask me what I was doing. But still she influenced me. I used to admire the sculpture of Kofi Antubam, which was at the Young Pioneers' headquarters where I was a member. Then I came in contact with this man and he influenced my work. I used to go the museum to look at his work."[13]

Like Onobrakpeya, Mettle-Nunoo has mastered the intricacies of intaglio and other printmaking techniques, such as embossing. Also like Onobrakpeya, he draws on traditional art forms, using them in rich embroidery-like patterns in etchings like *African Heritage, Ancestral Liberation,* and *Arrow of God*—the latter inspired by Chinua Achebe's novel of the same name. He points out that his art evolved through studying "the visual documentation of old African art, seeing it in museums and galleries, and then finally [finding] my own interpretive style. I therefore am able to work independently of my 'roots'."

Mettle-Nunoo points out that African artists are now often "cosmopolitan." However, he says that "as a Pan-African artist," his art still relates to the past, and is "ethnographic in form and spirit." Some of the older artists, he explains, were "Euro-centric" and "not Pan-African artists, but definitely of the pre-independent

mold . . . even though the[ir] subjects were generally African."[14]

He describes the aims of an artist: "a creator whose primary goal is to satisfy a curious visual need," who has "the desire to reinterpret nature or environment—natural or otherwise," and "whose work reflects a functional or spiritual purpose." But as an African artist, he says, "I see my work as a continuation of the past—a conduit through which our present generation can appreciate and understand traditional art, bearing in mind that the medium of interpretation is different." He believes that contemporary African art must carry a message. "It may, however, take any form to meet our own individual intellectual and sensual needs."[15]

There are, of course, numerous other artists—Kobina Bucknor (1924–1975) and Charlotte Hagan (1938–), for example, who specialize in textile design; and Meshack Asare, who writes and illustrates children's books for which he has won several prizes. Asare exhibits in London as does El Anatsui (1944–), an artist who works in wood, clay, and glass, using them in new contexts. Anatsui's exhibitions occasionally incorporate photography as "visual interpretations and enhancements" of his work.[16]

Anatsui slashes wood with a power saw, an idea that came to him at an art retreat in Cummington, Massachusetts. He then carves it, and sometimes employs a "pyro-technique" to engrave it. His sculptures, suggestive and evocative, have an organic flexibility that allows for the re-arranging of individual segments within a composition. He has discovered in roughly sawed pieces of wood an exciting medium that responds to his feeling for natural, traditional materials: "Nature's materials to me have more authenticity and substance than synthetic ones, which seek to imitate anything, have neither a culture of their own nor identity. . . . An intimate acquaintance with wood as an art medium makes one feel it must have a soul, a resident spirit, force. It certainly has a clear identity, a language, a presence which is entirely its own. . . ."[17]

One group of his works explores "decay, break up, delapidation. These phenomena are looked at not from the negative . . . perspective but rather as prerequisites for re-creation and growth."[18] Anatsui belongs to the Aka group of artists in eastern Nigeria, where he exhibits, and he also teaches at the University of Nigeria. In 1990 he was one of ten African artists whose work was chosen for The Studio Museum's Contemporary African Artists: Changing Tradition exhibition. He and other Ghanaian artists are branching out, experimenting with media and establishing precedents.

A new medium and direction characterize the work of Christian Lattier (1925–1977), who originated a unique African-inspired style. Born in Grande Lahou, Ivory Coast, Lattier was educated in Catholic schools. In 1947 he entered the École des Beaux-Arts in Paris, where he studied sculpture and architecture. In 1953 he began to create sculptures with rope and metal armatures, winning a prize for a giant panther figure fabricated with these materials.

The prize reimbursed his five years' tuition at the École des Beaux-Arts. Subsequently hired to work on the reconstruction of French Romanesque and Gothic cathedrals, he took part in the restoration of Chartres in 1956. In spite of his long years abroad, Lattier's sculptures, like the paintings and prints of El Loko, are inherently African.

Lattier's first one-person show took place at the Beaux-Arts Gallery in Paris in 1959. The same year he participated in the Salon de Jeune Sculpture at the Musée Rodin in the Paris Biennale. Other exhibits in Munich and Rome followed. In 1962 he finally returned to Ivory Coast where he became professor of sculpture at the National School of Beaux-Arts of Abidjan.

In 1963 Lattier had his first exhibition in Ivory Coast in the Hotel de Ville. The following year he was invited to make a study tour of the United States. Lattier had a second exhibit in 1965, and in 1966 he won the grand prize for all disciplines at the Dakar World Festival of Negro Art.

Primarily a sculptor, Lattier invented his own medium. Using fiber—usually associated with baskets, blankets, or rugs—he crochets rope over iron armatures to make sculptures that are African in appearance and spirit, but new in concept. His pieces enclose space, spread outwards with looped feelers, and rise to life-size or larger. They often incorporate several figures that function together in an intricate association of volumes and linear elements. The fact that the larger forms are not closely wound with rope allows for the involvement of inner space as well.

These organic qualities suggest an analogy with music. Lattier's interest in jazz is consistent with his sense of improvisation. One figure spawns smaller figures; one form generates other adjunct forms, resulting in a total complex of interdependent but fluid images that have a dynamic, kinetic presence. Tautly constructed of graceful, buoyant shapes, the iron armature and the natural texture and color of the rope counter the buoyancy.

Although they are three-dimensional and monochromatic, their forms relate to those of neighboring Senegalese tapestries and to familiar Ivory Coast traditions: a Dan Ngere mask surrounded by a ruff of raffia, the lines of a Korhogo cloth image, the projecting forms of a Senufo mask, the linear structure of cast metal, a network of strip loom threads, the tall shape of a woven granary, and the total effect of a costumed masquerader. Lattier creates fiber sculptures that evoke these known elements, but his work, in spite of its inferences, has created a unique precedent.

Lattier has as his memorial his public works, which include the exterior decoration of the City Hall in the capital city, Abidjan; a bas-relief mural in wood at la Caisse de Stabilisation, a major bank also in Abidjan; a low-relief sculpture in metal for the Maison des Ingenieurs in Treichville; and two murals in the Abidjan airport, one of concrete and the other of rope. However, many of his smaller works are not being preserved.

Like Lattier, Kofi, and El Loko, Omar Al Shabu of Liberia has traveled widely. He too translates his experiences into African structures with intimations of nature. He sees the canvas, in much the way that Lattier sees his materials, as the basis from which forms grow.

His loosely arranged shapes are congruent parts of a carefully conceived whole. Sometimes forms touch; sometimes they miss, or jostle each other, creating tensions. Often shapes appear broken or disconnected, but related like parts of a puzzle that are slightly awry.

In *Festival of Ancestors, Ancestor,* and *I Beg You* forms that look like piles of volcanic stones—some soft and rounded, some crumbling at the edges—generate energy. The result is like an ancient cairn which, although tilting and ready to topple, is a sculptural entity.

A deft colorist, Al Shabu uses color to build these entities, identifying each form by means of color. He organizes forms in swatches, close in value or closely related, such as black, brown, and gray. Then, as if to underline the tension, he introduces a sliver of bright, contrasting color and small patterns, like shreds of fabric.

Omar Al Shabu, *Festival of Ancestors,* date unknown, oil, 43" × 43". Collection of Yvonne Clark, Detroit.

Omar Al Shabu, *I Beg You*, date unknown, acrylic on canvas, 30″ × 20″. Collection of Dr. Eugene Hancock, New York City.

Reminiscent of musical counterpoint, which grows to a crescendo and then dissolves in a riff, his forms build and coalesce with a result suggestive of jazz, or of the process and juxtapositions of painter Romare Bearden. But Al Shabu's works do not share the same definition one sees in Bearden's works. A certain ambiguity tempts interpretation, but also defies it. With these loose formations, Al Shabu intimates and refers, ultimately allowing multiple meanings to emerge.

Much smaller than either Liberia or Ivory Coast, Gambia has produced few visual artists. Alhaji Bai Konte, a master musician who plays a twenty-one-stringed instrument, the kora, is probably Gambia's most famous musical artist. Also, in spite of the geographical affinity of Senegal, which has produced many contemporary artists, and Gambia, and the political federation known as Senegambia, there is a dramatic difference between the work of artist Momodou Ceesay (1944–), a Wolof and well-known Gambian painter, and the artists of Senegal. The Wolofs are also the majority people of Senegal, and their art, with its sense of solidity, seems designed for architectural purpose. Ceesay's painting is gentle, bucolic, almost ethereal.

Filled with the lilting tracery of leaves and tree branches, it is intended for close, intimate viewing.

Threads of color and wisps of design in a painting like *Njabot (Family)* give Ceesay's watercolors a romantic feeling of leaves rustling and air moving. His sensitivity to line and space contributes to the balance. The patterning, so prominent in modern Senegalese works, is here subjugated to the other elements and at the same time seems to flow from them.

Ceesay was educated in England at Suffield Academy and in the United States at Wesleyan University, where he received a bachelor of arts degree in literature and languages. Later he was artist-in-residence at the National Center of African-American Artists in Boston. He has had one-person shows in the United States, Nigeria, Senegal, Ghana, Jamaica, Colombia, Thailand, and Formosa.

His definition of the arts does not "acknowledge any basis for rationality. . . . Much of Western art, he feels, attempts to make a definitive statement, to distinguish itself, to be original. Ironically, such restrictions inhibit the freedom of expression, and spontaneity becomes impossible. In other words, that which strives to be original can never be." He sees the function of modern African art as representing the changing values in African life, and in "defense of cultural rather than political identity."[19] His own visions have as their basis a fundamental agility, which should allow him to express his principles.

These ever-present issues of freedom of expression, changing values, and African identity—the preoccupation of all African writers and artists—are discussed by South African writer Es'kia Mphahlele. Like Vincent Kofi, he describes the African predicament, but adds, "The African, even while seeking an equilibrium, as indeed he must, can accommodate change. Here lie both the strength and the weakness of our humanism. . . . We often have to use the foreigner's techniques and art forms to enrich our art, to release it and thus make it available to more of our people. In the process we make the techniques ours. . . ." He also quotes Ghanaian poet Kofi Awoonor, "'stop at the house of the moon/And pause to relearn the wisdom of our fathers.' For we daren't despise 'the magic of being ourselfs.'"[20] This balancing feat is one which El Loko, Vincent Kofi, Nii Ahene-La Mettle-Nunoo, Christian Lattier, Omar Al Shabu, and Momodou Ceesay have confronted and more often than not resolved.

III

Crescent in the Hand

8 Artists of the Image and Loom

Senegal

The World Festival of Negro Arts was held in Dakar, Senegal, in 1966, and it had an enormous impact on contemporary art in Africa. Reviewing the festival in *Nigeria Magazine,* editor Onuora Nzekwu called it a jamboree. It was a celebration and an opportunity to emphasize the contextual nature of African art; it brought together, socially, culturally, and politically, Africa and the diaspora. For the first time a world- and continent-wide gathering of artists from Africa and of African descent took place. It featured a spectacular display of their creative accomplishments in the performing and visual arts as well as a colloquium of scholars, including such luminaries as Aimé Césaire and Alioune Diop.[1] It was also a pulling together of the diaspora, a time when American ambassador Mercer Cook, introducing Duke Ellington and his band, recited the poetry of Léopold Sédar Senghor, the then-president of Senegal: "Just play me solitude, Duke,/And let me cry myself to sleep."[2]

For a number of reasons Dakar was an appropriate place for this celebration, not least among them the influence of the Negritude movement and its spokesman, President Senghor. The fact that Senghor himself saw emphasis on the arts as a necessity for development, defining development itself as different from economic growth, has helped create an atmosphere conducive to artistic activity.[3] The evidence exists in the 1979–80 exhibition that included 170 works produced during the previous 15 years by 73 Senegalese artists and that traveled to Canada, Mexico, France, and the United States. The ongoing support by the government and the personal encouragement of various artists by President Senghor are important reasons why Senegalese arts are now flourishing.

A number of new institutions have also encouraged artists in Senegal. Early contributions were made by the Musée Dynamique, which displayed art from around the continent; the Daniel Sorano Theatre Company; and the National Arts Institute. Prominent now is the Manufacture Nationale des Tapisseries at Thiès; its forerunner was the Plastic Arts Center, which Pierre Lods (see chapter 10) started with government support in 1957 as a village of artisans at Soumbedioune in Dakar. The Manufacture Nationale des Tapisseries is a complex composed of a school of fine arts, a gallery, a cultural center, and a workshop with many looms and forty weavers, and a number of resident painters, among them Papa Sidi Diop, Mamadou Niang, Abdoulaye Ndiaye, and Ousmane Faye. The complex, which has an impressive production, is the source of a movement that trains artists and weavers. The weavers execute designs of artists in residence as well as designs by others.

The modern expressions fostered by these institutions and those that have developed in various other ways are rich in association. They blend elements of Islamic, Euro-Christian, and indigenous African traditions. Art historian Peter Mark, writing about the delicate process of selecting Western elements—technology or media, for example—believes that this fusion is one of the most important dynamics behind the new movement. He also sees the movement as based on two traditional forms: music and fabric dyeing.[4]

The region has always had a variety of artistic traditions. During the thirteenth and fourteenth centuries there was some influence from the great eastern empires of Manding and from the Wolof Empire of Senegal. An Islamic order, which continued to spread, was established in the late 1600s, and in the late 1800s French incursions began. Some pre-Islamic masquerades, legends, and other rituals, however, are still extant, and some have re-emerged, having been hidden during the centuries when indigenous culture was beleaguered by foreign encroachments. These encroachments included attempts at de-culturalization by the French; interventions from Christian missionaries, for whom traditional carving was a sign of heresy; and influences of Islam, which discouraged representation of the human figure.

While the immediate past does not offer the same imagistic influences that exist in some West African cultures, the Islamic heritage is reflected in the rich patterns and forms of silver and gold jewelry, leather, pottery, embroidery, printed and woven cloth, and in the decoration on sea-going pirogues. The markets are, and always have been, centers for these crafts as well as for artifacts from surrounding countries. Clothing and women's elaborately sculptured hair styles are also important art forms. The men are famous for their flowing boubous and the women for their gold bangles, head ties, and billowing gauze, voile, or silk gowns.

Hundreds of Islamic symbols and calligraphic characters form a visual vocabulary for Senegalese artists, just as early Coptic symbols and Amharic calligraphy do for Ethiopian artists. Even the most modern imagery has these ancient sources. The paintings and tapestries of the accomplished artists in their twenties and thirties are proof of a creativity that has burgeoned into a prolific modern movement in a short twenty years, gaining international notice in the sixties.

The imagery of these artists is closely related to traditional West African forms, for example, Yoruba, Senufo, or Dogon carvings. Aware of the distance between traditional art, which could not be separated from a whole life system, and contemporary art, with an aesthetic raison d'être, the artists used Negritude as a cornerstone in an effort to reflect in modern expression those "essences" considered most profoundly African.[5] The philosophy of Negritude provided elements of mutual identification among Senegalese artists. Founded by Léopold Sédar Senghor of Senegal, Aimé Césaire of Martinique, and Léon Damas of French Guiana, it was a reaction to the injustices of colonialism and to the policy of de-culturalization and French acculturation.

As a tool for the affirmation of what were considered African values, Negritude identifies its tenets most specifically as the spiritual values associated with ancestors, the supporting role of the extended family, the beauty of the African woman, the presence of rhythm defined by Senghor as "the architecture of being," and the maintenance of balance—all of which were the anchors of the new movement.[6]

The policy of acculturation and assimilation practiced by the French revealed the fallacies on which it was based. When African intellectuals aspired to parity in French society, they found instead alienation. Gerald Moore and Ulli Beier in *Modern Poetry from Africa* speak of the "acceptance [of the African]—on certain terms—by a metropolitan white society. This society was quite prepared to forgive him his colour just so long as he would clothe it decently in the culture, religion and manners of a Western civilization. . . . Thus the policy of assimilation was to turn the attention of the assimilé back upon the one factor which the colonizer wanted him to forget—his blackness." The movement of Negritude was "simultaneously one of rejection and assertion."[7] The assertion helped foster a new awareness, a climate sympathetic to the arts.

The philosophy of Negritude is articulated in poetry, especially that of Senghor, who uses images such as "hands gentler than fur," "the soft flowering of lips," "the ancestor whose stormy hide is shot with lightning and thunder," and "your blue metallic eyes, your frosted smile"[8] to praise both the African woman and the ancestor and to reject the values of the West. His poetry also came to preface, with a kind of synaesthesia, the visual artist. Senghor, Césaire, and others in the movement inspired a generation of writers and artists both inside and outside the country.

However, Negritude, which was not the only force for inspiration, also found opposition in Senegal and in the African world, especially from English-speaking countries where intellectuals Wole Soyinka and Kofi Awoonor took exception to the idea that the African artistic sensibility could be contained in a formula.

Another strong force for inspiration was the need for social revolution articulated by writer-filmmaker Ousmane Sembene, who opposed Negritude. His films and others from Senegal are now internationally recognized. In fact, *The Christian Science Monitor* on February 23, 1978, published a review by David Sterritt headlined: "Hollywood's Unlikely New Cinema Rival—Senegal." In the same year the Museum of Modern Art in New York held a film series, "Senegal: Fifteen Years of an African Cinema, 1962–1977."

Among the earliest of these filmmakers, Ousmane Sembene was described by Jack Kroll of *Newsweek* as "one of the most remarkable artists in the world."[9] In addition to strong social content, Sembene's films, with an insistence on cultural references and symbols, offer interesting insights into the feeling for these elements also characteristic of Senegalese painters and tapestry designers. Sembene says, "We're now trying to create films on two levels—a simpler level and a more profound one."[10]

Sembene's film *Cheddo* is an example of this effort: interspersing the narrative action with sequences, which are dream states, during which the characters focus on imaginary episodes in the future. Another of his films, *Tawo,* depicts a young job-seeker whose dreams manifest his anxiety about what is going to happen to him, with several possibilities such as confinement in a jail or a mental hospital as envisioned scenarios. His film *Emitai* includes visions of the gods coming to participate in a ritual held while an old chief is dying. In Sembene's *Xala* a mask is turned upside down and passed around the table at a board meeting as a receptacle into which votes are cast. In this out-of-context situation, the mask as a symbol of traditional values underlines the corruption of some entrepreneurs. In the same film a lifeless mannequin, dressed in a bride's wedding gown, is a satiric comment on the husband-to-be's impotence.

Although Sembene's cinematic style has been characterized as neo-realist, the use of symbols is a profound element in all of his films. The mask, for example, recurs throughout *Black Girl* (*La Noir de . . .*), a black and white film, to emphasize the black-white dynamic that is central to the film's theme. Sembene also uses black and white visual elements to stress the conflict and ultimately to illustrate the destructive impact of white domination. "Through image rather than dialogue, Sembene exposes their interpersonal relations. . . ."[11] The most powerful illustration of this function is the depiction of the suicide at the end of the picture: the camera frames a white porcelain tub in which the body of the black woman floats as blood from her self-inflicted wound stains the water.

In contrast to the obvious political and social concerns inherent in many Senegalese films, the work of Senegalese painters seems apolitical, and often decorative. The artists, especially those designing for the Manufacture Nationale des Tapisseries, create a modern mythology, using symbols, bold colors, and highly stylized forms. Generally, however, it is the filmmakers of Senegal who have produced work that has the satirical power of Nigerian Demas Nwoko, the poetic strength of Sudanese Ibrahim El Salahi, and the emotional impact of South Africans Msabla Dumile and Cyprian Shilakoe. Nevertheless, the visual artists have created a style that is easily recognized as Senegalese. This style, which frequently reveals the tenets of Negritude, reflects its African origin, and within it there exists a wide range of expression.

Senegalese glass painting illustrates one facet of the range of expression. It came to Senegal via Islam from Europe and Persia during the nineteenth century. At first its subjects were religious, from the Koran or Bible.

Many of them were traceable to Persia, and they included legendary heroes Cheikh Amadou Bamba, the founder of the Mouride Brotherhood and the subject of many miracle stories, and al-Burāq, the Prophet Muhammad's winged horse.[12] Glass painting has now become a popular art form that uses other topical subjects; although threatened by a tourist public, it is still some of the strongest and most interesting art in the country.

However, the history of contemporary art in Senegal can be said to begin with artists who, like other early West African artists, were born in the early 1900s before the Negritude movement began. Although these artists did not start to exhibit their work until the sixties and seventies, one of them, Cheikh Mahone Diop (1918–), was already self-taught and making sculptures by the lost-wax process in 1944. Another, Mbor Faye, who was born in 1900 and created portraits such as his *Chef de Canton* and *Marabout Portrait I,* first exhibited in the Art Senegalais d'Aujourd'hui exhibition at the Grand Palais in Paris in 1974. His boldly designed paintings radiate the same direct beauty of early Senegalese glass paintings. He has since participated in many group shows and finally, in 1977, had a one-person show in Dakar.

Other early artists who bridged two worlds, Alpha W. Diallo and Mafaly Sene, were born in 1927 and 1935 respectively, and died in the seventies. Diallo painted historic episodes that were carefully composed and call to mind, because of their mood and drama, the work of African American Horace Pippin. Diallo's painting *Cheikh Ahmadou Bamba* has an impressive sense of the moment and the authority of documentary film. Sene's painting *Slave House in Gorée* is a tableau closer to the films of Sembene than to the work of most other painters.

Another pioneer, Iba Ndiaye, who was born in 1928 in Saint-Louis Island and has lived in Paris for many years, returns periodically to Senegal to teach. Having special insights into the non-African world, he has articulated the position of the African artist clearly and eloquently. "Curiously that Africans who study abroad are no longer considered 'authentically' African. . . . I have no desire to be fashionable," he says. "Certain Europeans seeking exotic thrills, expect me to serve them folklore. I refuse to do it—otherwise I would exist only as a function of their segregationist ideas of the African artist. These ideas confine the artist to the domains of the naive, the insolite, the surreal and the art du bizzare. . . . Above all painting for me . . . [is a way] of combat, a way of expressing my concept of the world."[13]

Ndiaye's work does not parallel any of the styles associated with most Senegalese artists. His canvases have a thick painterly texture and evoke a feeling of tragedy, desolation, and the loneliness of nomadic existence. His art is not self-consciously African in style;

Mbor Faye, *Ndaanaan Portrait II*, 1978, oil on canvas, 24" × 20⅝". Private collection, courtesy of Embassy of Senegal.

many talented artists ever since, and says that "the young artists" of Senegal "regard no Western art movement as primary sources of inspiration."[14] "He feels that young painters attach too much importance to details, and encourages them to be freer, to interpret nature without attempting to reproduce it."[15]

Tall's facility for line is one of the most prominent features of his drawings. In contrast to the sense of calligraphy one sees in the work of Ibrahim El Salahi (see chapter 9), Tall's *Lac Interiere* presents a network of lines that move, flow, and tumble. References to waterfalls, to clouds, and to outer space abound; and sometimes god and goddess-like figures emerge. His drawings are decorative explorations.

When Tall paints and designs for tapestry, his imagery expands. It is easy to understand his affinity for jazz; in *Judu Bu Rafet*, he uses color in the way that a musician improvises with sound. In explorative forays, he embellishes the overall design with finials, spirals, and decorative arabesques of color. Sometimes detail is sharpened

Mafaly Sene, *Slave House in Gorée*, 1975, oil on canvas, 48" × 32¼". Collection of the Government of Senegal.

rather his style is expressionist in character and African in content.

Papa Ibra Tall, like Ndiaye, has played an important role as teacher. Tall, whose contributions include the founding and directorship of the Manufactures National des Tapisseries at Thiès from 1965 to 1975, is considered the dean of Sengalese artists.

Born in 1935 at Tivaouane, he exhibited an artistic bent at an early age, winning prizes in secondary school, and finally obtaining a scholarship to study architecture in Paris. After spending hours reading about African art during a hospital stay, Tall began his study of painting at the École des Beaux-Arts in Paris. Later he explored tapestry, ceramics, and graphic arts at the Centre Pedagogie Artistique de Sèvres.

Returning to Senegal, Tall became a professor of art and, finally, head of the department of research in black plastic-arts at the École des Beaux-Arts of Dakar. He has been active in encouraging, teaching, and promoting

Papa Ibra Tall, *Projection Spatiale III,* date unknown, pencil drawing, dimensions unknown. Location unknown.

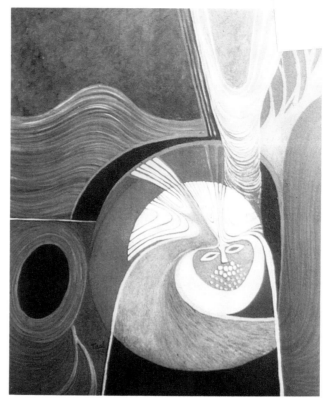

Papa Ibra Tall, *Cosmic Vigil,* 1978, oil, 47⅛″ × 39⅜″. Collection of the Government of Senegal.

and color is heightened by the use of a black ground. However, his art is primarily decorative, lacking the profundity associated with the work of artist Ibrahim El Salahi.

In 1975, Papa Ibra Tall retired from the directorship of the tapestry center at Thiès and became a technical advisor to, and painter for, the Ministry of Culture. He has exhibited on five continents and works in many media, including serigraph, and is a book illustrator as well. One of his major tapestries is at the United Nations headquarters in New York, and others are owned by the World Bank.

Tall believes that "African art is best expressed in a decorative mode, that it ought to be popular like mural paintings seen in the streets in black American communities." He sees tapestry-making as an appropriate step in this direction. Like Iba Ndiaye, he feels the perspective afforded by his foreign experiences has increased his respect for and understanding of the talent, needs, and potentials of African artists.[16]

The rhythm so evident in Tall's work characterizes that of other Senegalese artists like Souleymane Keita. Born in 1947, Keita is a painter, printmaker, and ceramicist who was head of the ceramics workshop at Soumbedioune, Dakar. In his work he interprets life on the island of Gorée, once a notorious slave-trading station and now a picturesque retreat where he lives. Like Tall, Keita is inspired by jazz, using color as a tool for improvisation. His obvious talent during his early schooling admitted him to the École des Beaux-Arts, Dakar, without having attended secondary school. He has completed a group of large murals for the airport in Libreville, Gabon, and for other government buildings in Gabon.

Richly patterned surfaces, strong designs, brilliant colors, sweeping lines, and rhythmic forms characterize the work of the other artists who work with, or design for, the atelier at Thiès, where tapestries are woven in the Aubusson manner. Mamadou Wade, one of the designers, and Ousmane Faye, who has his own workshop, were both trained in France at Aubusson. Prominent linear configurations, bold images, and a bold scale are also typical of the tapestries, as is the iconic authority of imagery based on African classical sculpture, especially Senufo. These tapestries are often enormous; when they

Bacary Dieme, *Couple,* 1978, tapestry, 78⅞" × 115". Collection of the Government of Senegal.

streams to dig for crabs. Later he began to paint designs on the walls of his house."[18] Although Dieme studied under Iba Ndiaye at the École des Beaux-Arts, Dakar, and under the Brazilian painter Wilson Tiberio in Senegal, his work shows little influence from either artist.

In *Couple,* the quality of line and pattern inherent in Dieme's drawings translates effectively to tapestry and retains a certain transparency. This characteristic is enhanced by soft edges associated with hand-woven ikat thread. Freely drawn outlines allow the background to merge or alternate with the imagery. Dieme has exhibited at the Elan Gallery in Washington, D.C., as well as in the major exhibition of Senegalese art, which traveled internationally in 1980 and 1981.

More architectonic, the tapestries of Ansoumana Diedhiou illustrate the principle of rhythm by the repetition of color and by the juxtaposition of straight lines and sweeping curves. In *Les Courbeaux* (*The Ravens*) patterns are relieved by large uninterrupted spaces, which heighten the soft texture of the yarn. Straight lines radiate from the central bird figures, which also revolve

Ansoumana Diedhiou, *Les Courbeaux* (*The Ravens*), 1977, tapestry, 103⅛" × 74⅞". Collection of the Government of Senegal.

were shown in the New Orleans Museum of Art, some hung the full height of the walls and had to be partially draped on the floor.

Given this grand scale, the function of the patterns is apparent: they strengthen the power to project. The availability of imported dyes, according to Peter Mark, also reflects the influence of Papa Ibra Tall and Pierre Lods, who in 1957 started the Plastic Art Center in Soumbedioune, Dakar. Mark argues that color and pattern function to create rhythm in the absence of music and dance, both of which were always integral to traditional art forms.[17] Most of the artists associated with Thiès are both painters and tapestry designers. The best work is exciting and many are overtly African in spirit.

For Bacary Dieme, forms as much as colors are the rhythmic medium. A Bainunk born in 1947, he grew up among the Diola, and his imagery reflects the traditions of both peoples. In 1978 he explained to Peter Mark that as a child he would "sculpt pottery and figurines out of clay when he and his friends went to . . . tidal

Ansoumana Diedhiou, *Khounolba,* 1977, tapestry, 85¼" × 58". Collection of the Government of Senegal.

Abdoulaye Ndaiye, *Bamba et Lat Dior,* 1973, tapestry, 87⅜" × 146½". Collection of the Government of Senegal.

around the original axis of the tree trunk or limb. Bright though the colors are, they are combined with elegant subtlety: purple shapes outlined with fine red-orange lines and lavender shapes with fine white lines are thrown into relief by the sharp black heads of the birds. In Diedhiou's tapestries *Khounolba* and *Le Diamate,* complex networks of forms are animated by the contrast of dark velvety areas and brilliant white details.

Born a Diola in the Casamance areas in southwestern Senegal, Diedhiou (1949–) played an important role at the Manufacture Nationale des Tapisseries. He said in an interview with Peter Mark in 1978, "I draw inspiration from my dreams, to build my compositions." And like Bruce Onobrakpeya of Nigeria, he seeks "to show things about [my people] because these are important and powerful things. And I worry. I don't want any of our customs to be forgotten. I would like the deeds of our elders to be known and to be seen as good."[19]

Like Ansoumana Diedhiou, Boubacar Coulibaly (1944–1982), who was born in Dakar, has a style that is recognizably Senegalese and, like Diedhiou, his use of color is a major distinguishing factor. Nevertheless there are great differences between the two. While Diedhiou's work is crisp and architectural with each area defined by a color, Coulibaly's is soft with numerous colors within one area, and has a lively impasto surface. Each color contrasts with an adjacent hue or is intensified by glimpses of underpainting. Like jazz themes playing off each other, color and classical African forms are ingredients for his innovation. Pieced together like a mosaic, color is vibrant and jewel-like. Both *World of Masks* and *Meeting of the Masks* have the mystical quality of script in a Persian miniature.

Abdoulaye Ndaiye (1936–), like Tall, was born in Tivaouane. Ndaiye was a member of the generation caught between the worlds of East and West. He has a pronounced feeling for pattern and design, and his success in creating mural-like tapestries is evident in *Bamba et Lat Dior.*

Ibou Diouf (1953–), like Tall and Ndaiye, was born in Tivaouane, and he has been called "the young wolf of painting."[20] The large and intricate designs of Diouf's tapestries, which are similar to Tall's in style, demonstrate how scale itself acts as an important aesthetic element. The impact of *Les Trois Épouses,* with a soft fibrous texture, brilliant color, and enlarged images incorporating classical forms of African sculpture, is that of a mural.

Diouf describes his meeting with Tall and his influence, "I know that this will surprise you, but I was never attracted by painting. You see, then I was a child. I loved to draw, no matter what, no matter where. In 1964 I met an instructor [Tall] who was in some way my Pygmalion. It was he who demanded of me many drawings for the purpose of illustrating his course of

Ibou Diouf, *Les Trois Épouses,* 1974, tapestry, 143⅜" × 186".
Collection of the Government of Senegal.

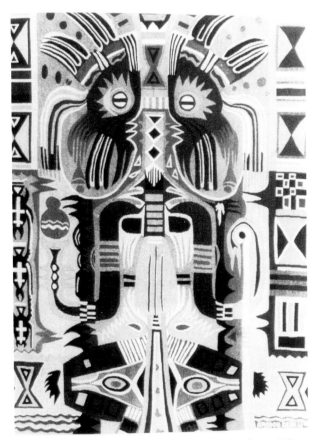

Amadou Dédé Ly, *Kocc Barma,* 1977, tapestry, 93" × 70½".
Collection of the Government of Senegal.

lessons." While working for Papa Ibra Tall, Diouf did substitute work for him on a stage set project Tall had undertaken at the Daniel Sorano Theatre, a major institution supporting the arts, and thus discovered an occupation that came to him quite easily. "I would never have come to painting, if it had not come to me, in the person of Papa Ibra Tall," he says. Instead he had dreamed of being a doctor or lawyer. In 1966 Ibou Diouf, who designed the symbol for the first World Festival of Negro Arts, was awarded the festival's grand prize for tapestry. It was at this time that he began to work directly for Sorano, and also developed a passion for painting.[21] Though the imagery in Diouf's painting is different from that in Tall's—humorous, for example; decorative characteristics are common to the work of both artists.

In an article in the *Sénégal Carrefour,* Diouf at twenty-two is described as the leading Senegalese artist after Papa Ibra Tall and Iba Ndaiye.[22] His inclusion in numerous exhibits all over the world indicates that he is fulfilling his early promise.

Amadou Dédé Ly has also had a meteoric career. Born in 1955 in Dakar, he was already exhibiting at the age of eighteen. His large tapestry named for the early Wolof philosopher, Kocc Barma, shows an impressive grasp of design elements, combining them in fascinating interlocking ways, much like the geometry of an oriental rug. In fact design elements join with other, more figurative forms in an imaginative synthesis.

While the work of these artists has figurative or sculptural forms, several artists combine them with another African sensibility: the integration of aspects of one or more creatures to create zoomorphic archetypes. Those invented by Cherif Thiam, born in Louga in 1951, and by Maodo Niang, born in Tivaouane in 1949, have mythical qualities like the images of Uche Okeke or Samuel Ojo Omonaiye of Nigeria. In *From Reality to Mystery,* Thiam creates a crocodile on top of which are two masklike heads. Though working in ink, his drawings have thickly patterned surfaces typical of tapestry design. His oil painting *The Third Was a Witness* is less tightly controlled; color is handled generously, like watercolor, and the work, like his others, projects an enigmatic quality, which recalls the paintings of Valente Malangatana of Mozambique (see chapter 11).

Niang's tapestry *Ndiougoup (Bat)* is a cluster of prickly forms—an abstract arrangement that imbues the subject with nervous energy. Niang employs a certain restraint; in contrast to the dynamic qualities of the image, the background is a simple complementary space.

Amadou Seck, born in 1951 in Dakar, is another artist who combines forms to create archetypal images. Seck's tapestry *Horseman and Bird* and his oil painting *Bird-Man* feature composite figures that recall the zoomorphic and metamorphic sculptures of the Shona artists of Zim-

Cherif Thiam, *From Reality to Mystery,* date unknown, ink, 26¼"
× 20⅜". Collection of the Government of Senegal.

Badara Camara, *Invitation,* 1978, tapestry, 63⅛" × 111¼".
Collection of the Government of Senegal.

babwe (see chapter 13). Fierce and imposing, they are
constructed of blocklike forms cut across by linear bands
of color. Pattern is a tightly constructed integral element,
not superimposed. Seck emphasizes texture and natural
colors, which he obtains by mixing organic ingredients
with pigments.

"There is no doubt we are using a mix of Western
and African ideas," he says. "However the borrowing is
not conscious. We are not uncomfortable with this
because African society always had many contradictions.
Dakar, for example, is a modern city but the villages
continue to hold on to the old customs. The important
thing is that our artists have not lost their identity. They
are still whole in themselves."[23] "We have returned to
our own sources, to our own personality," he goes on to
explain, reiterating, like Mphahlele, the idea that there
is an openness to select from "the good values of the
West."[24]

The work of most Senegalese artists is so unmistaka-
bly African in style, form, composition, and color that it
is difficult to point to influences from the West. Badara
Camara, Samba Balde, and Daouda Diouck create abstractions that might be compared to Western painting,
but their source is Africa. The use of empty space in a
complementary way is characteristic of their work.
Badara Camara (1947–), a native of Thiès, is the head
of the Technical and Artistic Division, Decorative Arts
Enterprises at Thiès. His abstract designs for tapestries
are striking in their simplicity, a deception in that it
relies on a subtle arrangement of forms. His *Invitation* is
visually balanced with colors, proportions, a precise
division of elements, and carefully conceived relationships, which carry obvious references to classical
African forms.

Samba Balde, born in Botto in 1950, was graduated
in plastic arts from the Plastic Arts Research Section,
National School of Arts. His work has some of the same
boldness as Camara's and a sense of freedom like Seck's.
He also often reduces imagery to elemental terms, using
strokes with the authority of a calligrapher. Unlike
Ahmed Mohammed Shibrain of Sudan, who works with
calligraphy alone and explodes the forms (see chapter
9), Balde begins with a subject like a mask or Tjiwara
(antelope) sculpture, which he then evolves into calligraphic forms. The designs present a challenge between
the subject and the calligraphic forms.

Like Seck and Balde, Daouda Diouck also uses a solid
ground to enhance his sweeping line. Born in 1951 in
Dakar, Diouck has exhibited widely since 1974. In his
tapestry *Tann,* he encloses a rich aggregation of forms
within an image, as does Adebisi Fabunmi of Nigeria. In
contrast to the intricate division of space typical of
Fabunmi's compositions, however, Diouck's imagery is
vigorous and expansive. In *Tann,* the firm outer bound-
ary intensifies the pressure of the swirling forms within.
The uncluttered, soft gray background conveys a directness of statement not always found in works of the
other artists who use pattern throughout their compositions. He also restricts his palette and, in so doing,
exploits a strength acquired by accepting limits. In another tapestry, *The Lonely One,* pattern is minimal and
subtle. A silhouetted, attenuated torso with superimposed jagged woundlike designs dominates the space.
Brittle edges and skewed forms define the image as
fragile and vulnerable. The adjacent white areas sharpen
the sense of desolation.

A number of artists escape categories and might be
described as having a more impressionistic style.
Ousmane Faye, born in 1940 in Dakar, is one of these.
The imagery in his painting *Forêt* and in his tapestry *Le
Bourgeon (The Bud)* is personal, with gentle lines and
fluid forms. The styles of Phillipe Sene, Babacar Seye,
Diatta Seck and Amadou Sow, characterized by less

Samba Balde, *Mask (Tjiwara),* 1974, tapestry, 76⅜″ × 43¼″.
Private collection.

particularily, has perfected a highly decorative style in which shapes are dovetailed to fit like pieces of a puzzle. Though forms are sometimes superimposed, the effect is flat. He studied under Pierre Lods, and some of the exotic effect associated with the Poto-Poto School (see chapter 11) seems apparent.

Mamadou Gaye, born in 1945 in Rufisque, teaches at the École de Beaux-Arts and is known for his engravings. He says "Today's artist makes pictures which are only for seeing. Although he has gained technique he has lost some of the atmosphere, spontaneity and mystery that imbued the village artist."[25] Both Mamadou Gaye and Amadou Seck emphasize the fact of function in traditional art and feel that the modern artist is aware of the past, uses its sources, but creates art that is "contemporary in spirit and execution."[26]

It is the particular talent of these artists that they have accepted other influences and other technologies, and

Daouda Diouck, *Tann,* 1979, tapestry, 121¼″ × 78⅝″.
Collection of the Government of Senegal.

structured forms and compositions, are a little like those of the Oshogbo artists.

Of the many others who deserve mention, several have an approach that is highly decorative. *The Sacrificed Ones* by Mohamadou Mbaye (1945–), *Horseman on Wheels* by Amadou Ba (1945–), *Bird of Paradise* by Boubacar Goudiaby (1946–), and *Sadiaba* by Bocar Diong (1946–) are all works in this vein. Diatta Seck (1953–), like Amadou Seck, constructs his paintings of thick architectural shapes. The work of Amadou Wade Sarr (1950–) is similar to that of Diatta Seck and Amadou Seck, but there is a sense of the topographical, of the earth as seen from above.

It is not possible to characterize all according to style, however, because style is often dictated by medium. Many artists have mastered different mediums and have developed a surprising variety of styles over a period of years. Diong, for example, paints canvases that seem awash with color and loosely formed figures. Goudiaby, have integrated them into their own vision without being overwhelmed by them. Their own perspective permeates their work, which communicates with brilliance of color, cadence, and form.

Senegalese minister of culture Assane Seck describes their position, "It is as if [the artists] were interpreting arcane writings. Without losing touch completely, they live on the edge of a cosmic vertigo."[27] Just as ancient sources inform oral tradition, a major art passed on by the minstrel poets, they are also integrated into the works of modern poets and, by the same mysterious force, into other modern art forms of Senegal. Senghor himself describes this process when he says: "The poem is bird-serpent, marriage of shadow and dawnlight/The Phoenix rises, he sings with wings extended, over the carnage of words."[28] The remarkable thing is that the phoenix has spread its wings and has flown so high in such a remarkably short time. A whole movement recognizably Senegalese has emerged and unfolded.

Ousmane Faye, *Le Bourgeon (The Bud),* date unknown, tapestry, 75" × 62". Location unknown.

Daouda Diouck, *The Lonely One,* 1978, tapestry, 56" × 42". Collection of the Government of Senegal.

9 Desert Light

Sudan

Across the continent from Senegal the artists of Sudan have responded to their traditions with very different results. Their imagery contains a haunting emotional presence. The delicacy and architectural precision that underlies this presence has its source in inherited forms, not the least of all Arabic calligraphy, which was surely a part of their earliest art-making experience. Vestiges of an archaeological past, elements of Arabic calligraphy, and structures that are mathematical or musical exist in varying degrees in the images of Ibrahim El Salahi, Kamala Ibrahim Ishaq, Mohamed Omer Bushara, and Salih Abdou Mashamoun and in the abstract forms of Ahmed Shibrain, Amir I. M. Nour, Shaigi Rahim, Mohammed Omer Khalil, Musa Khalifa, and Mohammed Ahmed Abdulla. These Sudanese artists demonstrate the qualities and profundity that characterize the modern movement in Sudan.

The traditions, religion, and geography of Sudan confer a certain sense of destiny. These artists were born in the land of the White and Blue Niles, where history reaches back at least four thousand years, and forward into Anglo-Egyptian Sudan, where Mahdist saints fighting the British welcomed death as a passage to paradise. In today's Republic of Sudan, the muezzin calls the faithful to prayers five times a day, and Koranic tablets present the first magic patterns and poetic imagery to the child. With desert, savannah grasslands, hills, and tropical landscapes extending from the Red Sea to Zaire and from Wadi Halfa to Juba, Sudan is the largest country in Africa, sharing borders with eight other nations. With an Afro-Arab heritage and remnants of early Christianity, it is the home of a hundred different peoples, Afro-Semitic and Nilotic—the Nuba, Nuer, Dinka, Shilluk, and Berber among them—the locus of five times as many languages as peoples, whose wide array of special artistries include the majestic stone temples and monuments of ancient Meriotic architecture, the refined decorative arts of heraldry, weaponry, armor; the calligraphy of Islam; and the bold and brilliant abstract designs of Nuba body painting.

All of these historical elements bring a variety of influences to bear. Scholar Richard Ettinghausen speaks of Islamic artists as having a strong relationship to abstract forms that leads them "as if drawn by some deep psychic force to the creation of pattern. . . . [t]hey invariably reduce and reshape . . . natural forms into delightfully complex configurations of pure design." He believes that the use of color and ornamentation is a response to the landscape, which is often barren and dry, and the unifying "network" of the faith itself spreading belief, iconography, and custom over vast areas. He says, "A language of abstract decoration developed" and became "a hallmark of Islamic creativity."[1]

Another scholar, Rene Bravmann, finds Jacob Bronowski's explanation of the close association between mathematics and design particularly appropriate: "Both fields of creativity demand clarity of vision, precision of thought and considerable organizing capabilities. . . . Not only were their methods and dispositions akin but, as has been suggested, within Islamic civilization the artist and mathematician became one."[2] These qualities might easily refer to the artists in Sudan today.

This synthesis of mathematics and design, which finds expression in calligraphy and which is, in turn, the basis of much contemporary expression, has the traditional arabesque as a major form. The arabesque expresses "its own canon of ornamental space. . . its own environment and its own measure, revealing itself not serially, not in depth, but within complexes of continuous curves and balances that secretly articulate the plane, render it active." Because the tenets of Islam grow from the realization that there is an immutable ordering of the universe, the adherent, says art historian Denis Williams, accepts the "belief in world forms [that] have been established once and for all" and therefore also accepts a sense of space that is timeless, and "carries no spatial connotations. . . . The Arabesque is reason liberated from space and exalted by poetry. . . . The strict, the pure, the lofty, official, Art of Arabia springs from a belief more inflexible, a restriction more exact, an imagination more fertile in pure formal construction, in free geometric invention and sensuous finesse."[3] The strongest Islamic influences in Sudan—calligraphy and the abstract shapes it has spawned—are those that many artists now probe, expand, reduce, and change to produce new art forms.

This extremely rich heritage became background for the contemporary art movement, which began in the late fifties. It developed "through accident, eccentricity and personal fortitude," says Sondra Hale, who has made an extensive study of the artists and cultures of Sudan.[4] The center of this movement was, and is, the College of Fine and Applied Art (formerly the School of Fine & Applied Arts), Khartoum Technical Institute, founded in 1946. Having graduated there gave an artist a stamp of approval.

The early artists forming the nucleus of this school were Ahmed Mohammed Shibrain, Ibrahim El Salahi and M. H. A. Rabbah. The first two began to have an impact in the late fifties; they now have many followers. While the work of their followers bears a general resemblance, the best have unique styles and directions.

Ahmed Shibrain (1932–) and Ibrahim El Salahi (1930–) are considered the progenitors of modern painting in Sudan. Shibrain, a devout person, is firmly grounded in Islamic philosophy and is, in fact, descended from the Mahdi, the spiritual and military leader who defeated the Anglo-Egyptian forces in the nineteenth century. Shibrain has been teaching since 1956 at the Khartoum Technical Institute where he is now director. He studied in London at the Central School of Art and Design from 1957 to 1960, and in 1964 he won an art competition sponsored by UNESCO.

Shibrain's imagery is primarily calligraphic and, although it breaks free of convention, it does not neces-

sarily obscure meaning. In his watercolor *Mosque Impressions,* he abstracts and simplifies the script to form a single overall image. Working primarily with pen and ink, he creates strong shapes that, while they retain their kinship to traditional forms, bring to mind Hans Hartung and Pierre Soulages.[5]

His broad, thrusting strokes do have something in common with expressionist painting of the West. However, his approach is disciplined by its links to calligraphy and its mystical religious significance, described by Rene Bravmann as "God's secrets," or "the explicit combination of the rational and magical."[6]

His preoccupation with both the meaning and the decorative aspects of Islamic calligraphy has as its legacy the beautiful old manuscripts and decorative wall paintings associated with Islamic tradition in Sudan. "The purpose of the decorative bits of writing that have adorned Sudanese houses for centuries was not only to convey the message of the text and to pay homage to the sacred language, but also to serve as ornaments and pictures in their own right."[7]

In works that are calligraphic abstractions, Shibrain sustains this visual poetry and enhances the power and immanence of the suras, chapters of the Koran, and their verses by expanding and simplifying shapes. As Denis Williams says, "He has extended the concentrated and intense idiom of Islamic tradition by the trimming away of form to its most austere essentials: straight and curved lines, contrasts of pure mass. At this level the Arabesque all but disappears, but the work remains charged with the traditional complexity. With these experiments . . . the implications are infinite."[8]

With similar inspiration, Ibrahim El Salahi has created

Ahmed Mohammed Shibrain, *Calligraphy,* date unknown, ink on paper, dimensions unknown. Collection of Sondra Hale.

Ahmed Mohammed Shibrain, *Calligraphy,* date unknown, ink on paper, dimensions unknown. Collection of Ulli Beier.

ning of each section, you decorated your wooden writing board. We used to make our own inks for this. . . . Strangely, it was African rather than Arabic in character . . . because we used crisscross patterns and sharp triangles and squares.[9]

Describing the decoration of houses as a fundamental influence, he continued,

It's a long standing thing. You will find that when people return from the Haj they paint their houses blue and they decorate [them], . . . probably with writing, and they might also draw some flags. They would write some forms of greetings like: 'He who is coming to this house, may he praise the Lord.' . . . Occasionally people painted animals onto their houses or even made sculptures. I don't know where the custom came from.[10]

He went on to explain that Islam takes on elements from indigenous cultures.

In addition to the classical education of the Khalwa, and his own sensitive observations, El Salahi's education included study at the Gordon Memorial College, the predecessor of the University of Khartoum. There he was delighted, for each day began with two hours of calligraphy, and one of his first teachers was Jean Pierre Greenlaw, who "wanted to have an art school based on Islamic philosophy." After this El Salahi became a teacher, first "for two years in Khartoum at a secondary school, then at the Institute of Design."[11]

Finally in London at the Slade School he was surprised at the taboos he found:

If you make a drawing that uses light and shade, you can not introduce a flat surface. . . . [c]olour is seen through light and, therefore, with colour you must have light and shade . . . everything stays neatly compartmentalized. Nothing should be pointing out of [the pictorial field]—other wise it might empty the whole scene and you'll be left with nothing![12]

He explained his assessment of the Western approach to the arts: "Those who analyse works of art give names to styles and devices and invent rules and in the end they give the impression that the artists themselves worked with this terminology, whereas the artists never thought about it. . . . Yes, you must have your freedom to choose! And you have within you your own sense of balance."[13]

In London El Salahi had the opportunity to study Islamic art at the British Museum. He was fascinated by what he found there, and in addition, he studied ancient hieroglyphics. "I kept wondering about the possibility of trying to bring that into my own work,"[14] and describing his own origins, he explained: "I am a mixture of Negro and Arab. I have always been fascinated by the richness in Arabic calligraphy's patterns."[15]

a modern language from the ancient one that was his birthright. He studied at the Slade School of Fine Art in London and on his return to Sudan found that his learning had become an avenue of estrangement. To reforge the links with his own culture, he looked at life around him and studied the forms and decorative patterns of handmade objects in the house and in the marketplace.

His father was an Islamic theorist whose religious teachings were a strong influence during El Salahi's childhood. At the age of two he was already learning to read, write, and create decorative elements in a Khalwa, an orthodox school. In an interview with Ulli Beier he said,

I was virtually born into that Khalwa. . . . We learned what is called the Sudanese hand . . . very similar to the North African or Moorish hand; . . . at the begin-

Ibrahim El Salahi, *Faces,* early 1960s, wash, pen and ink on paper, 14⅝″ × 20⅞″. Collection of Ulli Beier.

In a review of his early work Ulli Beier speaks of El Salahi's images as "introspective,"[16] and recalls that the artist sometimes resorted to quiet meditation in the desert as a way of searching for direction in his work.

> I needed to be with myself and emptiness. . . . The desert helped me to be myself; to clarify my thoughts. I can only find that in a place that has emptiness and is yet so full. I did not usually paint there. I went to meditate, to see with the inner eye, I was often quite ill in those days. . . . I really did cure myself just by sitting there very quietly. . . . [m]editation is the real unity with God.

But he also roamed throughout the entire Sudan studying the people, their customs, and their artifacts and empathizing with their vicissitudes. "I wanted to see what they accepted as beautiful. . . . to see where man's creativity went." He found handicrafts of wood, leather, fiber, metal, and houses "decorated to the hilt." There were verses from the Koran and lithachrome prints from Egypt, and pictures "of saints, califs, and folk heroes."[17]

El Salahi made dramatic changes, leaving behind what he had learned. He felt like he "was being a medium for a spirit of some sort. Something was working through me. . . . I never made any attempt to stop it . . . or even to control it; I am not the creator; I am not the one who is doing these things. I am merely preparing myself to accept what was coming. . . ."[18]

His re-discovery efforts led him to Islamic calligraphy.

> I realized the value of these two things about the word, it has a value as a vehicle to meaning and it has its own value, its own shape. . . . At first I wrote them [words] as they are with the meaning; I thought that was why the letter was made in the beginning.

But then gradually I started to break dow̲ of the letter. Sometimes I used letters with ̲ ing, putting Os and Rs and things together j̲ their relation. Gradually I started to abstract t̲ itself—to break it away into pieces, then resha̲ see the possibilities that could come out of this.[1̲]

In this way he finally evolved a style that was evocative, continuing and yet complete with each image; continuing in that it was also organically capable of generating another image.

In contrast to the use of line as a purely decorative feature in the service of exoticism, El Salahi began to improvise with line as a musician improvises with a theme, using it as a vehicle of meaning and enhancing its character. It moves like a thread delineating, elaborating, and circumscribing his images, which are delicate and ethereal, or taut and powerful in concert with the line itself.

He speaks of the process: "Through the abstracted rhythmic shapes of calligraphy, I have been led to visualize the presence of objects, the human figure, and a whole world of imagery."[20] Calligraphy formed the structure of his early work and was inherent in the primary elements: intense, staring eyes—sad, poignant,

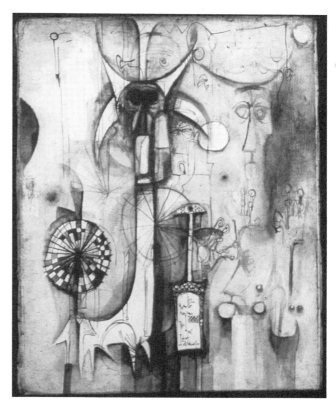

Ibrahim El Salahi, *The Donkey in My Dreams,* early 1960s, oil, dimensions unknown. Location unknown.

and hypnotic—and austere skeletal bodies with large knotty joints.

Twenty illustrations incorporating such images are contained in a 1962 Mbari edition of *Brush Fire,* by Congolese poet Felix Tchicaya U Tam'si. In a gesture on behalf of the poet, El Salahi asked that the illustrations, ink-wash drawings, not carry his name. Reflective and visionary in character, they extend the surreal quality of the poetry.

El Salahi's writing, like these illustrations and other drawings and paintings, is reflective.

> Islamic scholars . . . say there is nothing at all to restrict you from reproducing the human image as you want. In a way it's a kind of prayer too, because you are appreciating God's creations and trying to think about them and meditate on His creativity. . . . Their meaning is prayer mostly. Some are prayers which we hum when chanting, some of it is poetry, some of it is directly from the Koran, and some of it [is] just things which come into my head which have no meaning at all, just words put together. And they seem to come through me and appear on the canvas.[21]

His use of Arabic script is a means, not a theme in itself. Words extend his visual imagery and are also integral to it. Each is an aspect of the other. He says of his painting *Revolution,* "It made me sick to hear about things in South Africa. . . . They had to rise or die. They rose like a whirling sandstorm against the hot sky of the desert to burn up the shame of the past and the sad, painful memories that are still present through tyranny."[22]

Like eulogies to such painful memories, his figures often express sadness. They are connected to the past by archaic references and anthropomorphic forms, qualities revealed in his description of one painting: "In my dreams I used to see a donkey standing in the sun. Standing still and thinking. A donkey with a long drooping face and sad, vague eyes. The donkey's face becomes mine. My face becomes long and I stand in the sun thinking in place of the donkey."[23]

He depicts a mystical space, a kind of distance; although the faces he creates are intense and omniscient, seeing through and beyond the viewer. For the painting *Head* he wrote,

A man lost in his introspective visions,
Looking in and into himself,
Sitting in the shade of a cracked mud wall,
Gazing as the shadows creep over his toes,
Staring into the blaze of the sun.
Gazing into nothingness,
Until his two eyes become one,
Gazing into the empty horizon of far away dreams,

Into a mirror that I hold before my hands,
To paint a portrait for me.[24]

And for the drawing *Totem* he wrote,

This is my voice in the night. A torturing
experience of suffering with those who suffer.
A long continuous cry.
A spirit for those who suffer.[25]

His images, like driftwood on the beach, are strokes in space that also delineate that space. There is in this world that is at once strong and fragile, an equation that has to do with real life. Though often weighted with tragic purpose, that world is still imbued with the act of discovery and generation.

Indeed, he has learned firsthand how to turn tragedy into positive experience. Describing his experiences in jail where he spent six months and three days wrongly accused and without trial, he explained, "You try to pin the blame for your situation onto many external elements." But on arrival he met a learned man who helped him to accept his plight.

> It took me two days . . . for two days I felt terribly miserable, because I was resisting, because I felt I am

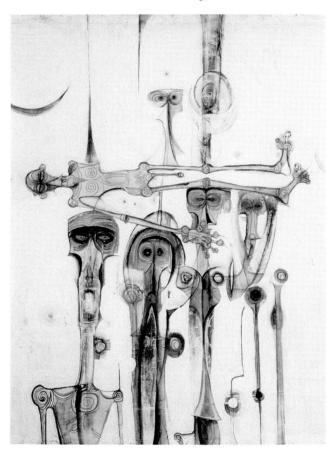

Ibrahim El Salahi, *Funeral and Crescent,* 1963, oil on hardboard, 37" × 38½". Collection of Mr. and Mrs. Ralph Marker.

me, and I have my right, and so-and-so has done me wrong and I cannot accept this. But after two days I understood: what this man is saying is the Truth. Whatever happens—even if does not seem to make any sense at all, is just a test for you as a human being. Once you believe, that whatever happens—however terrible—can only be to your benefit in the end—then the whole thing has a different taste. And something told me: I accept; it's an insult, it's hardship, it's difficult, it's unbearable, but I accept it. So I had the meaning of destiny explained to me just in time. . . . [J]ail became a very positive experience to me.[26]

He explained further that purifying oneself:

. . . needs a lot of hard work—but without a struggle, without tension. Because when you have tension you are distracted. . . . [w]hen you are that anxious, you are a Don Quixote; you are fighting, but you are fighting in vain. You create nothing. With acceptance, awareness sets in and peace of mind and tranquility.[27]

El Salahi translates this philosophy into both life and art. It has enabled him to integrate such elements as Tantra into his latest works using "painting as a platform for meditation." In these he is exploring the dynamics between the circle and square, and also releasing long contained feelings for color.[28]

Referring to a recent large work composed of a series of drawings, El Salahi sees it as embracing hope for the future—the "idea of growth and death, growth and rot, living so closely together." He went on to explain that this idea is also maturing in color and mentions that he is inspired by the luminous color of Georgina Beier's latest work.[29]

Ibrahim El Salahi has gained strength from assessing and defining himself and his culture. From a mixture of humanism, Islamic liturgy, and forms reminiscent of—but not mimetic of—African sculpture, El Salahi has created images that are indelible, lingering, and imbued with a sense of struggle. Now inspired by Tantric art, his present work carries new meanings and energies, and has an intensity, the nuances of which range from terror to trance. Because he is open to experience and growth, he keeps pushing beyond what he and others have done in a search to understand struggle and inequity.

In 1961 El Salahi's art was exhibited in Oshogbo, Nigeria, at the Mbari Club. In 1963 he was the recipient of a Rockefeller Fellowship, which brought him to the United States to work. In 1965 he exhibited at the Museum of Modern Art in New York. Since that time he has participated in many exhibitions throughout Europe and the United States, and is represented in major museum collections such as the Metropolitan Museum of Art and the Museum of Modern Art in New York. He has held posts in the Ministry of Culture, as a diplomat overseas, and with UNESCO, as a cultural advisor.

Amir Nour's connections to Sudanese culture are similar to El Salahi's in that both artists have drawn inspiration from indigenous art forms. They both reflect humanist concerns and specific insights into their culture. "Abstract thinking is not just a western thing," he points out, "Look at Islamic art. . . . Islamic art became abstract because of the religious taboos on worshipping idols and statues. So Islamic art was mostly geometric shapes; it came out of calligraphy."[30]

His own sculpture is so modern in appearance that it is often criticized as non-African, but Amir Nour affirms his links to Sudanese life and tradition by showing how the forms of utilitarian objects and architecture are related to those he juxtaposes:

There's nothing wrong with using technology; we need it. But the forms and shapes have to come from within the society itself—from the tradition and background we have.[31] In Sudan forms such as the crescent and horns of cattle are shapes used in the architecture of the Nubian house, and they are present in my sculpture *Protected Gate*. The dobe house with its oil lamps resembles a face at night. All of these elements are inspiration to me.[32]

Amir I. M. Nour, *Protected Gate*, 1973–74, bronze, 22" × 11" × 7". Collection of Miriam Wolford.

Amir I. M. Nour, *Ferocious Portrait*, date unknown, bronze, 19"
high. Location unknown.

He further articulates his convictions:

> However, technology is sweeping away tradition, so
> my work is an attempt to use the two. My sculpture
> has been criticized for its abstract quality—this idea
> that the West has a monopoly on the abstract. Muslim
> culture tends toward abstractions—architecture and
> calligraphy, for example. African art has a cool, serene
> quality, as well as a hot, ferocious one. You can see
> this contrasted in a firespitter mask, cool in the face
> and hot in the horns and teeth. Traditional sculpture
> often exaggerates shapes, distorts proportions for sym-
> bolic reasons. For example, the head is larger because
> it is the house of wisdom. I exaggerate some shapes
> for aesthetic reasons, and use the inorganic to depict
> the organic.[33]

The amalgam Nour creates is a subtle one and might
easily escape notice without his explanation, especially
because his work is also related to those twentieth-
century cubists who have consciously incorporated the
same diverse influences. About them, he remarks,

> You can't have a culture isolated from the rest of the
> world. Cultures have always developed by being fer-
> tilized by new elements from other cultures. I mean
> the whole modern art movement came about because
> some artists saw African art.[34] And yet Moore, Picas-
> so, Modigliani are never labeled Africanist, as I am
> labeled Western.[35]

Nour first studied at the Khartoum School of Fine and
Applied Art, and for three years was director of the
sculpture department there. He completed his under-
graduate work at the Slade School of Fine Arts, London
University, and continued his studies at the Royal College of Art. He then obtained a bachelor of fine arts and
a master of fine arts degree at Yale University. In 1968
his dramatic sculpture entitled *Ancestor* was awarded a
$1,000 prize for graphic and plastic arts by *African Arts*
magazine.

From 1974 to 1976 he had several one-person shows:
at the African-American Institute in New York, at the
Carnegie Museum of Art in Pittsburgh, and at the
International Monetary Fund in Washington, D.C. In
1980 he spoke at the International Sculpture Conference
in Washington, D.C. In Chicago, where he has been
teaching for a number of years, he recently completed a
large commissioned piece for the city. Entitled *Calabash
4*, it consists of four cold-rolled steel hemispheres each
with a black matte finish.

Nour says that he really happened into art with a
prize in intermediate school as the first push in that
direction. He was originally interested in architecture,
but missing the opportunity to study abroad, he pursued
the visual arts. He sees a connection between architecture and sculpture, but explains that as a sculptor he is

Amir I. M. Nour, *Calabash 4*, 1980, cold-rolled steel, 276" long.
Commission for the City of Chicago, 4th District Police Station
Plaza.

Salih Abdou Mashamoun, *The Memory,* 1969, ink and watercolor, 14″ × 11″. Collection of George Corinaldi.

His career in the foreign service, while perhaps constraining this more revolutionary approach, added a certain richness. Steeped in Islamic and Coptic history and culture, he began to work on goatskin as did the Coptic illuminators in ancient Ethiopia. In works created when he was in Damascus, he conveyed a sense of antiquity by manipulating texture. Interested in the surface of old walls and their graffiti, his paintings evoke the graphic images that remain. Unlike the use of calligraphy by Shibrain, vestiges of calligraphy created by Mashamoun mystify, rather than clarify, meaning.

In his most compelling works shrouded bodies, crypts, catacombs, and figures that look like medieval martyrs in sackcloth and ashes doing penance seem fixed in time and space. A static image with an open mouth against a rough-textured graffiti surface is like a petitioner at the wailing wall. The wall, as an image of the past, and the human face, as a saint or saviour, are two major symbols that express Mashamoun's preoccupation with human destiny.

He describes his work as prompted by a feeling of loss, but sees it also as a search, a search for a face that he has seen and is trying to find again. The sadness and

grieving finds a parallel in the works of South African artists, but the faces in Mashamoun's paintings reveal fatalism and relentless atonement suffered in the catacombs of the mind.

Similar traces of antiquity characterize the pottery of Mohammed Ahmed Abdulla, who creates modern forms with the colors, encrustations, and patinas found in ancient archaeological treasures. The sense of age they manifest is the product of fine craftsmanship and a sensitive aesthetic. Like antique amphorae in texture, the forms seem organically related one to another. And indeed, Abdulla explains that each piece is "a synthesis of those before" it.[62] Like Amir Nour's sculpture, Abdulla's pottery is inspired by and related to the domes, arches, animal horns, and various calabash and basket forms indigenous to Sudanese culture.

Abdulla speaks of his pots as though they were living, breathing organic entities.

Mohammed Ahmed Abdulla, *Vessel,* date unknown, ceramic, dimensions unknown. Location unknown.

I like pots to breathe or sweat or feel young or old, fruitful or fruitless. I like them to possess living feelings, so that when one looks at them, one is moved. They should feel generous, active, elegant, strong, but never passive. I do not like them being weak; I want them to be quiet, not noisy. I never want anything to interfere with what is in them.

He continues, describing the predicament of the artist in search of that organic vitality.

I do not ever think I have hit the nail on the head. Maybe I will stop if I ever hit it with the desired precision. It appears one is constantly involved with an elusive image.[63]

Abdulla was the student of El Salahi at the Khartoum Technical Institute. He also studied in London at the Central School of Art and Design, then taught at the Camden Arts Centre. His approach to pottery is an important indication of the integration of the arts in Sudan, not just on a superficial level, but on a philosophical level.

This deep philosophical attitude of Sudanese artists toward their art reveals burning ethical concerns and is apparent in their observations on the artist's role. Their creativity grows out of an aesthetic nurtured by intellect, and their interpretations are individual assessments of such questions as the relationship of art to country; of art to social and political themes; and of art to religion and tradition. The expression of thought in abstract, calligraphic, or figurative forms draws inspiration from Sudanese poetry, architecture, and craft, as well as from the desert. The Sudanese artists' devoted attachment to the mystical and poetic aspects of Islam runs through their work and defines it.

African audience.[8] "The responsibility for all occupations in the arts is that of storyteller. I thought film was the most positive way of assuming this responsibility, a perfect medium with its visual and audio specifications, lending these dimensions to metaphorical purpose."[9] Haile's films and ideas parallel the work and thought of his colleagues in the other arts. In the past the various arts were generally linked by religion and tradition. A comparison of the work of Haile Gerima and that of Gebre Kristos Desta and Skunder Boghossian reveals similarities. They have in common the fact that history, anger against poverty, and often ideology rather than religion are principles underlying their motivation.

However, before the emergence of painters in the sixties, the first three contemporary artists, like others who followed, turned to the West for their education, and became involved in art education. These artists, born just after the turn of the century, were Agannaw Engeda, Zarihun Dominik, and Abbaba Wald Giorgis. Agannaw, who started the first albeit short-lived school of art, did work of a conventional nature. Zarihun, who eventually became a school administrator, also taught drawing for one year at Makwemen School. In 1941 Abbaba, who studied in France in the twenties, taught an art section in the Ministry of Information.

Finally the effort was firmly centered when the Fine Arts School, the major art school in the country, was founded in Addis Ababa in 1957 with Alefellega Salam as director. Alefellega, who was born in 1929 (more than twenty years after the other three), studied at the Art Institute of Chicago and became instrumental in the thrust toward modern creative expression in Ethiopia.

The first painter of prominence was Afewerk Tekle who, born in 1923 in Ankober in Shoa province, also went abroad. He returned to Addis Ababa in 1953 after having studied in London at the Slade School of Fine Art and having traveled throughout Europe. When his paintings celebrated the church and royalty and he was accorded honors and commissions from those in powerful positions, he assumed the mantle of court painter. He was, like Ben Enwonwu of Nigeria, an artist who moved back and forth from one style to another with an ambivalence that suggested an inability to cope convincingly with all the varied elements assailing the modern creative sensibility in Africa today. Nevertheless, he defends his stance by saying that he chooses the style to suit the subject. One of his most important and most successful accomplishments is the large stained-glass window in the United Nations Economic Commission's Africa Hall in Addis Ababa.

However, the real beginning of contemporary expression in Ethiopia was in the 1960s with two important artists at the forefront as major influences: the late Gebre Kristos Desta (1932–1981), who returned from studies in Germany in 1962, and Skunder Boghossian

(1937–), who returned from successes in Paris in 1965. These men, as painters and teachers, inspired students and fellow artists, and pursued distinct artistic directions.

In spite of the allusions to tradition found in the work of later artists, Gebre Kristos made a complete break with the past in his own work, although he stressed the study of traditional culture in his teaching. Skunder, who had found ways to incorporate certain elements of ancient Ethiopian culture in his art, encouraged students to work toward a synthesis. The effects of the imagery of these two men and their philosophies are apparent in what has become a new generation of modern Ethiopian artists, many of whom are now living abroad, and even though in exile, still articulate elements of their traditions.

Gebre Kristos, perhaps more than any other Ethiopian painter, "kicked over the traces." His iconoclastic paintings are forays into abstraction, often using assemblage techniques to deal with such emotional themes as love, death, poverty, and dignity. In some paintings he incorporated tin cans, rope, sand, and other materials, which he referred to as pop, to the canvas, embedding them in thick impasto color.[10] His preoccupation with color as a major expressive element is appropriate to an artist born in Harar, one of Ethiopia's most colorful and exotic cities. Circles and skeletal forms, prominent recurring structural ingredients, seem part of a struggle to assert principles. Across these forms, slashing lines, which might be attributed to the influence of calligraphy, cut into the paint and add a forceful and deliberate dissonance. They reinforce the sensation of attack and the effort to complete the break with the traditions of religious art.

Gebre Kristos's anger against poverty and deprivation was released in the painting *Golgotha*, which is the antithesis of early Coptic paintings. The cross, represented by a series of crossing perpendicular and horizontal strokes, creates a density of form and color behind the figure of Christ. Like prison bars, the strokes reinforce the feeling of entrapment. The figure of Christ is defined by red paint trickling like blood down the length of his body, creating, in its flow, His form. The paint appears to take its own course governed only by gravity, and in its descent increases the sense of tragic destiny.

The son of a calligrapher and manuscript illuminator, Gebre Kristos first exhibited his work in 1954. From 1957 to 1961 he studied at the Academy of Art in Cologne, Germany. After travel in Europe for a year, he returned to Ethiopia to coordinate the first exhibition of abstract art in the country. It created an ongoing controversy within the less progressive segment of Ethiopian society. This is not to suggest that there were political inferences in his paintings. "I am not attracted by political or religious aspects of art," he stated.[11]

Stanislaw Chojnacki describes him as "unassuming, gentle and generous . . . one of the most independent and forceful personalities on Ethiopia's artistic stage. He stubbornly follows his own way, apparently completely departing from the traditional beliefs of what a good painting should be." Without attempting to integrate historical references or revive old forms, he earned respect, even though he did evoke disagreement. At first his approach seemed to grow from anger. In later years the anger seems to have mitigated, even as he continued to find more radical solutions. He said, "I think emotion comes first, then logic can follow."[12]

In 1965 he was awarded the Haile Selassie I Prize for introducing non-figurative art into Ethiopia and for having "outstandingly contributed [to] the growth and evolution of Ethiopian art."[13] He was also involved in multimedia productions utilizing his own poetry and art on videotape. For twelve years he taught at the Fine Arts School in Addis Ababa, where his impact was profound. Those who studied under him—Acha Debela, Falaka Armide, and Tesfaye Tessema—credit him with giving them inspiration, motivation, and direction.

Gebre Kristos summed up his direction and philosophy: "Ethiopian church art, . . . I am sometimes accused of discarding in favor of foreign styles—this supposedly indigenous style is actually Byzantine. . . . It, too, incorporates 'foreign' elements and arrives, perhaps, at a characteristically Ethiopian synthesis. . . . Fifty years from now we may see a new Ethiopian tradition evolving, one which draws on what the rest of the world has to offer, but which is more than the sum of its parts."[14]

After traveling to the United States for medical assistance, a lingering illness finally caused his death in 1981. His legacy survives with his own memorial in those artists he taught and encouraged, as well as in the paintings he left behind.

In contrast to Gebre Kristos, the career of Skunder Boghossian is firmly rooted in ancient culture and spans generations as well as geographical boundaries. Born in 1937 of Ethiopian and Armenian parents, he spent his childhood in Ethiopia and his young adulthood in London and Paris where, studying at the École des Beaux-Arts and Académie de la Grande Chaumière, he mingled with other African artists, adherents of Negritude, and Parisian surrealists, including André Breton.

Returning to Ethiopia to teach in 1965, he spent the next four years there. Later living in the United States—first in New York City, then in Atlanta, and Montgomery, Alabama, and finally in Washington, D.C., at Howard University, where he was appointed artist-in-residence in 1972—he witnessed the rise of black consciousness and was, in spirit and fact, part of it. His paintings are a fascinating kaleidoscopic encounter with a broad panorama.

Unlike the various directions taken by Afewerk Tekle, Skunder's work evolved according to his own personal growth. His focus carried him through a number of changes to develop a distinct and articulate style, one that reflected a deep concern for the traditions of his culture, and which, when translated into modern visual symbols, was a poetic statement about the complexity of that ancient history, of its conflicts and of its deep religious mysticism.

Some of these changes were, however, profound in nature. Critics have even suggested that his Paris work has a surrealist orientation.[15] The neo-African poetry of Aimé Césaire, Léon Damas, Birago Diop, and Léopold Sédar Senghor had been embraced by André Breton and other surrealists in Paris, and " 'Negritude' was celebrated as the consummation of surrealism,"[16] an assessment considered presumptuous and inaccurate by many Africans.

Skunder's Paris-era paintings, with delicate embryonic imagery, do have a mirage-like quality, but they also contain persistent references to antiquity. Many of the qualities mistaken for surrealism can just as easily be related to a sense of history. Those in the series he calls The Nurturers, with such titles as Inside the World Egg and Cosmological Explosion, have an implosive energy. In Explosion of the World Egg atom-like forms shoot into space like meteors in the firmament. A soft incandescent aura surrounds images that can be construed as either cetacean mammals, tiny fetal forms in swaddling clothes, or shrouded mummies; all of which suggest genesis and antiquity. By inference the images are symbols of death and resurrection. This series of paintings, which is visionary and visceral and suggestive of outer space, never loses the feeling of the ancient liturgy of his heritage.

When these works were shown in Paris at the Galerie Lambert in 1964, they received enthusiastic reviews, but it was for Skunder an uneasy success with no sales. Feelings about the revolution in Algeria were strong, and Skunder was sometimes mistaken for an Algerian. These difficulties and the feeling that he needed to be a part of his own culture again prompted his return in 1965 to Ethiopia.

Teaching at the School of Fine Arts in Addis Ababa during the next four years, he played an important role by encouraging beginning artists to create a contemporary movement. His dramatic compositions, called "xray [sic] visions" by Stanislaw Chojnacki,[17] triggered debates. Soon, however, he became an inspiration and catalyst for his students. The Addis Ababa showings of his work were landmark events and he eventually won the Haile Selassie I Prize.

Skunder's work by this time had developed a new luminosity, as though the paint itself contained a light source. It seems appropriate to identify this rich glowing

Yusuf Grillo, *Mendicants* (detail), ca. 1967, oil on canvas,
48" × 24". Location unknown.

Erhabor Emokpae, *Olokun*, 1967, cowries, manillas, and
coins, 144" high. Standard Bank of West Africa, Lagos.

Demas Nwoko, *The Adam and Eve Series*, 1963–65, oil,
25″ × 17″. Location unknown.

Adebisi Fabunmi, *Missionary Activity in West Africa*, 1969, yarn
tapestry, dimensions unknown. Location unknown.

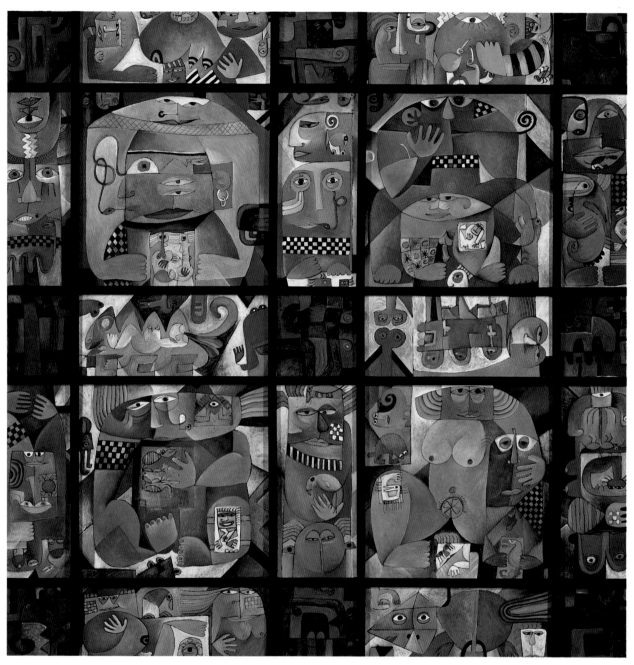

Georgina Beier, *Untitled,* 1985, oil on hardboard, 25 panels, 33½″ × 33½″. Collection of the artist.

Muraina Oyelami, *Newly Weds*, 1971, oil on paper, 30″ × 19¾″. Location unknown.

Twins Seven-Seven, *Queen Oranmiyan the Mother of All Future Teller Ghosts*, 1967, varnish, ink, and gouache on wood, 27″ × 24″. Private collection.

Sangodare, *Festival of the Creator God Obatala* (detail), late 1970s to early 1980s, batik, 85″ × 67″. Collection of Georgina and Ulli Beier.

Middle Art (August Okoye), *Painting of the War—Bombed House*, 1976, oil on board, 24¾″ × 35¾″. Private collection.

Samuel Ojo Omonaiye, *Wall Hanging,* 1972, appliqué on cloth, 56″ × 70″. Private collection.

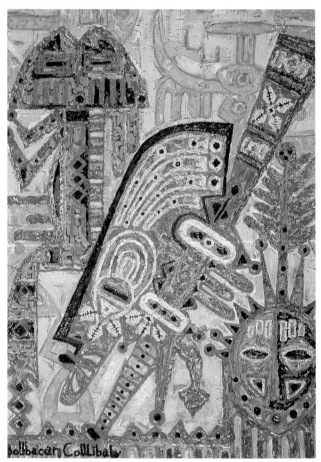

Mbor Faye, *Portrait I Marabout*, 1978, oil on canvas, 24″ × 20⅝″. Private collection.

Boubacar Coulibaly, *Meeting of the Masks*, 1976, oil on canvas, 45¾″ × 35″. Collection of the Government of Senegal.

Skunder Boghossian, *Rhonda's Bird*, 1974, mixed media on board, 13¾″ × 22″. Location unknown.

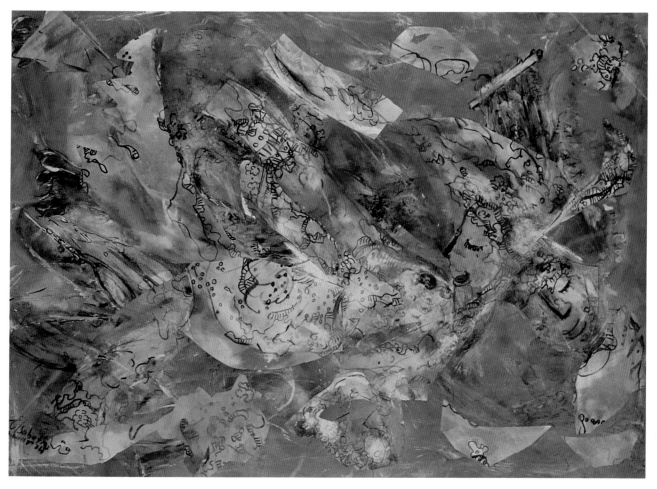

Elisabeth Atnafu, *The Year of Love,* 1984, mixed media, 60″ × 40″. Location unknown.

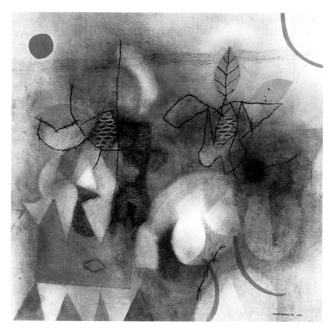

Louis Maqhubela, *Untitled,* 1970s, early 1980s, watercolor on paper, 28″ × 36″.

Valente Malangatana, *Nude with Flowers*, 1960s, oil on canvas,
dimensions unknown. Location unknown.

quality with the light in Ethiopia. The colors on his canvases became more iridescent and translucent, and at times revealed layers of forms below the surfaces.

In many of his paintings there was a feeling of agitated motion and often a swirling mass of small molecular forms. A dense crystalline and highly organized clutter conveyed the sense of an infinitely complex universe, a Byzantium in constant motion. In *Nubian Princess* he orchestrated a collection of symbols to support the bier on which the body of the princess rests and to suggest both the fragments of her individual life and the relics of an antique past.

Conflict seems inherent in most of Skunder's work and is derived from the deft and intricate juxtaposition of shapes and symbols as much as from narrative elements. In *Axum, The Battle of Adua,* and *Union,* created after his return to Ethiopia, forms join like myriad facets of a jewel. The fusion of tiny forms in *The Battle of Adua* is dramatic and energetic, and prompts critics to use such words as "violence," "struggle," "cosmic," and "creative force" to describe his work. In *Union* shapes collide, one form dissolves into another, and tiny molecules flow from image to image to diffuse edges in some instances and reinforce them in others. The result is a sense of upheaval, of a confrontation with the cataclysms of history.

Some of his paintings include icon-like images directly related to early Coptic manuscripts and talsam, or magic scroll paintings. As a part of his own iconography, they appear as anchors reinforcing an idiom that is the result of a deliberate confrontation between the forms of tradition and those of science and technology.

One especially interesting drawing done in 1974, *Rhonda's Bird,* illustrates conflict in a more literal way. It combines a delicate white bird—luminous like a prescient spirit—a leopard, and a warrior-animal. Through the dramatic use of symbols, the portrayal of space as infinite, the counterpoising of elements in conflict, and the display of great technical facility, Skunder creates motion, light, and tension, and brings to life implications of an ancient past.

Skunder's approach to his work finds a parallel in Sudanese artist Ibrahim El Salahi. Both El Salahi and Skunder find direction in tradition, and both have discovered sources in religion and in the calligraphy of their indigenous languages. After traveling abroad, both returned to their own countries to integrate foreign elements, and though their visions are very different, both have sought solutions that retain some of the ancient symbolism and mysticism of the religious past. As with El Salahi, it is Skunder's own reinterpretation and reorganization of symbols that places them in a new framework with new meaning for the viewer. Chojnacki describes Skunder's accomplishment: "Between his world of constant change, and the flat immovable world

of medieval Ethiopian illuminators, there is an abyss. Whereas the old masters captured a petrified eternity of the moment, Skunder captures the suspense of uninterrupted change."[18]

At Howard University in Washington, D.C., during the seventies and eighties, Skunder influenced Ethiopian student artists, both in and outside the university, who were drawn to this country because of his presence. By this time his work was in important collections including those of the Museum of Modern Art in New York and the Musée d'Art Moderne in Paris, and he had already had one-person exhibitions at the Merton Simpson Gallery in New York in both 1962 and 1965.

By the seventies his work had begun to change. He experimented with other materials including metal, parchment, and goatskin. The influence of the magic scrolls was pre-eminent. While many of the forms were recognizable, the concept was different. Instead of paintings that depicted long scrolls, his work included three-dimensional assemblages of scrolls. A large piece entitled *Suspension of Belief* illustrates this further evolution of his iconography. Describing it, Skunder says, "It's just like a plant. It interacts with space. It's alive. It wants to move out of the building."[19] Constructed of fifteen scrolls and banners made of parchment, canvas, burlap, leather, mirrored glass, wood, and shingles, the major portion of the work hangs from the ceiling on an arched bamboo rod in such a way that it moves subtly. Other smaller accompanying units can be hung in various configurations; for example, he invites the curator to participate by creating the arrangement of pieces for an installation. This flexibility and the organic relationship of each element to the whole suggests that the work represents

Skunder Boghossian, *Illumination,* date unknown, pen and ink, dimensions unknown.

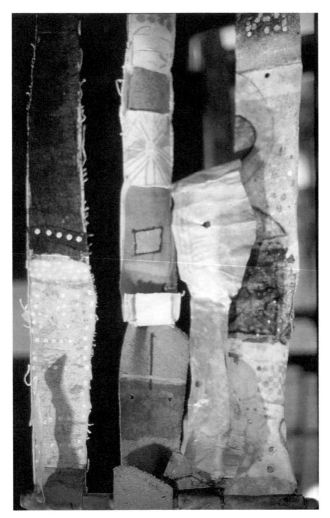

Skunder Boghossian, *Suspension of Belief,* 1986, acrylic on parchment, canvas, burlap, leather, mirror, wood, and shingles, 60" × 53" × 2". Collection of the artist.

is an important element in Sheriff's art. Ethiopian critic and poet Solomon Deressa writes:

> Colour, which is Sheriff's strong point, seems to have been what bothered his German teachers most. . . . What might have seemed the wild exuberance of the Fauve to teachers who live in the grey tonalities of Nordic light is an inner world that the Ethiopian painter carries with him, whether by choice or in spite of himself.

Deressa also comments on Sheriff's secular approach and describes the contrasts that make up his vision.

> Sheriff's art may be expressive of new Ethiopian possibilities in that the frontiers of religious and social background and even tradition are both unworriedly crossed and ignored as irrelevant. . . . Ultimately his individual vision of the world of forms gains its significance from an imperturbable outer calm and unrelenting inner tension.[21]

Among the other artists of Sheriff and Skunder's generation are Theodros Tsige Markos (1936–), Zerihun Yetemgeta (1941–), and Endale Haile Selassie (1945–1968), all of whom became accomplished artists with distinct styles. Theodros, who was Skunder's childhood friend at the Teffari Mekonnen School, already had another career with the Ministry of Foreign Affairs when Skunder's presence stimulated his interest in painting. He began a new career at the age of thirty-two, leaving his position at the Ministry to become head of publications for the Department of Commerce. It was at this time that he began to paint seriously.[22]

Shapes in Theodros's paintings often seem the result of a spontaneous flow of color reminiscent of the patterns on marbled paper. In the painting *Masks* the small shapes cluster together, like lichen on a tree, to form larger masses leaving interstices of mysterious configurations. Looking at them is like studying the forms of clouds to find those hidden images that only long meditation reveals.

Chojnacki describes Theodros's approach: "the process of painting appears to be an intimate experience of tension and self-discharge, in which his laying-on of colour on canvas acquires the potency of the physical act." He too sees the same relationship to cloud images: "This playing with colours is also the dreamer's experience. In the same way as observation of clouds will always result in the perception of figures and objects, a closer look at Tewodros' [Theodros's] paintings will reveal a wealth of human shapes and forms which the artist allows to emerge from a fluid, blurred mass of colour." Chojnacki further explains that Theodros thinks of his work as surrealist and proceeds by allowing the imagery to "develop spontaneously in the process of painting."[23]

an ongoing direction; with it Skunder has opened the door to infinite possibilities. He uses the word "evolution," stating that "*The Scroll Series,* has traveled through the entire distance of my vision to this time."[20]

Born two years after Skunder in 1939 in the area of the Addis Ababa market, Abdel-Rahmam M. Sheriff was a student at the Commercial School and graduated from the Fine Arts School. He then studied for one year with El Salahi at the Khartoum Technical Institute beginning in 1958. Moving to Germany in 1962, he attended both the Kassel and Berlin academies, where he graduated in 1968. While there he developed a sophisticated style that involved using several media in one work. Returning to Addis Ababa, he eventually taught graphics and art education at the Fine Arts School, where he has served as director since 1975.

His technical facility is expressed in the skillful way in which he uses newspaper and other printed surfaces to create reverse prints that have the effect of collage. Color

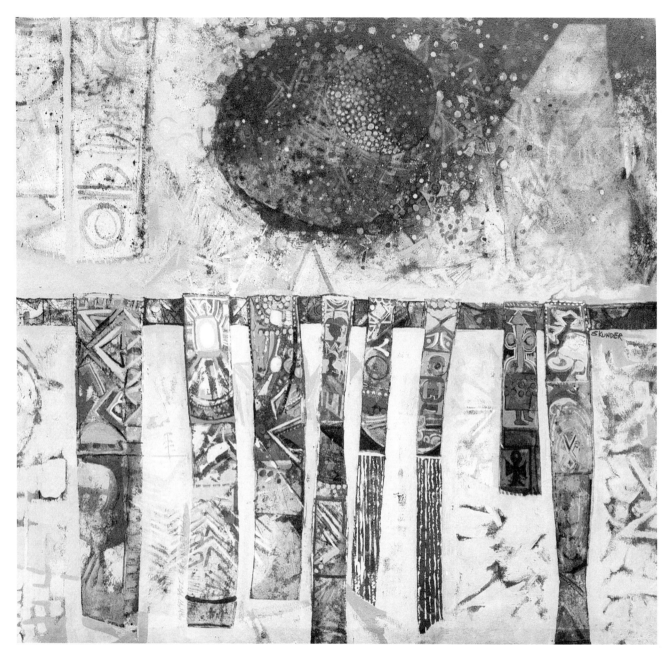

Skunder Boghossian, *Climatic Effects*, 1984–85, acrylic on canvas, 72" × 50". Collection of George Corinaldi.

Zerihun Yetemgeta, who graduated from the Fine Arts School in 1968, was also influenced by Skunder, but soon became independent and self-directed. While his use of Biblical images is quite different from his use of older Coptic forms, there are certain underlying references to talsam and their diamond and triangular shapes. In his works angular shapes form jagged diagonals like streaks of lightning, and create a surface that is alive and restless. In place of the more formal icons of the magic scrolls, the imagery, because of these diago-

nals, has an exciting, explosive sense of movement. In *A Cave Painting* there are cryptic, totem-like figures with archaeological references, but the background moves with agitated tracery.

Skunder said about Endale Haile Selassie, "The moment I saw his works, I knew that he had talent and quality, and I was really happy about it." Very soon they were working together in Skunder's studio in the compound of the Fine Arts School. Skunder was amazed that Endale quickly learned his techniques, and then he

Theodros Tsige Markos, *Masks,* 1970, acrylic on paper, dimensions unknown. Collection of Ambassador and Mrs. William D. Hall.

exigencies of alien surroundings while managing to retain a strong Ethiopian identity in their work. They and other Ethiopian artists exhibit together in the belief that in this way they can establish their presence and make a strong impact as artists who are Ethiopian.

Acha Debela arranged such an exhibition, Ethiopian Artists in America, in 1973 at the Department of Health, Education, and Welfare, in Washington, D.C., and another, The Ethiopian in America, at Morgan State University in Baltimore. Acha, who was born in 1947, says he owes a debt to Gebre Kristos Desta, under whom he studied and in whose studio he worked from 1966 to 1968. "Gebre was like a friend rather than a dominating teacher. His spirit shines through our paintings. He was my most important influence."[26] Acha is currently documenting Gebre Kristos's life and plans to install a memorial collection of his works. Acha received a diploma with honors from the Fine Arts School in Addis Ababa in 1967. He was awarded a scholarship to attend Ahmadu Bello University in Nigeria, where he earned a bachelor of fine arts degree with honors in 1972. The same year he was appointed curator of the Morgan State University Gallery of Art in Baltimore. He obtained

began to create his own style. The two men made a pilgrimage to the stone churches and other historic sites, traveling "by foot and mule and bus" and upon their return had individual exhibitions at the Belvedere Gallery in Addis Ababa. In fact many of Endale's paintings were hanging at the Belvedere Gallery at the time of his death. He took part in 1966 World Festival of Negro Arts in Dakar, where his work was highly praised.[24]

Endale's career ended abruptly at twenty-three when, frustrated by his inability to travel abroad for further education, he took his own life. He is revered and credited with having contributed "artistic goals" and "critical spirit, which were indispensable to the life of our culture and to those of us who carry the responsibility of the role of the artist in Ethiopia."[25] While an art student, he undertook extensive research recording the art of the island monasteries in Lake Tana. This was of major importance because he recognized the potential cultural sources revealed to him and integrated references to ancient religious art into his modern painting, a practice other painters now continue.

Like Skunder, other Ethiopian artists traveled to the United States, most of them to pursue their studies. Tesfaye Tessema and Wosene Kosrof arrived in 1971, Acha Debela in 1972. Like Skunder, they adapted to the

Zerihun Yetemgeta, *A Cave Painting,* 1977, oil on canvas, 21" × 16½". Collection of George Corinaldi.

Acha Debela, *Journey to the Unknown,* date unknown, acrylic on canvas, 30″ × 40″. Collection of the University of Maryland, College Park.

Acha Debela, *A Song for Africa,* 1989?, acrylic on canvas, 40″ × 30″. Collection of the artist.

in 1976 a master of arts degree in art history and museology from Morgan State University and in 1981 a master of fine arts degree from the Maryland Institute College of Art. A lecturer and a curator at the University of Maryland Eastern Shore, he continued to arrange exhibitions until 1989, when he began to pursue a doctorate in computer art.

Some of Acha Debela's strongest paintings constitute a series entitled *The Refugees.* These paintings incorporate shadowy figures with blurred profiles, empty shapes groping for some substance. In *Journey to the Unknown* the figures have a ghostlike transparency, and the soft pastel colors and passive blue-gray outlines become electric when juxtaposed against other inanimate objects—a solid blood-red street, for example—and bring them close in feeling to Haile Gerima's film *Harvest: 3000 Years* as well as to the tragic figures of South African artist Cyprian Shilakoe (see chapter 14). They are surreal evocations of the same desolation and despair.

Even the musicians in Acha Debela's paintings seem lonely and bereft. Sometimes the geometric treatment of the non-figurative elements in these works is reminiscent of the paintings of Nigeria's Yusuf Grillo. Acha Debela's use of blue is similar to Grillo's use of blue, but his forms are less angular and more rhythmically flowing.

In a recent development Acha is finding a new synthesis between his ancient heritage of Coptic symbols and calligraphy and his former more figurative work. Drawing on the myriad forms of the talsam scrolls, illuminated manuscripts, and architecture, he has turned them into dazzling areas of crisp shapes and combined them with softly rounded human forms. Colors also go through changes as heavily patterned forms cluster in brilliant prismatic and light-refracting arrangements. This new breakthrough holds promise of rich possibilities.

Tesfaye Tessema's work has an iconic quality that conveys his Coptic-Byzantine heritage in ways that are, in form and spirit, convincing. He is also a colorist who works with color to exploit its intensities. The result is a loosely formed, interlocking collection of splashy shapes. They have the appearance of brilliant abandon, punctuated by eyes and heads, and occasionally a shape like an ancient obelisk from Aksum or a series of windows like those in Lalibela's twelfth- or thirteenth-century stone churches.

His paintings are testaments to crises evoking revolution and bloodshed, depicting soldiers and guns, images that record the moment. Sometimes the imagery is more controlled, closer to Skunder's intricacies. Tesfaye says that his works are also landscapes of meditation where, for him, colors change from morning to night according to the light. "The Ethiopian church is one inspiration that keeps our art going," he explains. "And Gebre Kristos was another. He taught me to be free with my colors, and not to be suffocated."[27]

Born in 1952, Tesfaye graduated from the Fine Arts School at the age of eighteen. He attributes the achievements of the modern movement to Gebre Kristos and other professors as well as to the atmosphere at the school, which encouraged individual freedom and originality of expression. Seeking further education, Tesfaye went to Washington, D.C., in 1971. He attended Howard University at a time when members of Africobra, a group of black American artists from Chicago, had begun teaching there.

Some of their stylistic elements, such as the division of space into small color swatches, are also a part of Tesfaye's stylistic approach, but his unique sensitivity for

Tesfaye Tessema, *The Red Flying Paper*, 1979, oil, 36" × 19". Location unknown.

color puts these elements to use as soft and luminous mosaic foundations for bold icons reminiscent of those in the talsam. A critic, noting these icons, suggested stylistic similarities to Paul Klee; rather than indications of influence from Klee, the similarity of the two artists' works are more properly attributable to Klee's use of Coptic imagery.[28]

But he also uses his iconography in a topical manner. In his painting *An Artist in Jail,* he divides physical elements with color swatches, that is, the bars frame the figure so that color functions not just as pattern but as structure. The framed figure also reinforces references to antique illuminated manuscripts: the artist imprisoned in a cell is analogous to the composition of a saint at work in a scriptorium. *The Red Flying Paper* is another instance of topical subject matter. It is inspired by "students who were passing red flyers just before the change. I had never seen such flyers before."[29]

He explains this tendency toward topicality by stating: [An artist] "is someone who uses his ability . . . to document events and ideas in the society and to run

Tesfaye Tessema, *An Artist in Jail,* 1970s, oil, 40" × 32". Location unknown.

commentary on what he sees and hears in the society. Therefore, the artist, to me, is a philosopher, a historian, a documentor, a commentator, a seer, and a prophet who uses the visual language to fulfill his obligation to the people."[30]

While in Washington, D.C., Tesfaye worked on the National Museum of African Art's courtyard murals (at the old A Street, Northeast location), which were painted as a tribute to South Africa's Ndebele culture. His work *The Ancestors* hangs in the College of Fine Arts at Howard University. He now lives in New York.

A sense of time and history defines Wosene Kosrof's canvases. In addition to canvas, Wosene, like Skunder, sometimes uses goatskin stretched to a thin membrane. In his works one can observe strong "wax and gold" references to Coptic manuscript painting. Building a patina of colors and shapes, he conveys inner and outer meanings in the same manner as do the layers of calligraphy on slates used by Islamic scholars. With visual allusions to Coptic imagery, he creates a feeling of the sinopic quality of the past. Crisply defined red, gold, and black letters on a white ground look as if they were cut out of paper, or floating in space; some contours are stencil-like and fashioned by the ground itself; some forms are opaque with metal-sharp geometric edges. He counterposes these elements against rough, energetic strokes and thickly textured underpainting. As a result of this approach, his work finds a parallel in the shifting imagery of traditional Amharic poetry.[31]

In an interview in July 1985, Wosene said,

The fact that I use Amharic calligraphy is an obvious connection with my cultural past: the monks applied the church language, Ge'ez, written with red and black paint, to underscore the visualized Biblical or religious story. . . . One major difference between the writings on my paintings and the writings of the monks on theirs, is that what I write is intelligible to all Ethiopians. Few understand the church language which is comparable to Latin in the West.

He explained that he believes that

. . . art always has a message because it arises out of a culture. Each artist is a part of his or her own culture, and uses his own particular understanding or reality when producing a work. . . . [t]he attitude that separates art from culture is the kind of attitude that perpetuates the view of an artist as superior, special, detached, inspired by muses, etc. I personally can not accept that attitude. . . . I explore the present continuously and this is reflected in my work. My paintings are about where I was, and where I am.

He also explained that he is not far from his roots.

It's only geographic distance that separates me. I carry my culture with me wherever I go. . . . Two ex-

Wosene Kosrof, *Prayer,* 1984, mixed media on canvas, 30″ × 15″. Private collection.

pressions that have greatly influenced me are graffiti from all parts of the world, and jazz. This great American music form is a constant inspiration to me. I try to capture rhythms of jazz on canvas, the moods the instruments create, the movements, the silences, their pacings. . . . I talk with artists as much as I can; I observe the American landscapes, clothing, and then I translate all this in to my own personal expression.

But my African, and in particular, Ethiopian, roots are always visible in my work.

In addition, Wosene states that an artist must "learn to let go of logic: by that I mean he goes beyond accepted 'reality' and, through his works, offers new ways of seeing, new possibilities for perceiving."[32]

Drawing on the wealth of calligraphy in the ancient liturgical languages of Geez and contemporary Amharic, each with alphabets of several hundred symbol characters, Wosene uses them like tracers to re-assert the authority of history. His works also document his own life. Childhood memories and neighborhoods give his work an autobiographical shape; in spite of the feeling for history, there is a conspicuous contemporary presence. In *The Blues* he documents the contemporary experience in the United States. In *Bag Women* he expresses the abrasive elements in modern life. Like other contemporary artists, Wosene feels compelled to describe the frictions generated by contact with a diverse mixture of peoples, reflecting the tensions, the frustrations, and the anger of the outsider.

The expression of this friction is the most dramatic and disturbing element in Wosene's work. Wild, unbridled strokes surge across the surface over finely wrought calligraphy, like graffiti scribbled in willed disharmony over pre-existing concepts, uniting anarchy with order.

Like Shibrain of Sudan, who uses the forms and literary meaning of calligraphy, Wosene also makes aesthetic use of calligraphy's meaning and form, and is one of the first Ethiopian artists to do so. In his works, painting and writing become one. He also often incorporates folk songs and poems in his calligraphy.

Born in 1950, Wosene obtained a bachelor of fine arts degree from the School of Fine Arts in Addis Ababa in 1972, and then taught painting and drawing there. He received a master of fine arts degree from Howard University, which he attended from 1978–1980. He has exhibited his works in Africa, Great Britain, Europe, the Caribbean, and the United States.

Another artist who works in the eastern United States is Falaka Armide. Although first a sculptor, he is now one of the most important East African printmakers. Born in 1935, he obtained a bachelor of fine arts degree from the Fine Arts School in Addis Ababa, studying under Gebre Kristos and Skunder, and later obtained a master's degree in art at Howard University, where he specialized in printmaking.

Falaka carries a sense of sculptural form into his printmaking, creating birds, horses, and human figures in which he emphasizes strong anatomical forms. He uses design patterns and swirling configurations to delineate muscles and limbs in motion, especially in the woodcut *Freedom*. Linear configurations build up quivering masses of great power, creating a feeling of violent

Wosene Kosrof, *Talisman* (detail), 1984, acrylic on canvas, 38" × 21". Private collection.

Wosene Kosrof, *Almaz*, 1984, acrylic on goatskin, 12" × 16". Collection of Kiros W. Selassie.

Wosene Kosrof, *Prayer II*, 1980, mixed media on canvas, 52" × 32". Location unknown.

agitation and conflict. Horses, twisting, contorted, are expressionist symbols as are his depictions of vultures with flamelike wings.

In *Struggle, Netakee,* and *The Vulture,* the bird is a metaphor for evil. *Struggle* depicts an old man with a vulture on his head, and refers to the struggle to survive under the Italian occupation, a time when vultures attacked those who were starving but still alive. Falaka's images seem bred in a crucible of pain, and indeed they are intended to reflect his anger with the inequities he perceives in Ethiopia. Falaka now teaches printmaking, drawing, and restoration at Howard University. He has had numerous one-person shows in the United States and Ethiopia, and in 1971 he won an *African Arts* magazine award.

Two other artists who studied at Howard University and were given their first impetus by Gebre Kristos and Skunder are Seleshi Feseha and Alemayehou Gabremedhin. Both attended the Fine Arts School in Addis Ababa before going abroad. Seleshi, who was born in 1944, studied for two years at the Museum School in Boston, and obtained a bachelor of fine arts degree with honors from Howard University. After returning to and spending five years in Ethiopia, he traveled to Warsaw, Poland, where he successfully earned a master of fine arts degree, again with honors, at the Academy of Fine Arts.

According to A. B. Spellman, director of Expansion Arts at the National Endowment for the Arts, Seleshi began to look deeper for meanings while working under Skunder at Howard University. Describing Seleshi's work, Spellman said "Symbols move in and out of reality." In the painting *Ten Billion Dollars,* "A casually destructive Lion of Judah, oblivious of the hooded form, which represents the aspirations of the Ethiopian people, carries a crown across the carcasses of the

victims of the State. Thus, the multi-million dollar looting of the nation's treasury by the late emperor, Haile Selassie, is conveyed." Spellman goes on to interpret other paintings that express the "excesses of the Menghistu [*sic*] regime."[33]

Seleshi captures, as does Skunder, a sense of antiquity. *Axum,* glowing with pale red luminous color, repeats, like visual echoes, old Coptic symbols such as the outlines of windows in the ancient orthodox churches of Lalibela. Also like Skunder, he uses delicate molecular forms to create a crystalline atmosphere. Edges are fused and color is soft and muted. In this atmosphere he sets small geometric constellations; they suggest an eternity of time and space. Such treatment, as well as reflections of history and contemporary issues of justice, distinguish his work from that of his colleague Alemayehou Gabremedhin, whose forms and color are more robust.

Seleshi says that although modern African art is separate from culture, it shouldn't be philosophically separate. He sees an artist as "a witness of his times" who "opens" himself to society, which in turn learns from his work. Although he believes that art does not necessarily carry a message, he says that his own work depicts political oppression.[34]

Alemayehou Gabremedhin, a recipient of a trustee scholarship at Howard University, also has a master of fine arts degree from that school. Now working in Maryland, he says,

Why do I paint? I ask myself that question often. I basically paint for myself. I feel satisfaction when I

Wosene Kosrof, *Gunda Gunde,* 1988, oil on canvas, 12" × 12". Private collection.

Falaka Armide, *Freedom*, early 1980s?, woodcut, 30″ × 45″.

express joy, as well as anger in my work. I live in my paintings. My most rewarding moments are when I paint my inner feelings. I do not seek a style; I do not want to become restricted by such conventional ideas and not be able to express my feeling naturally.[35]

My subject matter conveys impressions and concerns about my own part of the world. I use concepts and visual images from ancient Coptic-Christian art and architecture, traditional and modern music of Ethiopia, and contemporary African-American cultural patterns such as jazz rhythms. I employ a variety of bright colors to produce forms and shapes such as the crosses, the Axum obelisk, the churches at Lalibela to transmit visual messages that have a philosophical content, are aesthetically remarkable, and create a feeling that is Africa.[36]

Some of his most omnipresent images are the narrow scroll shapes, the forms of traditional musical instruments, and the patterns inspired by the borders of women's woven shawls. About the latter, he says,

I like using the basic visual vocabulary of circles, triangles and squares, so I can create rhythmic patterns on canvas. The rhythmic feeling I communicate through repetition of these geometric shapes has been inspired by the brilliant overlapping patterns found in the clothing of Ethiopian women, by musical counterpoint and by the precision of mathematics. I purposely work in series to express continuity and to emphasize the single motif which, supported by numerous interacting symbols, will eventually become the spiritual force needed to activate the energy of the African people.

He continues,

I draw inspiration from the black American experience and use color to express the violence and oppression of the black dilemma. I feel the survival of African traces in African-American culture is important: survivals are positive examples of the strength of our traditional art systems.[37]

Alemayehou creates thick, dense formal patterns and organic designs with the texture of snake skin or feathers. Using acrylics and watercolors he builds prismatic effects by transposing symbols to form narrow, undulating bands of color in kaleidoscopic focus. In all his work there is a sense of restless motion, an upward thrust, and a controlled, but tempestuous force.

Elisabeth Atnafu, also a graduate of Howard University, demonstrates that modern Ethiopian expression is not totally a male preserve. She has exhibited in New York, Washington, D.C., Los Angeles, and Guadalajara, Mexico. Now working in New York, she combines a fascination for delicate pattern—a part of the visual grammar of most Ethiopian painters—with broad, slashing strokes. She defines transparent forms with these

Seleshi Feseha, *Axum*, 1970s, acrylic on board, 19¾″ × 27⅝″. Collection of Jeff Donaldson.

Alemayehou Gabremedhin, *Untitled*, 1985, watercolor, dimensions unknown. Collection of the artist.

Elisabeth Atnafu, *Lovers in Love*, 1984, mixed media, 40″ × 60″. Location unknown.

strokes, revealing layers of intricate linear symbols in high-key colors.

Her process seems related to that of Wosene Kosrof. Both take advantage of the possibilities for complexity that underpainting allows; both make use of graffiti-like patterns and expressionist strokes; but Atnafu's imagery is ethereal. She creates a sense of illusion, of shifting space, and of soft diaphanous draperies which, while enclosing a clutter of agitated shapes, seem constantly wafted by rhythms. She paints in a large format, and the major shapes suggest dancers and the influence of music. Indeed, she designed two album covers for Ornette Coleman.

These Ethiopian artists, representative of many others, use their Coptic-Byzantine heritage in ways that underline their inherent sophistication, illustrate the great diversity of culture on the continent, and at the same time disclose their very Africanness. That so many are in exile only seems to make them reach deeper into their past and their own psyches for their cultural identities. From this sensitivity and searching grows the panoptic splendor and subtlety that characterize their work. Their fresh interpretations break out of the mold, but their genesis is at the profound core of "wax and gold." As individuals and as a group, they are giving us glimpses of Ethiopian antiquity in concert with today's reality.

V

Creators of Myth

11   Between the Natural and Supernatural

A renaissance in the visual arts of the sort that occurred in Nigeria, Senegal, Ethiopia, Sudan, Zimbabwe, and South Africa has yet to unfold in East and Central Africa. Writers and poets, however, perhaps as precursors, have found an "African" voice, and have created new images to address contemporary issues. Authors Ngugi wa Thiong'o and Joseph Kariuki of Kenya, Okot p'Bitek and Taban lo Liong of Uganda, and Tchicaya U Tam'si of Congo Republic, respond to today's exigencies with language that is powerful. Although foreign—French or English—it is transformed to serve other cultural canons and needs.

While a number of outstanding visual artists have appeared, their numbers are small. One of the reasons is a demographic one: the total population of Kenya, Tanzania, Uganda, and Zaire is less than that of Nigeria alone. In addition, recurrent migrations from Ethiopia south across savannah lands to graze herds or to escape slave traders resulted in the periodic shifting of peoples, and the disrupting of patterns of continuity.

The stability of farming communities, which provided a consistent structure for the arts, and the proximity of nearby rain forests, which created environments for the great traditions of West Africa, didn't exist in East Africa. Art forms in East Africa consisted of items worn or carried such as jewelry, basketry, vessels, rugs, and the arts of adornment. And architectural relics such as tombs and mosques along the Swahili coast demonstrate the early artistic and religious influence of Islam, ex-emplified by the carved doors of Lamu, and the arts of calligraphy and body painting.

Although wood carving was practiced in Kenya, Tanzania, Uganda, Mozambique, and the Central African Republic, only in Zaire and Congo do these classical arts parallel those of West Africa. The variety in central Africa spans a gamut from some of the greatest carvings in the world to delicate Kuba cloth and sacred emblems of authority including crowns, armlets, and knives, which are of great artistic merit and have been a source of inspiration for artists in other parts of the world for six decades.

One factor that hampered the development of a modern art movement was colonial education, which emphasized European values, employed European methods and curriculum, and generally neglected to encourage indigenous expression. Makerere University College in Kampala, Uganda, served several countries, but instruction followed the British pattern. While Margaret Trowell, the British artist and teacher who founded in 1937 the School of Fine Arts, now a part of Makerere University College, refused to give painting demonstrations, easel painting did develop, and a number of artists created works that reflect this approach. The direction there could not compare with that acquired at the Technical Institute at Zaria, Nigeria, or the support given the arts by the government of Senegal. Also no artist-professors with the vision and experience of Khartoum's Shibrain and El Salahi or Addis Ababa's Gebre Kristos

Desta and Skunder Boghossian emerged under this system.

Except for Pancho Guedes in Maputo, Mozambique, and Elimo Njau in Nairobi, Kenya, there were no extraordinary catalysts and mentors like Georgina Beier and Frank McEwen (see chapters 12 and 13) to encourage fresh directions, rather than impose European criteria and aesthetics. Most importantly, traditional values and, in logical sequence, contemporary cultural expressions were undermined by the presence of colonial settlers. Coupled with exploitation for tourist markets, the psychological vestiges and physical strictures of colonialism continued to operate after independence in the form of economic imperialism, which hampered the free development of original expression.

One should add that artistic expression in East Africa has a major ally in nature, itself. In Kenya, Tanzania, and Uganda, the grandeur of the landscape—plateaus, majestic mountains, waterfalls, lakes, and the national parks (six million acres in Kenya alone)—may well be the source of the transcendental quality in the arts. Creatively interpreted, it reflects not only its own magnificence, but the variety of life cycles, religions, and peoples whether Bantu, Nilotic, Judaic, Indian, or Arabian.

In contrast, with tropical rain forests Zaire and Congo have numerous sculptural traditions of the many indigenous peoples. Unfortunately, instead of serving as a basis for growth, their incomparable legacy has become a seductive force encouraging sentimental attachments to the past. The results of instruction under the aegis of three institutions—the Desfosses School in Lubumbashi (later incorporated into the Académie des Beaux-Arts and des Metiers d'Art run by Laurent Moonens), the École St. Luc founded by Frère Marc-Stanislas in Kinshasa (later also Académie des Beaux-Arts), and the Poto-Poto School in Brazzaville—were mixed. The new art, frequently lacking in purpose and content, took a decorative turn. In this atmosphere romantic rhetoric substituted for fresh vision.

While many artists have suffered the restraints of Western academic schooling, the following selection consists of artists who create works that draw from the past, yet address the present. They suggest the future talent of Uganda, Kenya, Tanzania, Mozambique, Zaire, and Central African Republic, demonstrating remarkable originality, consistency of direction, and technical facility in an artistic climate of dull tourist art and Western academic painting.

These individuals, reviewed in a sequence that loosely parallels their age and appearance on the modern scene, are Gregory Maloba, Sam Ntiro, and Elimo Njau, all of whom studied with Margaret Trowell. Their art is often affected by European or Eurocentric teaching, but they are particularly important because of their historical position and the encouragement they have given to others.

Their influence began in the forties, the early days of contemporary art in East Africa. Maloba, one of the first students at Makerere University College School of Fine Arts in Kampala, developed concurrently with the school, and soon became an instructor. Displaying a talent for handling massive form, recognized by Henry Moore and reminiscent of Jacob Epstein, he occupied a role like Nigeria's Ben Enwonwu by creating public works, such as the *Independence Monument* for Uganda, for example. As an early modern artist, he bridged foreign and indigenous cultures.

Working in stone, wood, bronze, cement fondue (a luminous cement used in casting), and terra-cotta, Maloba eventually moved from portraiture, which was formidable but Western in style, to equally imposing, but more contemporary concepts. These more recent pieces represent a triumph over his academic background. Of monumental proportions, they might be compared to the work of Henry Moore, but they have a distinct African presence, a description not altogether inappropriate to Moore's work.

Born in Mumias, Kenya, in 1922, he also studied at four different institutions in England, including the Royal College of Art from 1956 to 1957. He taught at Makerere University College for more than twenty years and, from 1966 until his retirement, was head of the Department of Design at the University of Nairobi. Exhibiting extensively, he has served in many other capacities in support of the arts.

Sam Ntiro (1923–), born in Machame, Kilimanjaro, Tanzania, also graduated from the Makerere University College School of Fine Arts and, like Maloba, taught there. He too studied in London at the Slade School of Fine Arts at the University of London, and spent a few weeks in the United States on a Carnegie traveling grant, and later as an artist-in-residence at Southern University in New Orleans. As an early teacher, he had a seminal influence. His paintings, which depict landscapes and people at work, however, are limited by a highly stylized approach.

The contributions made by Elimo Njau (1932–), who studied with Ntiro, are different. For years he has worked to encourage artists at a grass roots level in Tanzania as well as in Kenya. Njau, born in Marangu, Tanzania, near Kilimanjaro, was graduated from Makerere University College with a degree in fine arts and education. He supports and encourages artists because he is concerned about the channeling of talents into Western educational systems. He has established two nonprofit galleries: the Paa-ya-Paa in Nairobi and the Kibo in Marangu. Here East African artists, and sometimes artists from abroad, work and exhibit.

Njau explains that "Paa-ya-Paa" means "the antelope

rises" and is a symbol of new "creative adventures." As a gallery it "seeks to be 'just a place' away from lecture halls and away from experts, a place where creative ideas and thoughts may flourish and flow freely between persons in the spirit of equality and in a relaxed and casual atmosphere. In such a place and atmosphere we hope artists, musicians, architects, writers, playwrights, actors and critics will gather momentum for further creative work."[1]

Elimo Njau sees the countryside as a source of creativity waiting to be developed. "Excessive use of cultural material imported from abroad for television and the arts . . . is not only expensive but [it] gradually kills our confidence in indigenous material let alone our awareness of original local possibilities and experimentation in the use of local material to cut down costs and boost the local image of our indigenous artists' work."[2] Many of his own works, stylized landscapes, like those by Ntiro, hang in prominent places, some as murals in public buildings in Kenya, Uganda, and Tanzania.

Also a product of Makerere University College is Louis Mwaniki, a professor, sculptor, painter, and printmaker. Born in 1934 in Nyeri, Kenya, he studied in Turin, Italy, from 1961 to 1963. Returning to teach at the University of Nairobi, he left again in 1967 to study in Montreal, Canada, for two years. Later, with a doctorate in art education from New York University, he returned to Nairobi, where he teaches at University of Nairobi's Kenyatta College.

Mwaniki's artistry has a focus that is distinctly African in spite of his foreign experiences. Unlike the work of some artists that bears the stamp of colonial imperatives, he turns the medium to his own purpose; as a result, his work becomes African.

Mwaniki, one of East Africa's fine printmakers, has contributed graphic illustrations to a number of East African publications, and his prints have been included in numerous exhibits abroad. In *Things Fall Apart* and *Despair* crisp blacks and definitive forms demonstrate his technical proficiency. *Watching over People of the City* is a painting that reveals his capacity for striking imagery. His sculpture, like that of Francis X. Nnaggenda of Uganda (also discussed in this chapter), combines metal and rough-textured wood bearing marks of the adz. Rounded corners and solid rocklike forms give his sculptures the appearance of large talismans and amulets. Coordinating individual sculpture images, he creates assemblages in which they function as integral units.

Another carver, Athumani Omari Mwariko, after an apprenticeship to Elimo Njau, opened his own art gallery, Mwariko's Art Gallery, in 1967 in Moshi, Tanzania. There he showed his own works. When the gallery suffered a fire, he restored it to house a variety of artifacts. Born in 1944, in Handeni, Tanzania, he studied at Makerere University College School of Fine Arts. He

later attended Haystack Mountain School in Maine. He has exhibited in London, Japan, the United States and East Africa, and has contributed illustrations to numerous publications.

His carvings have the energy of quick, spontaneous drawings. As in the work of Mwaniki and Nnaggenda, the rugged strokes of the adz remain. The resulting strength is reminiscent of work by Ghana's Vincent Kofi. However, there is an important difference. Though generally smaller than Kofi's giant pieces, and in contrast to the calm strength of the latter's sculpture, Mwariko's work expresses emotion that is volatile, and the figures seem to cry out in despair.

Suffering and despair are frequently expressed by East African artists, especially in reaction to political oppression. Athumani Mwariko, like Francis Nnaggenda and Musani Muyinga of Uganda, Kiure Msangi of Tanzania, Hezbon Owiti of Kenya, and Henry Tayali of Zambia, makes strong statements, frequently leavened with humor, about personal and communal tragedies.

Athumani Omari Mwariko, *Wrestler,* date unknown, wood, 12" high. Collection of Donald Bowen, courtesy of Commonwealth Institute.

A combination of tragedy and humor also describes the work of Samwel Wanjau. When Wanjau brought carvings to show Elimo Njau in 1966, Njau saw a special talent that deserved encouragement, and he responded: "I found that even in his antelopes there was a sense of movement which made the animals appear not static like so many . . . done for the tourist market." Njau then encouraged him to "create stories and anecdotes instead of doing small individual animals," and to make use of the grain and bark.[3] After two years of working under Njau's aegis, Wanjau held a one-person show in Njau's gallery.

Born in 1936 in Nyeri, Kenya, Wanjau has had a hard life. His father was a blacksmith, and he was fascinated by his father's workshop. Living through the Emergency, he carved stocks for the guns of the Mau Mau, and "was arrested and thrown in jail. His father's hut was burnt down by the Home Guard and everything was destroyed." He was shot in the arm as he tried to escape and was returned to jail.[4]

In 1957 Wanjau joined a group of Wakamba carvers at the Gikomba Center in Nairobi, but further vissicitudes included his arrest for not paying a poll tax, and being sent back to his birthplace. In 1961 he returned to Nairobi and joined the Wakamba artists a second time. He already had an individual direction as an artist, and although he felt the Wakamba work too limiting, he stayed. There he became technically proficient.

With the help of Elimo Njau, he was able to work in new ways with larger pieces of wood. He defined areas of the carvings with various textures instead of with the glassy smooth surfaces of the tourist pieces. The strength of his forms must be forged by his own odyssey, and considering its harshness, the humor in his work is all the more moving.

Terry Hirst, in an article in *African Arts,* says that for Wanjau "the conviction with which he expresses himself in both word and wood grows out of long silences." Hirst suggests that Wanjau has a close tie to his own culture because he has not been "educated away from . . . tradition" and that because his Kikuyu village is central to his life, it is the "foundation upon which he constructs his creative assault upon the city."[5]

Hirst goes on to compare Wanjau with a singer or storyteller who is reflecting his experiences through tales about a farmer and forest fighter, or rebel. Hirst also comments on Wanjau's fresh perceptions of older themes and cites as an example "the hare ingratiating itself with the tortoise by putting on a tortoise shell [an act] which has wider implications in" today's Kenya. He invents timely modern themes as well: "paratroopers," "beauty queens," and "forest fighters."

Hirst explains that Wanjau "once told a group of students that he has only to see a piece of wood, and he realizes the complete sculpture within it."[6] While each of Wanjau's creatures projects specific traits, each is the quintessence of its species, and they convey human characteristics as well. In a typically African synthesis Wanjau, like the Shona sculptors of Zimbabwe (see chapter 13), also depicts metamorphosis. He distills these characteristics, both human and animal, and creates uncanny references to both. Moreover, he maintains the original quality of the medium itself—so often lost in the process of carving statues for tourists.

Although they relate to everyday life and people, his carvings are never rote. Each carvings leaves no doubt that it expresses closely what Wanjau sees. With vigor and directness, they provide metaphors for and insights into myth and nature.

Francis X. Nnaggenda, born in Uganda in 1936, makes striking statements with sculpture that is radically different from the work of both Wanjau and Maloba. Endowing his work with suggestions of myth, he arrives at a subtle synthesis. Like Maloba, Nnaggenda has taught for a number of years at the University of Nairobi, and his pieces are installed at the National Culture Center in Kampala.

Nnaggenda is a Baganda from Bukumi, and one of the few East African artists not to have attended Makerere University College. First attending the Technical Institute in Kampala in 1959, he later became an apprentice at Freibourg University in Switzerland. He then attended for three years the Bayerische Akademie der Schönen Künste in Munich, where he completed in 1967 a five-year course.

Nnaggenda's foreign experience and the years of turmoil at home have served as catalysts to bring together elements of conflict. In his large pieces, as in Skunder Boghossian's paintings made in the sixties, the ancient world appears to confront the modern world. Nnaggenda accomplishes this by combining various kinds of wood with hand-hewn surfaces and jagged textures— the marks of the adze still in evidence—with vestiges of smudged paint, daubed colors, and fabricated metal. Such startling juxtapositions invest his pieces with a rugged power. Generally quite large, some of them combine a variety of found objects including old saw blades, nails, and metal scraps.

His assemblages display neither the dilettante use of objet trouvé nor calculated artifice. One large piece, *Spirit Within Man,* recalls, as do Nigerian Jinadu Oladepo's small brass cast figures, the stoic stance of an icon with two large eyes as the dominant feature of three faces.

My Inner Trainer is reminiscent of the works of American sculptor Uzikwee Nelson, who constructs large welded sculptures based on African imagery. With its harsh grainy surface, there is something more strident and apocalyptic in Nnaggenda's piece—a foreboding

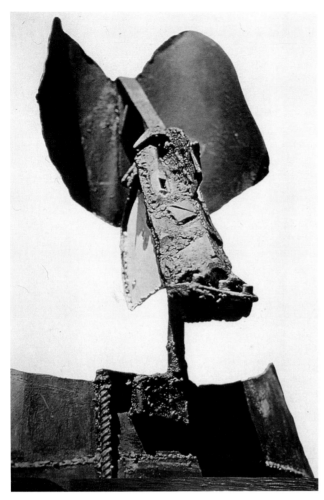

Francis X. Nnaggenda, *My Inner Trainer,* 1967, painted and welded metal, 84" high. National Cultural Center, Kampala.

figure poised as if for flight. *Blood Rain Dust* has a sense of battles, of scars, and of losses. Rough metal patches on wood, like scraps of medieval chain mail, and nails bent to close a woundlike crevice, suggest a maimed or brutally severed potential.

This maiming of human potential is Nnaggenda's theme, and pieces such as this one echo the stark, challenging poetry of his countryman, Taban lo Liong:

with lights we came on scene in time machines
and thought first generator toy
and dismantled wheel rod indicators
shaking cosmology out of balance.

. . . puny nietzches strut
bloated frogs
race of supermen has come . . . was auschwitz far
sacredness is dead
and hiroshima invented.[7]

A recent work, *War Victims,* integrates his concern for the ecology of the natural environment with suffering

endured in Uganda during the 1970s. Sidney Kasfir, in an article on Nnaggenda, addresses the conflicts that present a challenge to today's artists. She cites another: "Widespread belief in witchcraft, in what is now supposedly a Christian country, poses endless riddles and ambiguities for the sensitive artist responsive to his environment." And drawing attention to the difference between the works of Nnaggenda and other African sculptors who consciously adapt African classical forms, she points out that "there is no anthropological self-consciousness in Nnaggenda's work."[8]

In contrast to the organic nature of classical African sculpture and the images by Oladepo or Nelson, the works of Nnaggenda have elements that seem disassociated, or "added on," producing startling juxtapositions. Rather than accumulating or generating other forms, forms and materials function to jolt the viewer. Like Valente Malangatana of Mozambique (also discussed in this chapter), Nnaggenda grapples with the dichotomy between imported and traditional values, and in so doing, creates art that is passionately iconoclastic and suggests conflicts between the natural and supernatural worlds.

The supernatural and natural are joined in a more organic way in the prints of Hezbon Owiti (1946–). Born in Nyanza, Kenya, Owiti had his first major showing of prints and paintings in 1965 at the Mbari Mbayo Gallery in Lagos. An overriding sense of East Africa asserted itself despite the fact that Owiti, a Luo, created these prints and oil paintings in Oshogbo, and even included certain elements reflective of West Africa.

Describing his beginnings, he says,

I was born in Central Nyanza, Kenya. My parents were very poor, but my mother was a very good pot-maker. In 1956 I was sent to school to start my foundation in education through the little money of my mother's pots. I took an interest in art during this time and used water colours, pencil and my mother's clay. At the age of 15 I won the Young Artist Certificate of East Africa.[9]

His opportunity to go to Oshogbo came while working as a young artist on his own. Offered a job as caretaker of the Chemichemi Cultural Centre in Nairobi, Owiti was helped by the then director of the center, South African writer Es'kia Mphahlele. Through Mphahlele, Owiti obtained a six-month scholarship from the Farfield Foundation, enabling him to work at the University of Ibadan and in Oshogbo.

After his experience in Nigeria, Owiti wrote:

Artists are ever poor, I am one of the poorest. But I am just 24 years old. I have already achieved critical if not financial success. I have held one-man shows in Nairobi, Lagos, Ibaden [*sic*], Oshogbo, Dar es Salaam,

Addis Ababa, and Ohio. And my works have appeared in . . . museums in the United States, Great Britain and Canada. . . .[10]

In Oshogbo he was stimulated by atmosphere and artists. From the start, his canvases, thickly painted with brilliant color, had a strong African sensibility. One painting depicting a crippled person with large crutches and whose head is bent at a right angle to the body is especially touching. *Laughter at the Zoo* reverses people and animals in a burlesque comment on humanity. Owiti explains:

They came along to feed us
They threw their rotten uncooked
food to me
Their laughter was endless when
we chased it
The lines on their faces were
legible with hate
Oooo was their mouth and eyes.[11]

Owiti's interest in animals began as a young child when he started making figures of goats and cows, telling stories about them to other children.

I naturally and [*sic*] a self-taught artist. I became attendant and assistant gallery-keeper at Chemichemi Cultural Centre in 1963. Without any teaching I groped my way through using oil, ink, and pencil. Later in October that year I won a special prize for a carving at Nairobi's Freedom From Hunger exhibition, which subsequently toured the United States.[12]

His black and white prints, with stark silhouetted images and the barest details—like the chiseled planes of a carving disassembled and then reconstructed so as to be seen in two dimensions—are neither imitative nor nostalgic. Sharp-angled forms and elongated limbs

Hezbon Owiti, *Life Tree of All Animals,* late 1960s or early 1970s, linoleum cut, 10″ × 14″.

crowd against the frame. A sense of motion is further enhanced by the lines left when negative spaces were carved into the original block.

Motion is an inherent characteristic in Owiti's works, especially in his images of horses, which parallel a description of a wild Serengeti horse by Nairobi poet Tejani: "arched neck/and thick nostrils/quicksilver quivering, . . . he stood square/with gun-powder feet," and at the sound of an auto horn, "he exploded convulsively/feet limbs and body/boosting each other/and rose/rose."[13]

This energy has zoomorphic and anthropomorphic sources as Owiti depicts a spirit world, bringing alive trees that join with horses and human figures. Humorous or sad, they are always kinetic.

He explains the spirit transformations:

As an artist one quickly becomes used to this intense loneliness. There is no one for you to go to, and you must have total assurance and total honesty. . . . Suggest you are the only one in the world—you have everything you need—the loneliness comes and then death joins you—everything looks danger to you—suggest you join trees and skeletons.[14]

Hezbon Owiti, *Horse,* 1966, linoleum cut, 8¾″ × 11⅞″.

Depicting this metamorphosis (an integral part of East African belief systems, including that of his own Luo culture), and steeped in masquerade and myth, Owiti is like the stone sculptors of Zimbabwe (see chapter 13). His combinations of animals, trees, and humans, like the Shona's depictions of one creature changing into another, are powerfully evocative of trance. They become metaphors for the unity of conscious and unconscious life.

In his work a man and horse image; a multi-headed horse; a tree trunk, which takes on human form; and tree limbs, which become birds, animals and humans, reinforce the strength of the unpredictable, the sense of magic and transformation, and the connection between the natural, or physical world, and the world of the spirit.

Kiure Msangi (1937–) of Tanzania does not generally interpret subjects such as metamorphosis in his paintings. Addressing political inequities and grievances, he has used traditional symbols in powerfully expressive paintings to interpret the impact of tragedy. Motivated by the Sharpeville Massacre in South Africa, the assassination of John F. Kennedy, then by that of revolutionary Frelimo leader Eduardo Mondlane, and finally by the killing of a political leader and his neighbor, Tom Mboya, his paintings of these subjects illustrate Msangi's potential as an artist. The painting that depicted the funeral of Mondlane was purchased by subscription and given to Syracuse University where Mondlane studied.

In these works pattern and style are forgotten and the horror of a cosmic disaster is paramount. Brilliant colors and violent strokes are propelled by unbridled urgency. Slashing, thrusting, they shape the figures with thick impasto colors—reds, purples, browns, blacks—and form a powerful alliance with traditional masks. Among the paintings where this marriage is blatant, yet viable, the mask-like faces come alive in a macabre evocation of both history and the present. As recipients of violence, the figures represent the victimization of peoples swept up in history's malevolent floods.

In his depiction of evil and anguish, he is close to Malangatana of Mozambique: neither painter separates himself from feelings and worldly concerns in order to reach an objective state. In Msangi's paintings color and form plumb the depths of physical feeling; figures huddle in fear and are splayed like animals at the slaughter, their skeletal faces torn. They are the antithesis of images in which thought and feeling are distilled to serve as vehicles for meditation.

In the poetry of Kenyan poet Jonathan Kariara, Msangi's victims find their counterparts. Kariara's poem, "Vietnam," describes women whose babies have been slaughtered: "Women sat reclining/Monuments of peace/Sculptured by death, . . . winnowed/(The dross drifted with the river)."[15]

Kiure Msangi, *The Sharpeville Shooting,* 1970, acrylic on board, 24″ × 32″. Collection of the artist.

Msangi points out that his people, the Pare, are a group that is only 150 years old with a history of recurrent migrations in search of farming or grazing lands.[16] Growing up in a rural environment, he planted seeds and cared for yam vines when he was three years old. As a young adult he attended Makerere University College, where he obtained a bachelor of fine arts degree and a diploma in education. With a Fulbright Scholarship, he earned another bachelor of fine arts degree, this one at the California College of Arts and Crafts, and a doctorate in education from Stanford University.

While in California, he taught at a number of local institutions (Mills College, California College of Arts and Crafts, City College of San Francisco, and Stanford University), helping students understand African values and cultures. He deplores the fact that Africans have been defined by others: "scholars look at other civilizations as 'interesting' instead of as made up of human beings and human experiences." He points out that the Western world appears to be asking, "How long are they going to take until they get to where we are?"

Msangi believes that:

Western academia tends to look at humanity from its own angle, and if only people could lower their guard, when they study other people and really feel as one with them, they could begin to understand why people think and feel the way they do, and then all of that warmth that is African would be understood.

Msangi stresses the importance of humanist principles, which he sees as,

being dropped in favor of personal aggrandisement and personal pursuit of happiness which never really translates into happiness. . . . When people were less pursuant of materialism, they had less material things, but they pursued goals which were more long-lasting, which were humanly more beneficial.

Finally speaking on behalf of the preservation of differences among peoples, he explains,

> I think the world was intended to be a multi-racial, multi-lingual and multi-cultural globe. That way it has the potential for feeding and enriching all of us. I would hate to see all people black. . . . I would hate to see all people white or all people Chinese.
>
> Even one language, you see . . . I can use English in writing and speech to express my thoughts, I'm sure, as well as I can use Kiswahili, and I'm sure as well as I can use Kipare, and yet with my wife who is Pare . . . there are certain beautiful intimate things we can share in Kipare, we don't even have the concept for in Kiswahili, let alone in English. And there are certain things we can share in Kiswahili for which there is no equivalent in English at all and I would hate to think that I would be limited to English, or to Kiswahili or to Kipare because then I couldn't partake of all this wealth here and that wealth there.[17]

Because of his humanist concerns, perceptions of tragedy often form the basis of Kiure Msangi's work. In it he confronts the tragedy of Eurocentric attitudes and presumptions with an understanding sharpened by his many years abroad. He is now committed to working in East Africa, where he is on the faculty of Kenyatta College in Nairobi.

Conflict between current tragedy and past tradition is a characteristic of the work of Valente Malangatana Ngwenya (1936–) of Mozambique. His powerful imagery weaves together the strands of indigenous culture with those of an imposed one, so that they still retain all of the stresses and strains of their inherent dichotomies.

Like Msangi, Malangatana had humble rural beginnings, and worked hard as a child. His father kept leaving home to work in the South African mines. His mother had talents for beadwork and was a tattoo artist, and like many African children, for want of paper, Malangatana drew pictures in the sand. When his mother became ill, he went to live with his aunt. There he kept drawing—often religious subjects prompted by his Catholic schooling—and struggled with menial jobs to earn a living. He eventually went to night school to study art.

Although he received a lot of criticism from others who thought he was wasting his time, he threw himself into a flurry of painting. In 1959 Pancho Guedes, a Portuguese architect who had designed buildings in Maputo with a sculptural brilliance likened to those by Antonio Gaudi, met Malangatana, who was working as a ball boy in the Lourenço Marques Club. Guedes eventually arranged a stipend and studio for him.

Expressing himself both in painting and writing, Malangatana defines his approach to painting in a short biography,

> . . . I do paint for pleasure, not as a profession, but because I love art and poetry. Apart from this, poetry is art written on white paper without colour and in repeated letters, but poetry in a picture has life, smell and movement also . . . and I will even say that wherever I am, I shall be painting. . . ."[18]

This he has done, and twenty-seven years later, he paints consistently and has completed a prodigious body of work. He has also suffered incarceration, an experience that surely influenced his later work. His latest series cries out for change, and has earned him the role of revolutionary painter. His paintings have been exhibited throughout the world including Europe (at the Museum für Volkerkunde, Leipzig, Germany; and at the Secretaria de Estado de Cultura, Lisbon), the United States (at the National Museum of African Art, Washington, D.C., and at the African-American Institute, New York City), and Cuba (at the Havana Biennial). He has also received a scholarship to study etching in Portugal.

His haunting canvases, crowded with bodies and bursting with energy, communicate a feeling of crushing pressures in the barrios and streets of Maputo. Soldiers and sailors with weapons and flags consort with prostitutes; weapons, flags, freedom fighters, and pregnant women form a tableau conveying the texture of violence and love and the necessity for change.

His colors, rich reds, dark purples, intense cadmium yellows and oranges, are heavy but luminous like stained glass. He uses them to depict conflict, struggle, rape, seduction, religious ritual, witchcraft, and initiation rites. Some have said that his work is a kind of "black mass," and speaks of a vision not unlike that of Hieronymus Bosch.[19]

As human episodes of nightmarish intensity, painting itself became a kind of exorcism. Within his paintings a palpable aura of magic and evil coexists with love and procreation. His work not only reveals fundamental conflicts but also, because it draws from episodes in his life, contains an essence that is both painful and passionate. These episodes perform another kind of exorcism: they wrench attention from the commonplace to force concentration on life's intensities.

His drawings with delicately wrought outlines also articulate an almost tangible pressure. Space is crammed with rocklike sculptural forms of voluptuous nudes. Masses of heads, limbs, bellies, and breasts are compacted. Images of the cross, of possession, and various creatures with claws and fangs form an ominous alliance. Fascinating details shock, mesmerize, and exert

Valente Malangatana, *Youth Listening to Tales of Bunyale,* 1969, ink, 19¾" × 14⅛". Private collection.

fearful supernatural powers: a lizard-like monster nuzzles a man's head. In many of the paintings a self-portrait shows the artist with tears of blood, hands of monstrous size, and ubiquitous, staring eyes. While a sense of evil pervades, also inherent in this and most of Malangatana's works is the illusion of life, of abundance, and of overpowering sensuality.

In his drawings and paintings, women with cascading strands of hair and full rounded forms are bewitching symbols of refuge, love, salvation, and danger.

In his poetry, woman is sanctuary:

In the cool waters of the river
we shall have fish that are huge
which shall give the sign of
the end of the world perhaps
because they will make an end of woman
woman who adorns the fields
woman who is the fruit of man

The flying fish makes an end of searching
because woman is the gold of man
when she sings she even seems
like the fado-singer's well-tuned guitar

when she dies, I shall cut off
her hair to deliver me from sin.

Woman's hair shall be the blanket
over my coffin when another Artist
calls me to heaven to paint me
Woman's breast shall be my pillow
woman's eye shall open up the way to heaven
woman's belly shall give birth to me up there
and woman's glance shall watch me
as I go up to Heaven.[20]

"Woman appears here as a kind of redeemer," says Beier. Many of the women, he notes, "evoke strong religious associations. Malangatana's picture *Nude with Crucifix* shows the short compressed body of a thickset, reclining woman. The feet and most of the head are cut off by the margin of the picture. The huge breasts and belly form a kind of 'trinity' with dark nipples and navel as the focal points in the glowing, orange flesh. The cross lies embedded between the breasts . . . but the hand is a dangerous claw. . . ."[21]

Though his paintings are sometimes called surreal, they are not, as Julian Beinart points out, an "intellectual" surrealism. They take a kernel from his own experience, and add other dimensions described by Beinart as: "issues of universal importance—faith and love, jealousy, hate, mysticism and death." He explains that often it is difficult to tell whether figures belong to one race or another, one religion or another, noting "He seems able to avoid making those distinctions that exist so painfully between cultures and one senses in him the crosscurrents that must cause daily conflict to so many people. His paintings are for him the means of resolution, of showing things . . . that integrate and belong to all."[22]

Malangatana turns these crosscurrents into powerful dramas, elaborately wrought with symbolic clues and a very real presence of evil. With imagery that evokes the necessity for change, he has become a painter of the

Valente Malangatana, *Nude with Crucifix,* early 1960s, oil on canvas, dimensions unknown. Location unknown.

revolution. Betty Schneider, in an article in *African Arts* magazine, quotes him as describing a painting as "a vibrant thing, crying to the spectator, full of heat and life that makes him cry, or creates tremors in his body."[23]

Generally speaking, neither art schools nor artists in Central Africa have made a commitment to change, especially political change. The art schools have, however, produced technically accomplished artists who have created some important works. In 1958 one of Central Africa's most important students, Liyolo Limbé M'Puanga, enrolled in the Kinshasa Académie des Beaux-Arts, founded in 1943 by Frère Marc-Stanislas, a Belgian priest. Although including some references to African art, art instruction was based on the classical European model. Born in 1943 in Bolobo, Zaire, M'Puanga completed courses at the Académie and was admitted to the École des Arts Appliqués in Graz, Austria, graduating in 1965. In the same year he entered the Académie des Beaux-Arts in Vienna, finishing with a prize for his excellence and a masters in sculpture in 1969.

Liyolo eventually developed a classical approach to sculpture rooted in two worlds. While he incorporates certain shapes related to the dynamic forms of traditional carvings and castings, his images depict certain naturalistic attitudes associated with European sculpture.

Working in a variety of materials, he chooses classical subjects—mother and child, torso, musician—all monumental in their overall conformation. The legs, arms, and bodies are based on forms in nature and appear to be stylized rather than built-up of geometrical volumes. The neck is lengthened, the body streamlined. One can recognize sharply angled arms and legs and pear-shaped thighs as forms from African art, but the relationships between forms are different.

As the torso is arched or the figure is bent, a sense of motion is generated, and at the same time relates his work to some Western concepts. African carving often adheres closely to the axis and shape of the wood from which it is carved. Most African bronzes have a similar vertical axis, but because many of Liyolo's figures are in motion, they have asymmetrical aspects and do not conform to a central axis.

During the past thirty years his work has gone through many stages and so it can not be easily categorized. He has created pieces such as *Torse IV*, and *Le Criquet*, which are tour de force examples of a convergence of style, content, and material, and illustrate his mastery and diverse accomplishment.

Working with many different materials—brass, pewter, bronze, sheet metal, wood—and a master of all of them, he is best known for his work in bronze. The elegance of his bronze torsos echoes the deceptive simplicity of traditional African forms. Liyolo has exhibited throughout the world and teaches at the University of Zaire in Kinshasa.

In addition to the Kinshasa Académie des Beaux-Arts,

Ibanehe Djilatendo, *Deux Chausseurs*, 1931, watercolor, 14⅜″ × 28⅜″. Private collection.

there are two other major Central African art schools. One is in Poto-Poto outside Brazzaville, Congo, where Pierre Lods ran a studio workshop. The other school, which was developed from a workshop led by Romain-Desfosses, is the Académie des Beaux-Arts (founded by M. L. Moonens) in Lubumbashi, Zaire. Both schools produced a variety of artists, many of whom became commercial. The repeatedly copied neon-colored stick figures of Poto-Poto have become slick, stock items for the tourist market. The art of the Romain-Desfosses group is more decorative than it is expressive of feeling, and it is often identified by stylistic elements such as stick figures, long-necked birds, and snakes.

There are, of course, other exceptions. Both Ibanehe Djilatendo and Lubaki of Zaire painted to give form and meaning to stories. Among East and Central Africa peoples there are master storytellers and singers. Following these traditions, contemporary expression has become a vehicle for stories and myths, often supernatural in character.

Djilatendo's paintings, full of animals, hunters, soldiers, and feathery trees, are explicit narrative tableaux with action described in vivid graphic detail. Executed with great sensitivity, each shape appears as though created by a carefully controlled wash of color, perfect in its synthesis of profile and dimension. The animals are extraordinarily spirited: fierce, shy, quizzical, amused. Like the animals created by Samwel Wanjau, each is lively, humorous, and has a distinct personality.

Lubaki has a more carefree style. His people and animals are wonderfully humorous; elephants pick blossoms from the trees and cavort like puppies, and people are preoccupied with telephones. Both artists are visual storytellers who draw on proverb and myth with humor and verve.

The late Clément-Marie Biazin (1924–1981), a Yacoma from the Central African Republic, was an indomitable artist and raconteur. He had little education, but read about explorers who had undertaken long journeys to find out about other countries. "We don't have enough of that in Africa," he said.

"We should have books recording our past history and preserving the memory of our traditional cultures. But since we have achieved our independence, we have forgotten the traditions that constitute our originality. This is the thought that impelled me to start painting." Leaving home at 22, his odyssey became a twenty-year trek through Zaire (then Congo) and Uganda (then Burundi and Rwanda) from 1945 to 1955; and six months later in 1956 through Cameroon, Equatorial Guinea (then Spanish Guinea), Gabon, and again Zaire. Roaming "on foot . . . he worked at whatever jobs were available—as mason, cook, farmhand—until he had set aside enough money to go on to the next country," learning enough of eight or more languages to get

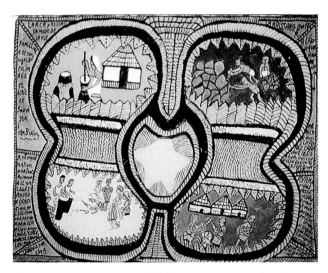

Clément-Marie Biazin, *Untitled*, late 1960s–1970s, drawing, dimensions unknown. Location unknown.

along. "Ultimately he covered an area as large as all of Europe. 'I had wanted to see how other people lived,' he said, 'and find out about their customs.'"[24] In 1966 he returned to his home in Bangui, and began as a self-taught artist to create a visual odyssey that culminated in 500 to 600 paintings.

His paintings are spirited mandala-like panels framed by decorative linear patterns that give them the look of embroidery. Through these paintings he transposed the disappearing customs and oral traditions of African peoples as well as the history of colonial imposition. While his work has important documentary value, the imaginative framework surrounding the illustrative elements and text is most interesting, suggesting a free translation of designs from a Koranic prayer board, an Islamic talisman, or an embroidered robe.

Robert Sève, a French filmmaker, met Biazin in 1967 when Sève was making a film about the Barthelemy Boganda Museum in Bangui. For fourteen years Sève helped Biazin, and also created a prize-winning film about him, the proceeds of which were used to purchase Biazin's art materials. Sève also taped fifty hours of Biazin's accounts. He arranged showings of Biazin's work at the Stedelijk Museum, Amsterdam, in 1978, and at the Stadtische Kunsthalle, Düsseldorf, in 1980. Michel Leiris of the Musée de l'Homme in Paris compared Biazin's work to "the old codex or modern comic strips," but without the usual "Occidental cliches."[25]

Leiris also comments on the "aesthetic and ethnological" importance of Biazin's art,[26] as does François Mathey, a conservator at the Louvre, who explains that Biazin avoids the "anecdotal," and adds that he is most impressed by the work's "purely artistic aspect" in addition to its "historical, political and sociological" importance. "I find back in those story-images all the invention, impetuosity and authority of the anonymous artists of the Middle Ages."[27] Robert Sève sees Biazin's work as painting and story telling with a moral base. His pictures, he points out, refer to the "extermination of ancient Africa," first by the Arabs and then by white colonialists.[28]

On a trip back to the Central African Republic in 1977 Sève found Biazin ill with leprosy and no longer able to work. He took the artist to France, but it was too late. "Clement remained alert and radiant with generosity until his death," in 1981 at the age of 57.[29]

Among the many artists of Central Africa who have developed from a workshop or from working on their own are Ancent Soi of Kenya; Hizza, Jaffary, S. G. Mpata, Ebrahim Said Tingatinga, K. H. Tedo, and Rashidi of Tanzania; and Pli Pli and Cheri Samba of Zaire; all have made original contributions to modern African art.

One of the most significant facts concerning the artists of Kenya, Tanzania, Uganda, Zaire, Congo, and the Central African Republic has to do with the variety of their styles and expressions, not a surprising characteristic given the wide range of peoples and cultures they represent. When their art is closest to its African roots, it weaves a fabric of spirit and matter, unifying the natural and mystical, and recreating myth with vitality and humor. When it addresses the present, it challenges the sources of conflict, especially the unhealed scars of colonialism.

Incorporating such qualities in an original body of work, Wanjau, Owiti, Djilatendo, and Biazin demonstrate directness, spontaneity, and sincerity, while Mwaniki, Nnaggenda, and Malangatana show the potential for greatness. All have managed to transcend the impositions of colonialism. Perhaps their energy, imagination, and independence of vision will inspire others to fulfill their promise and create major movements in East and Central Africa.

12   Sky and Land in Zimbabwe

Because artists among the Shona people, who number about four million, have been largely responsible for the modern movement in Zimbabwe, the country does not have the heterogeneity of expression found in East and Central Africa. A similar combination of spirit and substance, however, is present in their art. With depictions of metamorphosis, artists of Zimbabwe draw on deeply religious experiences. Their imagery combines animal, human, and plant forms so that each becomes a metaphor for the other. Just as the experience of trance—so intrinsic to the African universe—leads to a spiritual encounter, the Shona artists connect elements of the natural and spirit worlds in their work, and capture the essence of transformation.

Although much of Zimbabwe's artistic heritage is lost or unrecorded, the country (formerly Rhodesia) has had important periods of cultural and political strength in the distant past, including one in the 1600s during which Portuguese invaders were defeated. In warfare the Shonas, who live between the Zambezi and Limpopo rivers, have relied on their traditional religious systems for power. Their courage, resourcefulness, and persistence are well documented. Through the centuries strong elements of these same deep religious beliefs have sustained them and certainly remain to inform the work of their new artists.

Other sources of strength in the traditional Shona world, held in common with much of Africa, include the lack of a two-dimensional linear concept of time, and existence of a structured totality of traditional life rather than a categorized Western version. Just as in other African societies, the dead are honored and spirits are given their due that they may regenerate life and keep it flexible and dynamic. In spite of the fact that the artists are surrounded by a number of contemporary foreign or urban influences, they find symbolism in traditional mythos. Their reality belongs to a psychic, intuitive, visionary, and spiritual realm rather than to the largely institutionalized and anonymous domain of Western society.

The first stirrings of contemporary expression occurred in the late fifties. In fact the late fifties, sixties, and early seventies were described as the era of "great excitement" by Frank McEwen (1907–), an ardent supporter of contemporary artists in Zimbabwe.[1] It was a period of exemplary artistic production, which was, to a large degree, the result of McEwen's inspired leadership as the first director of the National Gallery in Harare (then Salisbury). The emergence of these artists, albeit a gradual process, was all the more dramatic given the fact that the last great period of Zimbabwean culture was several hundred years earlier.

At a time of colonial dominance and divisive racial policies, it was McEwen's vision that made possible the use of this modern, well-equipped institution as a gallery and workshop school. McEwen encouraged artists to work and exhibit. It is important to note that he recognized the need for the gallery to serve the whole community. By 1973, 155 exhibitions had been held; among these was the first exhibition of European masters in Africa and one of the first in Africa to illustrate the influence of African sculpture on post-impressionist European painters.

Encouraged by Sir Herbert Read to become director of the National Gallery, McEwen went to Harare, Zimbabwe, in 1954 for preliminary planning of the new gallery building and to advise trustees as to the future potential for the institution. In 1956 when he took up his post, he met Thomas Mukarobgwa, who came to the building site each day to eat his lunch. Mukarobgwa eventually became a prominent artist and the head attendant at the gallery, a position he holds today.

McEwen has an impressive background and important experience, particularly his history of close association with the great painters of Paris for whom African art had been such an inspiration. At the end of his second stay in France, as délégué des beaux arts of the British Council for which he had received the Order of the British Empire, he said he had become "less enchanted with what remained of the great School of Paris and more inclined toward Africa. This was partly through Africa's 'contribution' to Picasso and to contemporary art in general."[2]

In the beginning McEwen personally financed a workshop that was formally titled the Workshop School. After eighteen months of struggle, the school was formally taken over as a non-profit organization by the National Gallery with monies generated by sales of art created there. McEwen was able, often with great difficulty, through interested friends, museums, and collectors, to maintain artistic integrity without having to sell to tourists. Painting was first undertaken in 1957, then wood carving, which was laid aside because of the temptation for making quickly turned-out tourist items, and then in 1959 work progressed to stone carving. From 1956 to 1973 more than one thousand Shona took part in the Workshop School.

As many as seventy-five individuals, all with little or no previous training, worked regularly at the Workshop School. The philosophy McEwen espoused and the method he followed were those he had used years before in Toulon, and which he ascribes to Gustave Moreau. The non-didactic method, he says,

differs from the old model art-school treatment of talent. Instead of teaching, in the sense of cramming the unformed mind with foreign information, example, and imposed subject matter, it is accepted, from the start, that the sensitive, latent artist possesses the spirit of art to be brought out, respected, and nurtured. In this sense the non-pompous, non-authoritative teacher acts, not as a master, but as the aid and friend of his pupil who is, in a way, his superior in creativity.[3]

It is apparent that this confidence in the individual was a factor crucial to subsequent success.

McEwen calls the traditional art school "nefarious" and berates the process:

The Universal Art School had spread its arms with the touch of neutrality and sameness. . . . It is more accurate to state that art schools most frequently destroy art by smothering it at birth. Other destructive features are not only the out-dated curriculum and the obligatory hours of presence but the fact that any person with a degree of manual skill, whether creative or not, can remain in an art school and dilute and distort its collective atmosphere while promoting the general plagiary. In the Workshop School, on the contrary, the artists seek seclusion. They work in separate cubicles in which they jealously protect their own aura, or they work in the bush under their own favorite trees. They have no curriculum and no obligatory hours of presence. They come and go when they can or wish to do—when their moods are right.[4]

Thomas Mukarobgwa (1924–), as the first artist, became a painter who created bold and passionate landscapes. The sense of history and the mystery of a hardly fathomable past are echoed in his titles. They speak of a life still connected to nature: *The Old Man Afraid to Cross, Where I Used to Go with My Cattle, River Coming in the Middle of the Bush, Man Fetching Magic at Night, Very Important Bush, The Tree and the Sky in the Middle,* and *Beautiful Crossed Tree.*[5] He introduces the landscape and its lifeways in a manner that asserts its primal beauty as though discovered for the first time. Jacques Rabemananjara, a poet from nearby Madagascar, sees nature in the same way. In a poem entitled "Blue, blue, the eye of heaven," he says: "Life in blossom between

Thomas Mukarobgwa, *Where I Used to Go with My Cattle,* 1960s, oil, dimensions unknown. Collection of Frank McEwen.

Charles Fernando, *I*, date unknown, red-brown serpentine, 24″ high. Collection of Pierre Descargues.

my lashes./Unbroken sky between my lids./Innocence between the folds of my heart. . . ."[6]

A similar marriage of inner and outer visions is typical of Mukarobgwa's work. His landscapes are swept by storms of rain and lightning. The rhythms of the hills and valleys and the textures of trees and rocks are imbued with a lyrical presence that unites the narrative and the typographical. His brush hurries, moves in jagged, thrusting strokes. Tumbling forms of waterfalls rushing, waves crashing, and hills rising seem propelled by the force of genesis and by the awesome reality that connects humanity to nature. Both paintings and sculptures by him have appeared in *African Arts* magazine,[7] and his work has been exhibited in Africa, Europe, and America.

Painter Charles Fernando is also a jazz musician. Using the shapes of instruments as images, he translates music to color in rhythms by employing a system he invented as a kind of synaesthesia. Like Mukarobgwa, Fernando creates rich textures and vigorous movements with a flurry of brilliantly colored strokes. He occasionally makes sculptures, and has also exhibited widely.

Another colorist, the late Kinsley Sambo, constructed expressionist figures of strong ropes of color, and sometimes of colors, as delicate and transparent as a paisley shawl. Mukarobgwa, Fernando, and Sambo are represented in the collection of the Museum of Modern Art in New York. Zimbabwean painters Chris Chabuka, Victor Matinga, Joseph Ndandarika, and Lucas Ndandarika are noteworthy, but the major emphasis in the art of Zimbabwe became sculpture, and the major artists, sculptors.

13   The Sculptors of Zimbabwe

Artists with an Old Legacy

In traditional Shona families there was always a muvesi, or carver, who was empowered by a Mudzimu, a special ancestral spirit who became manifest in dreams. The muvesi was the creator of myriad household items executed in wood and clay with great skill and artistry. Although no recent tradition of religious sculpture exists, most modern Shona sculptors have strong traditional religious connections, but unlike the muvesi, their work is not created for a functional purpose.

With no immediate artistic tradition or formal stereotypes to guide them, the modern artists have great freedom and therefore, McEwen states, there is not the same struggle as might otherwise be the case. "They are not westernized with separate faculties of the mind, nor are they frustrated spiritually or sensuously by the materialistic inroads of puritanism."[1] There is "no apeing of tradition, no pandering to the Western pattern," he explains,[2] nor as in "airport art" (a term he invented to describe art produced for the tourist market), "which destroys many potential artists," a facile pictorialism.[3]

Powerful traditions of myth and ritual may very well link the work of new sculptors to ancient stone pieces estimated to have been created about 1500 A.D. These steatite carvings, with which modern artists were generally unfamiliar, were found at Great Zimbabwe, a formidable structure surrounded by massive stone walls that were partially destroyed by invading Zulus.

Some sculptors from Harare have had some schooling; but a number have an agrarian background, and stone is for them a natural environmental medium just as it was for the fifteenth- or sixteenth-century builders of Great Zimbabwe. Interestingly enough, both the ancient and modern sculptors have used images of the bateleur eagle, or Chapungu, a messenger of God and a sacred and powerful symbol. However, the ancient images were carried off to London and Cape Town museums early in this century. Relics of later sculptures have been found and hints of other long-hidden sacred pieces exist, but the work of the new sculptors represents a revival after hundreds of years of apparent dormancy.

Michael Peppiatt, writing in *Arts International*, describes the work of the present sculptors by saying, "The key to its extraordinary spontaneity lies perhaps in the great range and freshness of tribal memory. . . ." He goes on, quoting McEwen, to say that a "tribal historian can run off the Shona genealogy, ancestor by ancestor, for four days non-stop," an indication of a viable literary lore.[4]

Oral literature, therefore, provides an important clue to the sense of history and the poetry inherent in the perception of the Shona artists. Michael Gelfand, a scholar who worked directly among the Shona for some thirty years, says, "To the muvesi, carving is a means of talking, a way of telling what he sees in a dream. . . . I believe these men [Shona sculptors] are trying to tell us what life means and what in it matters! . . . the protecting mudzimu is evident. The key to life is the Family—Man and Woman with their issue."[5]

Music is also a way of communicating and an important traditional dimension for the Shona, who are described as "gentle and deeply reflective . . . with enduring patience."[6] The mbira, or thumb piano, for example, is an instrument for communicating with the world of the spirits.

The spiritual pantheon of the Shona includes a sky and rain god, Mwari, thought by some to be the creator god, though some scholars disagree and speak of Musikavanhu as the ancient creator god whose association is with water creatures and fertility, as well as with the hornbill, bateleur eagle, and fish eagle. The Muhacha, or ancestor tree, with indwelling spirits of the dead, is also an important thematic element in the new art forms.

Indeed spirits, which inhabit nature and which are observers always close at hand, are all visible in the imagery of the modern sculptors. They often indicate their spirits' presence with eyes, which may be integral parts of trees or figures. Sometimes a spirit is manifest in zoomorphic form, in a skeletal being, in the face of a baboon, in the ears of a hare, in the horns of a buck, in the wings of a bird; sometimes the spirit dwells in anthropomorphic or biomorphic forms. Often there is an integration of the characteristics of two animals in one, or the depiction of human duality. In addition, a Shona may have membership in a totem group, which accounts for the combination of animal and human forms, and for the feeling of metamorphosis that exists in many of their sculptures. The baboon, like the mythological Indian monkey, Hanuman, has a magical import. He can, as a spirit, inhabit a human being and impart skills and wisdom.

In the hands of these contemporary artists, their religious mythology brings with it some of the qualities of ritual sculpture, which functions to calm, honor, and appease heavenly and earthly deities. An intrinsic power grows from this combination of archetypal form and religious meaning. The presence of ancestors, incarnate in a medium in trance, for instance, testifies to the ever-present links between the living and the dead. The communication between Mwari and the ancestor spirits determines the welfare and serenity of their descendants. According to McEwen, the medium of the most important ancestor, Chaminuka, has "absolute power and authority."[7] "What the Westerner fails, or finds most difficult, to bear in mind is the undividedness of . . . life and thought—one cannot pluck out one aspect of it, whether cooking, agriculture, or art, and consider it meaningfully apart."[8]

Just as life and thought is undivided, so among the artists certain characteristics are shared. The artists begin with meditation or dream. The actual execution is simply the carrying out of the more important state of inspiration; perhaps even the polishing is done by others. And even the various styles seem the purview of all. Just as they share subject matter, the best artists change from one style to another without sacrificing individual

strengths. "The Shona artist continues to take all tribal myth and all constants of human life—birth, the duality of the human personality, marriage, creativity, etc.,—as his undevalued province."[9]

McEwen found that, although generally the forms of African art were not familiar to the new sculptors, they often developed features that coincided with those typical to classical African sculpture:

There was an emphasis on verticality, often a frontal stance, the enlarged head—seat of the spirit, evidence of the human in animal life, the facial expression of trance and the posture from dance described as "relaxed tension." The presence of myth and folklore.[10] . . . [T]he sturdy sculptural legs; the chevron; the snake and spiral symbols all came into carvings.[11]

In the beginning the contemporary Shona artists used the softer stones. "Wood was abandoned because it became the medium of mass-produced, trash-trade carvings for the tourists," McEwen said.[12] "At one time there were 17 quarries in operation producing wonderfully different (mostly serpentine) qualities and colors of stone." The artists handled "huge blocks of stone by . . . methods of leverage."[13] The use of material that is difficult to carve is one characteristic of the truly committed artist, for those working for the tourist market are interested in ease and quick results. Eventually developing techniques to block out and carve in fine detail the hardest granite, they also used soapstone, limestone, verdite, and lapidolite, carving in ways that seem to restate and intensify the energy, mystery, and the ageless power inherent in stone. These qualities were clearly strengthened by their association with religion, myth, and dreams.[14]

Their work reveals the properties of stone, and its essential nature remains undisturbed. A number of larger sculptures convey a sense that they were created to be sited out-of-doors, like outcroppings of rock, organic in form, but molded by human hands for the purpose of enhancing the environment. Their simplicity of mass evokes monumentality; the large head, as in other African sculpture, is the seat of the spirit.

Sometimes there is a touching kind of intimacy that seems to grow from the original rock itself; often artists with a particular expertise create the feeling that the stone has hardly been altered. These pieces are basically large rocklike shapes with areas of low relief and the barest glyphlike detail. The polished surfaces are highly sensuous responding to light and shadow, and this play of light brings them to life.

Jean-Joseph Rabearivelo of Madagascar, in his poem about the night, describes such artistry and captures the sense of light as life by depicting a stone carver who is a metaphor for night carving the dawn: "A dying lapidist,

Sylvester Mubayi, *Skeletal Baboon Spirit*, 1960s, light green serpentine, 7½" × 11¾". Collection of Frank McEwen.

the Night/ . . . with what loving care he cuts the prism./The craftsman on his own unnoticed grave/Sets up this monument of light."[15]

The most impressive and committed of this group of Shona sculptors are Sylvester Mubayi, Joseph Ndandarika, John Takawira, Henry Munyaradzi, and Amani. They have continued to grow and to express their spiritual and cultural matrix. While many others were productive and created important pieces, they remain the major artists. Thomas Mukarobgwa was the first artist; others, including Charles Fernando, Chris Chabuka, and Boira Mteki, followed. Those who should be mentioned and who have done memorable work are Moses Masaya, Phinias Moyo, Amon Mwarekah, Cornwall Mpofu, Clever Machisa, Bottom Mpayi, Louis Chipfupe, Paul Gwichiri, Makiwa Chimoyo, and Canisius Guru.

In 1962 the efforts at the Workshop School were enhanced by the success of an important event in the capital: the International Congress of African Culture. This congress encouraged others and a number of new artists emerged: Joram Mariga, Zindoga, Denson Dube, and John Vanji. Annual exhibitions were held and again artists emerged; some did not last, some did ster-

eotypical work or lost interest, but many continued and produced important work. In 1966 their entries in the Commonwealth Exhibition of the Arts received enthusiastic praise from the London press, and the major artists were established.

The most prominent, Sylvester Mubayi (1942–), created sculpture of undisputed eminence, and was the first to use skeletal imagery. Mubayi had worked in a tobacco factory and then in a brewery before becoming an artist. In 1967 he began carving at Sipolilo, a field workshop with connections to the National Gallery some 145 kilometers from Harare, and a place where McEwen spent weekends encouraging sculptors. (The field workshop at Sipolilo was later disavowed and links were severed when it was discovered that tourist carvings were being shipped in lots to South Africa.)

Mubayi developed to become one of the top sculptors, juxtaposing forms in a surreal defiance of anatomy, a direction stemming from the dream and visionary sources relied on by all the Shona artists. The skeletal spirits that Mubayi and others create are described by Michael Peppiatt: "Each work compresses an uncanny power within its great rib-cage which radiates out like a center of solar-energy . . ." and sometimes "resembles two sets of powerful fingers reaching into one another."[16]

His *Spirit Tree* also evokes fingers or petals, unfolding and growing from a jewellike eye at the root. In addition to single images, some of them ten feet tall, Mubayi has created complex compositions depicting Goyaesque scenes of disaster. In 1969 his accomplishments brought him the Ernest Oppenheimer Trust Award.

Joseph Ndandarika (1940–), who is known for intense, brooding, mystical, and sometimes humorous figures, worked for a wizard before coming to the Workshop School. His *Lovers,* two baboons, monolithic in concept like twin fetuses merging one into the other, is poignantly human, and yet paradoxically immutable. Another work also entitled *Lovers,* a black man and white woman, is a humorous and daring confrontation with the then-Rhodesian officialdom.

Generally his figures follow closely the curve of the original stone. Though emphasizing and sharpening de-

Sylvester Mubayi, *Eagle Bull, Spirit and Matter,* 1960s, black serpentine, 22½" long. Location unknown.

Sylvester Mubayi, *Spirit Tree,* 1960s, gray-black serpentine, 10″ high. Collection of Frank McEwen.

Sylvester Mubayi, *Magic Stallion,* late 1960s, dark green serpentine, 48″ high. Location unknown.

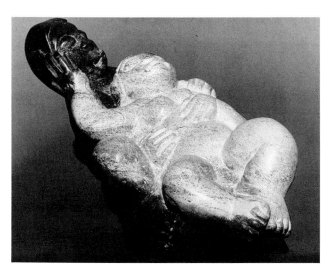

Joseph Ndandarika, *Lovers,* 1960s, red-pink serpentine, 20″ × 10¼″. Collection of Frank McEwen.

Joseph Ndandarika, *Lovers,* 1960s, red-pink-gray stone, 22″. Location unknown.

John Takawira, *Baby Chapungu,* 1960s, black serpentine, 15"
high. Collection of Pierre Descargues.

metamorphosis reflect his mastery as a sculptor.
McEwen, in fact, describes him as "the most powerful
master of mythical and magical themes."[17] Like Mubayi,
he has many shows and prizes to his credit.

Henry Munyaradzi (ca. 1933–) entered the Workshop
School in 1968 after having begun carving in Sipolilo.
He is a designer who can create with consummate
craftsmanship and unerring subtlety the grace of a stork
or the bulk of a rhinoceros. The large swooping *Insect-
God* is a dominating phallic-unicorn figure that demonstrates his technical expertise and stylized geometry.
Round heads, stelae, and figures with satellite volumes
exhibit a stylized control and stark geometric symmetry.
One of the most important of the Shona sculptors, his
forms are often abstract but his content is not. His work,
like the work of most Shona sculptors, is persistently
biomorphic and ideographic.

Amani's beautifully simplified forms are as powerful
as and may be likened to the work of Marino Marini,
especially his *Horse and Rider,* which condenses elements
to their simplest denominator, and in so doing enhances

tails, he allows the larger portions to simply reinforce
the basic shape. Also a ceramicist and a painter, he
creates richly colored, impressionistic landscapes, animated by waves of vibrating color. His paintings and
sculptures are in important collections, including New
York's Museum of Modern Art.

John Takawira (1938–), another major sculptor, began carving small utensils while still in a mission school
in Inyanga. However, his important work was done at
the Workshop School and in Vukutu, a retreat established by McEwen. He first exhibited in the Workshop
School's annual exhibition in 1963. Working with black
and gray serpentine, he polished its hard surfaces to
acquire a satin smooth glow. He also made pieces in
which he combined rough and smooth surfaces and
patterns. The feather patterns on his bateleur eagle, *Baby
Chapungu,* are natural extensions of the larger volumes,
and they expand into exuberant plumage.

A master of the baboon myth, Takawira carves
totems, uniting the human and baboon like two heads
of Janus. He also creates skeletal figures, some of which
are ten feet tall and appear to confront death with that
special life force referred to when describing African
sculpture, to symbolize connections between the natural
and supernatural. Such depictions of opposite forces and

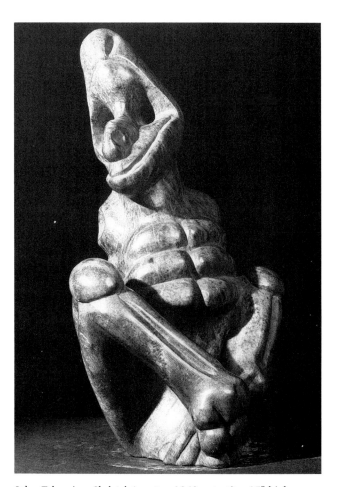

John Takawira, *Skeletal Ancestor,* 1960s, steatite, 15" high.
Private collection.

John Takawira, *Totem Protector,* date unknown, black stone, 51¼″ high. Private collection.

Amani, *Horned Head,* date unknown, gray-black serpentine, 11″ high. Collection of Frank McEwen.

Henry Munyaradzi, *Zimbabwe Stele*, 1960s, gray-green
serpentine, 13¾" high. Collection of Frank McEwen.

Zimbabwe Stele (opposite view).

Joram Mariga, *Medium Priest with Sacred Eagle*, date unknown, light green serpentine, 18¾" high. Collection of Frank McEwen.

small and are often carved from a rich green serpentine streaked and flecked with veins of a golden color.

Nicholas Mukomberanwa (1940–) arrived at the Workshop School in 1964 from a mission school. When he moved to Harare (then Salisbury) in 1961, he became a policeman. He resigned from the police force to continue his sculpture full time. His work is highly stylized and has a strong architechtonic sense, although it is more organic than architectural if contrasted to the work of Festus Idehen of Nigeria. Mukomberanwa has participated in many exhibitions including shows in Harare, London, Pretoria, Johannesburg, Paris, New York, Washington, D.C., and San Francisco.

Compared to Nicholas Mukomberanwa or Henry Munyaradzi, Makiwa Chimoyo is an impressionist whose pieces express the rough and grainy nature of stone. He achieves this expressive effect by an archaic method of rubbing the carved piece with a harder stone.[19] *Protective Bird, Two Birds,* and *Mother and Child* have a poignancy that calls to mind many of the graphic images by South African artists.

Boira Mteki, one of the early Workshop School artists, was a gem-cutter, and used this skill to make large monumental pieces whose rugged texture and huge size give them a primal power one associates with mono-lithic stelae. Mteki's forms are softly molded. His large

Nicholas Mukomberanwa, *Symbolic Head,* 1960s, black serpentine, 16" high. Collection of M. and Mme. Loudmer, Paris.

meaning and the surface beauty of the medium. McEwen says "Amani is a natural stylist with a superb aesthetic sense. So sophisticated is his work that it appears to belong to some unknown ancient tradition."[18]

The work of Joram Mariga (1927–), in contrast to the round monumental character typical of much Shona sculpture, is more natural and usually smaller in scale. Mariga, who was an agricultural specialist in Inyanga before he began to carve, was first encouraged by Pat Pearce, a sympathetic artist, who along with her two daughters, gave valuable assistance and put him in touch with McEwen. Mariga seeks beautiful colors in the hardest stones. In many of his figures there is a feeling of quest, and in *Nyakaturituri,* a totem-like image portrays one man carrying another, a reflection of a particular ritual. His most fully conceived works are

Nicholas Mukomberanwa, *Virgin and Child*, 1960s, black serpentine, 51¼" high. Collection of M. and Mme. Hagnauer.

heads with their impressive features have an archaic energy, reminiscent of the statuesque figures by Vincent Kofi of Ghana, and those at Easter Island. Godlike, ancient, and abiding, they are imbued with a trancelike intensity.

There are many more important artists and memorable images as well. Among them are Bernard Matemera, whose works depict fetal-myth figures, one of a standing rhinoceros; Bernard Manyandure, whose antelope with convoluted limbs manages to retain its morphic form and convey a transcendental state at the same time; Lemon Moses, whose rigid heads and figures are stoic and archaic; Paul Gwichiri, whose sculpture *Birth*, an arc with the head of the mother at one end and the child emerging at the other, speaks of anguish and wonder in one eloquent metaphor; Kumberai Mapanda, whose pieces seem to be made of assembled volumes as though they were individual parts of a three-dimensional puzzle; Zindoga, whose hen and chickens are fused into one compact entity, and Denson Dube, whose humorous *Mouseload* depicts a truck with a mouse in the back.

In 1969 after connections with Sipolilo were severed, the National Gallery obtained the right to use a "magnificent wild estate" called Vukutu in the mountains 256 kilometers from Harare. "Before settling there, some of the wise men including Thomas Mukarobgwa spent nights there to consult with the spirits for there are many important ancestor graves in the rocks." Hidden among the rocks are early paintings created by non-Bantus. The major artists chosen to work at Vukutu accompanied by their families were Sylvester Mubayi, John Takawira, and Joseph Ndandarika, and Amani. They were joined from time to time by younger promising artists including Amon Mwarekah, Bernard Takawira, Cornwall Mpofu, Phinias Moyo, and Moses Masaya.

Six round huts, or rondavels, were built to house the artists. It was to become a kind of "convent-monastery . . . the object was to go farther into pure great stone carvings. . . ."[20] The surrounding landscape, with its magnificent rocky outcroppings, or kopjes, is arrest-

Ask, *Plant*, date unknown, stone sculpture, 14" high. Collection of Frank McEwen.

Bernard Manyandure, *Strong Man,* late 1960s, stone sculpture, dimensions unknown. Collection of National Gallery of Zimbabwe.

Paul Gwichiri, *Birth,* 1971, green serpentine, 15" high. Musée Rodin.

ing. In various states of completion, the figures outside the rondavels made the site look like a man-made quarry. As though related, both the figures and the rock kopjes confronted each other, one a metaphorical witness for the other.

McEwen lived at Vukutu with the artists, not as a teacher, but as a participant and as a moving force. Mary McEwen also made important contributions. Other new and promising artists came on a trial basis. "This place became a 'Holy of holies' where we began to do great things and to which the artists aspired in an inspiring creative association. . . . Vukutu with its seclusion, its philosophical and spiritual atmosphere became the life and soul of our movement." McEwen's guide in all of his work was "Muchatera Majura, the medium of Chaminuka; there was no higher spiritual authority in Mashonaland."[21] As a medium, he could reach the creature-spirits in their natural shrines in the trees, in the water, or in the kopjes.

In 1971 Sculpture Contemporaine des Shonas d'Afrique, a major exhibition of more than one hundred modern Shona sculptures, some as tall as nine feet, and weighing as much as three tons (the second in Paris), took place at the Musée Rodin. The exhibition stirred enormous interest and inspired many collectors to purchase. Equally successful in 1972 was a major exhibition of Shona sculptures in London at the Institute for Contemporary Art. During the fifteen years following the opening of the Workshop School, almost seven thousand pieces were sold.[22] In 1973 at the height of pre-independence tensions, McEwen was forced to resign and activities at Vukutu came to a halt.

In spite of ensuing neglect amounting to suppression and lack of support under succeeding directorship, committed artists Sylvester Mubayi, Bernard Ndandarika, John Takawira, Amani, and Henry Munyaradzi continue to produce distinguished work. In the absence of McEwen, another interested individual, Roy Guthrie, supported and assisted artists who could not have survived without his help.

Considering the environment of the National Gallery and the availability of Western art influences, the Shona artists' accomplishment is unique and amazingly free of eclecticism. Contrary to Marion Arnold's opinion that Shona sculpture is not truly African in identity, it seems to have created a new Shona or Zimbabwean identity.[23] A comparison might be made with the highly stylized sculptures of some Europeans, Archepenko or Barbara Hepworth, for example, who like other European sculptors have not escaped influences of West African art; but it is the strong connections to both biological and spiritual worlds that is intrinsic to the best Shona pieces and that distinguishes them as having the same physical and psychic balance as the rock kopjes. It is apparent that most European art the Shona sculptors may have seen was rejected as irrelevant, for their work is firmly grounded in their own ethos, and is distinctly religious in character. Their personal interpretative sensibilities have merged with traditional values, views, and mystical energies in ways that, from artist to artist, neither sacrifice individuality nor the power now associated with modern sculpture of Zimbabwe.

Rather than a quality recognizable by style or material, the African presence in Shona sculpture is a special energy referred to by William Fagg, Frank McEwen, and others as "life force." Michael Peppiatt, speaking of the sculptures, describes them as "an instinctive and complete recording of vitality," as though "a powerful inner necessity . . . brought them into being. . . . Moreover their authors sense that this is an absolutely crucial moment for their culture; they feel that they have a contribution to make to world culture now—as they enter a world of imported values—more than ever."[24]

Winston Saoli, *Untitled,* date unknown, etching, 6⅝″ × 5″.

of mortality/and all immediate joys ephemeral,/angered and wounded, 'No!' and 'No!' I cried."[7] Love and death form an alliance in Mazisi Kunene's "Farewell": "O beloved farewell . . ./Hold these leaping dreams of fire/With the skeletal hands of death/So that when hungry night encroaches/You defy her stubborn intrigues."[8] And Bloke Modisane defines the unholy union most eloquently with: "incestuous silhouettes/to each other scream and shout/to me shout and scream/pry and mate:/inbred deformities of loneliness."[9]

This same torment permeates the work of the late Cyprian Shilakoe (1946–1972), whose death at twenty-six cut short a career of great promise. His etchings often suggest love and a denial of it: *Mma Koko,* which features two faces as close as lovers over tombstones. Indeed, the titles of Shilakoe's prints parallel the sense of loss and desolation voiced by the poets: *Nobody Loves Me; Loneliness; Labour Pains; He May Come, Mother; I Don't Want Birth Control;* and *Where Have They Gone To.* Keorapetse Kgositsile's *Requiem for My Mother* is an echo: "The roads to you/Lead from any place/Though I will never again/Know the morning odor of your anxious breath,"[10] or Kgositsile's poem that speaks of the dead who "cannot remember even the memory of death's laughter./But memory/defiant like the sound of pain/rides the wave at dawn. . . ."[11]

Shilakoe's burden-bent, hooded wraiths exist in limbo. In them a feeling of waiting, of mourning and of existing without hope is pervasive. The white faces in *Silence* suggest the association of white—as in some African societies—with death. Children, depicted as piteous waifs, are indelible images. Delicate tones and textures, feathery lines, and fluid forms contribute a feeling of vulnerability and innocence.

He intensifies the sense of loss, despair, and resignation by an enigmatic quality, for we are not told who it is that is awaited or why, or who it is that has gone. This quality defines his subjects as having unsurmountable problems and inscrutable destinies. In the etching *Follow the Footprints, You Will Find Her Sleeping* the reclining figure of a woman stretches across the horizon. Footprints lead to her. Is she awake? Is she alive? She seems too far removed for contact.

Although he is best known for his etchings, Shilakoe was also a sculptor whose pieces had some of the same haunting quality found in his prints.

Just before his death in a car accident in 1972, *African Arts* magazine announced that he had won the first prize for graphics in its annual contest, and commenting on his work, said, "The social comment is so bitterly clear. And yet there is no cheap theatrics of political posing here, only that surgical accuracy of the artist's eye recording the deepest kind of human truth. Within a highly personal idiom, an overall social context is effectively evoked."[12]

Cyprian Shilakoe, *Follow the Footprints, You Will Find Her Sleeping,* 1970, etching, dimensions unknown.

Cyprian Shilakoe, *Figure*, 1968, etching, dimensions unknown.

Lucas Sithole, *Wounded Buffalo*, 1970, liquid steel, 16½″ × 29½″ × 19¾″. Location unknown.

Shilakoe was reared by his grandmother at a lonely mission station at Barberton, and herded cattle as a boy. He went to school at Buchbeeskreich in northern Transvaal, and eventually attended the Swedish mission school at Rorke's Drift in 1968, finishing in 1970. The death of his grandmother was traumatic for him.

After Shilakoe's death, his close friend, artist Dan Rakgoathe, wrote in tribute: "He derived inspiration from anything he set his eyes on, e.g. the transient drifts of clouds across the infinite sky, the swaying ghostly trees in the caressing breeze, splash spots on carelessly painted walls, linen flapping desperately in the violent wind—all these gave him inspiration for shapes and forms reflected in his etchings and sculpture."[13]

Hal Eads, an American friend, said: "I found moments of sanity in the presence of Cyprian Shilakoe. In spite of the structures [of apartheid] he transcended his situation and lived beyond. . . ."[14] His art derives its strength from the fact that it releases its secrets slowly. An echo lingers, taunts, and endures. In his short life Cyprian Shilakoe left a legacy that expresses the wretchedness of apartheid with eloquence, and in ways never before articulated.

Other artists continue to create the new tradition. Beginning in the late twenties and thirties, the first black contemporary artists in South Africa began to work. Michael Zondi (1926–), probably the first, worked in a Western portrait genre like the early Nigerian artists. Lucas Sithole, born in 1931, took more original directions. Some of his themes parallel those of Shilakoe, but Sithole works only as a sculptor. Born in the Transvaal township of Kwa Thema Springs of a Swazi mother and a Zulu father who was a minister, he was first apprenticed to a carpenter. Eventually he went to work in a soap factory and began to carve on his own. He now works in wood, stone, and liquid steel, and has created a number of tall, slender sculptures that are elegant in form.

These elongated images are typical of his work, but he has also carved more solid sculptures of wood that are close to the biomorphic forms of the Shona. Some of his sculptures have a similar plasticity, especially one entitled *Fat Head*, but frequently the wood planes of a piece project into space or resemble slender tree limbs and snake forms, while those of the Shona are generally more contained, adhering closely to the natural shape of the stone.

One remarkable work by Sithole entitled *Wounded Buffalo* is of liquid steel. Bulky with sloping, fluid lines, appropriate to the material and conforming naturally to the pose of the dying beast, the sculpture speaks of tragedy as clearly as Shilakoe's print *Mma Koko*. This half-slumped buffalo steer conjures a hero-dragon archetype, the identification of which is clear. This one image conveys the doom of a fallen hero and of an oppressed people, and it combines a sense of power lost with the sacrifice of an innocent.

Lucas Sithole exhibited at the Venice Biennale in 1968, and in 1979 the Pretoria Museum held a one-person show celebrating twenty years of his work. Gallery 21 in Johannesburg has published a catalog, which includes a large portion of his oeuvre.

Another sculptor, Sidney Kumalo (1935–), born in Johannesburg, is of Zulu origin. He began his artistic career after working in the city's Bantu Men's Social Centre. In 1952 he entered the Polly Street Art Centre in Johannesburg to study with Cecil Skotnes and Edoardo Villa. In 1960 he was asked to teach and then for four years he replaced Cecil Skotnes as director when the latter retired. There he influenced many students.

Considered one of South Africa's finest artists, Kumalo has been exhibiting for more than twenty years, showing his work in many international exhibitions. Most of his pieces are built of clay then cast in bronze. They are highly stylized in ways that suggest classical African sculpture with which he is conversant. Like the Shona sculptors, Kumalo often integrates human and animal images. Demonstrating a powerful command of form, he constructs muscular volumes that twist and pull; and while he makes no overt political references, the anatomy of a figure may be tense with stresses and strains. The solidity and central axis of his forms convey strength, the interpretation of which ranges from protest to endurance.

Kumalo's *Seated Woman* has such intensity. Although a columnar piece, it is in dramatic contrast to classical African pieces with vertical axes. Here the axis arches, stretching the whole figure backward, suggesting resistance, supplication, and torment.

Sidney Kumalo, *Horse*, 1988, bronze, 8½" long. Location unknown.

The intensity and multiplicity of meaning in Kumalo's works find their parallels in the paintings of Louis Maqhubela. Although Maqhubela's paintings are not blatant statements about apartheid and oppression, these subjects are a profound part of the world Maqhubela creates, a world that is hauntingly beautiful, and transfixed in time and space. He, himself, states, "I do not seek to express apartheid. But if it's there, it's there."[15]

Describing his beginning as a painter, he says he came across the work of Sudanese artist Ibrahim El Salahi and was astonished. "For the first time I knew that we could paint. Before that I knew an African could carve, but I did not know we could paint! That convinced me of my direction."[16] He has received praise in a number of publications, and in 1973 was awarded a prize by *African Arts* magazine.[17]

Maqhubela was born in Durban in 1939. He moved to Johannesburg, and there was encouraged by Cecil Skotnes at the Polly Street Art Centre. His first one-person show was in Johannesburg in 1967. He has recently taken up printmaking at the Goldsmiths College of Art and Design, University of London, where he has also exhibited at the Picadilly Gallery and the Camden Art Centre.

The world Maqhubela paints is lonely, a place where the only living being may be a single bird, beautifully buoyant, and yet unreal, like a puppet on a string dancing the dance of death. Repeatedly in his works, a bird symbolizes the unfettered spirit, and yet is set in the context of a ravaged land or against a glowing sun, bringing to mind the imagery of the Madagascar poet, Jean-Joseph Rabearivelo. He too uses birds as symbols. About one bird he writes, "A bird without color and name/has bent her wings/and wounded the lone eye of the sun."[18]

Sidney Kumalo, *Head Leaning on Arm*, 1985, bronze, 10½" long. Location unknown.

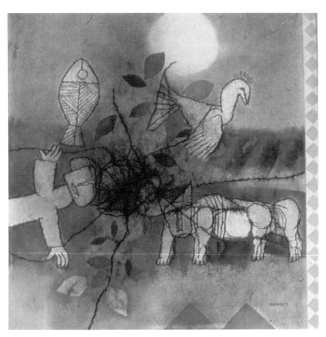

Louis Maqhubela, *Untitled,* 1970s to early 1980s, oil on paper, 28″ × 36″.

There are jarring implications in the anomalies he explores: a captive—an animal inside a corral or a human enmeshed in a snare of wire—and a figure that is seemingly free, but psychologically bound. They are macabre actors in a ghostly scene that combines an ethereal beauty with frightening imagery. Sometimes the figures seem bereft of power or will, and appear borne aloft by waves of color. The warrior-like figure is surrounded by a labyrinth of color or a thicket of clotted lines.

The imploded fiery red blossoms, the twisted threads that cut and confine, and the maimed bodies and truncated limbs all speak with tragic eloquence of destruction. In painting after painting these elements present a desperate landscape. The atmosphere is often as soft-spun as gauze and as translucent as porcelain, but it is an uneasy environment, criss-crossed by wire and repeatedly blurred and diffused as if by smoke or explosion. The blowing leaves, the shards of light, and the red embers are synonyms for devastation.

His luminous color spreads across the surface and shimmers through a maze of emblems and forms; red shines like lacquer, and black seems to pierce the paper. A black wire cuts across the dazzling face of the moon or sun; fine lines that look like hairs on a lens form a web. Frequently color, texture, and line merge in an impenetrable tangle, and often a dark core of color is the heart of the painting.

As Maqhubela scrutinizes morality, he conveys not a narrative mythology but a philosophical one. He combines his technical expertise with intellect and feeling to reveal content. The manifestations of oppression, not as narrative but as psychological dimensions, permeate the texture, color, and imagery of his work.

Here is an evanescent but ominous realm against which crisp details such as a black sun and wisps of barbed wire stand as witnesses to the struggle of a single bird, of a snake, or of a human being to exist. The bird cries, the snake bites, the man falls.

A Christ-like figure in this blighted world is a powerful image with all of its original meaning of sainthood, expiation, martyrdom, and sacrifice intensified by its correspondence, its contemporary identity. Maqhubela's paintings, because they evoke much that is presentable only in metaphor, tell of a destruction that is both physical and spiritual. They relate not only to the South African situation but to the immeasurable dimension of oppression itself. In their symbolic sense they stand for tyranny everywhere.

Maqhubela's eloquence is also verbal. He describes his purpose: "I do not wish to paint as a reaction to apartheid. If we only react, then they own all of us. They own our minds and our souls as well as our bodies."[19]

Like other South African artists, Dumile Feni, whose entire name is Mslaba Dumile Geelboi Mgxaji Feni, uses the human figure to express the tension and tragedy of South Africa. His artistic vehemence led Lionel Ngakane, writing in *African Arts* in 1970, to call him "angry and eloquent."[20] His anger and eloquence permeate his drawings and are his response to apartheid.

His drawings have a sculptural dimension and recall the fact that he is also a sculptor. His bronze figure of a baby won first prize in a 1971 *African Arts* magazine contest. Depicting an uncanny young-old child, it seems shrewdly perceptive.[21] Dumile began to draw and to carve when he was a small child, and when still very young, he obtained work at a pottery factory in Johannesburg.

Born in 1942 at Worcester, Cape Province, he was six when his mother died, and his family moved to Cape Town. At the age of eleven he went to live with an uncle in Johannesburg. Becoming ill there, he was treated at a sanatorium, where his talent was discovered, and he was asked to paint murals on the walls of the building. In 1965 he gained the support of Gallery 101 in Johannesburg, and in 1966 he had a one-person show. Considered a leader in the township art movement, his work has appeared in exhibitions in the United States and Europe, and in the form of illustrations in books and journals.

Today his drawings are often inspired by memories of his mother. Mother figures represent much that he has to say. His swooping graceful lines depict the mothers' fates in twisted limbs, contorted bodies, and swollen flesh. Pain, anger, and frustration pushes from within,

Dumile Feni, *Untitled*, date unknown, ink, dimensions unknown. Collection of Voices from Exile, Washington, D.C.

With two large charcoal drawings, *The Resurrection* and *African Guernica*, Dumile challenges society. The former is a sardonic comment on white authority. It shows his talent for catching nuances of character and social attitudes with expressionistic blunt lines, rough textures, briefly drawn forms, and the simplest of media. The latter work has two levels: underneath, sinopic drawings, and above, more clearly delineated figures. "The central figures are almost apocalyptic in appearance, screaming a message of warning and doom to the modern world," states historian E. J. De Jager, who calls the two works "perhaps the culmination of his art."[22]

Dumile's works have antecedents in his personal life. Although by 1968 he had a number of successes including three one-person shows to his credit, he was sent by government officials to Cape Town from Johannesburg because he could not prove he was employed. "In Cape Town he was given fourteen days to leave, and was endorsed to his place of birth, Worcester. Worcester also refused him a resident's permit and in turn gave him fourteen days to leave or be arrested and sent to a tribal reservation. Dumile, in desperation, returned to Johannesburg and applied for a passport to leave the country. He had to wait a year before he was granted a passport."[23] Dumile now lives in New York; to this day he has not returned, nor has he been able to see his two children. He says, "There is nothing they can do to surprise me. I am doing what I have to do."[24]

and lines wind round and round, adding containment and pressure.

Dumile was also inspired by music, especially jazz, and musicians figure prominently in his work. However, musically inspired images are cries of pain; even though the musicians are dancing, singing, and making music, they underscore a prophetic sense of struggle, a struggle that is perverse and turning inward.

This feeling of conflict is pervasive and is articulated by images of wringing hands, strained necks, bent heads, taut muscles, and contorted postures. Extremities are linked, as though grafted, to other body forms. Hands become heads, and heads become arms and grow out of limbs. Through carefully calculated distortions— elongated limbs, clutching fingers, tortured expressions, and screaming faces—his figures are metaphors for an aberrant quality of life, and so document the passion of South Africa in unforgettable terms.

Dumile Feni, *Young Men Fighting*, date unknown, charcoal, dimensions unknown. Location unknown.

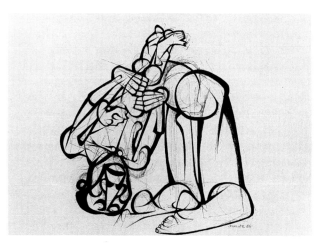

Dumile Feni, *Mother and Child*, 1986, ink drawing, dimensions unknown. Collection of Voices from Exile, Washington, D.C.

In contrast to the carefully delineated forms drawn by Dumile, figures created by Vumikosi Zulu, a skilled printmaker, have some of the wraithlike qualities of Cyprian Shilakoe's images. Zulu's images crowd together as though imprisoned by the frame. They represent fear, which is palpable in its intensity, and their vulnerability is reinforced by bumpy, seemingly malleable bodies. Large heads, scrawny arms and legs, and pleading eyes in the etchings *Who's Going to Speak for Us* and *Robbers and Robbed Man* are undeniable testaments. Gaping mouths and staring eyes that are reflective and penetrating, reinforce the pain and arrest the viewer. He is a master of conveying emotion: anguish, bitterness, terror, skepticism, and resignation.

Zulu was born in central Natal in 1943. During his school years he worked with clay and carved wood and bone. In 1970 he attended the Evangelical Lutheran

Dumile Feni, *Woman Being Carried Away by an Animal*, 1970s or 1980s, ink drawing, dimensions unknown. Location unknown.

Vumikosi Zulu, *Who's Going to Speak for Us,* 1974, etching, sheet: 23″ × 18½″; image: 17½″ × 13¾″.

Church Art and Craft Centre at Rorke's Drift, and for two years worked at graphics and sculpture; he then remained at the center as an artist-in-residence and weaver.

Eric Mbatha (1948–), also a printmaker, portrays the crippling effects of township life, and like Zulu and Shilakoe, portrays the pathos: children are like those of Sisyphus; women in his etching *African Queens* are sad but formidable and majestic.

John Muafangejo (1943–1987) conveys with linoleum cuts a very different mood. Exuberance and verve characterize his compositions, which are bold confrontations with the exigencies of life. His subjects, in everyday situations, are defined by large sharp-edged forms. *An Interview of Capetown University in 1971* is a portrayal of oppression, but his vigorous design, robust figures, and lively patterns project a strong inner freedom.

Not unlike Asiru Olatunde of Nigeria, Muafangejo illustrates with directness and humor stories from the Bible as well as scenes of hunters and farmers. He integrates titles and sentences, which describe events depicted, into the compositions.

In Muafangejo's *Adam and Eve* linoleum cut, Adam,

small and sturdy, has a jaunty appearance while Eve, a statuesque figure, dominates an ebullient garden of trees, animals, and birds. She appears as a symbol of fertility around which all the flora and fauna pivot.

An Ovambo born at Oshikango, Namibia, Muafangejo went to Rorke's Drift in 1967. After a year and a half, he became ill. Nonetheless, he managed to complete the three-year course on time. He then taught in Ovamboland, and created tapestries and prints. He returned to Rorke's Drift in 1974 as an artist-in-residence, but again became ill. Now devoting his life to his art, he works at his home in Oshikango. His prints have been exhibited widely and have appeared in *Studio International;* in 1983 his prints were included in the World Print Council Exhibition.

The prints and manifestos of Gavin Jantjes (1948–) of Cape Town, reveal an approach to the inhumanities of apartheid that differs radically from the approach of

Vumikosi Zulu, *Robbers* and *Robbed Man,* 1974, etching, sheet: 20¾″ × 15½″; image 12¼″ × 8½″.

John Muafangejo, *An Interview of Capetown University in 1971*, 1970s, linoleum cut, sheet: 17″ × 24″; image: 13¼″ × 15¾″.

John Muafangejo, *Adam and Eve*, 1968, linoleum cut, 20½″ × 25″.

Shilakoe, Zulu, Mbatha, Dumile, and Muafangejo. The difference lies not in feeling or intensity but in media, style, and symbol. Whereas the figures in Shilakoe's etchings are poignant, elusive, and their power is in understatement, the bold figures in Jantjes' prints provoke the viewer to confront brutality in its most patent form.

The human figure, says Jantjes, is central to "African artistic expression" rather than the "visual landscape," which "is almost anything these days . . . for the Western-European artist. For African artists MAN is the visual landscape."[25] And the men and women in his works document the humilities of apartheid with journalistic reality.

Using graphic images of guns, bullets, barbed wire, and the wounded and dead, made with techniques like photomontage, silkscreen, and collage, he makes forceful political statements. As major compositional elements, symbols and comments are always unerringly placed; Jantjes' precision is searing.

In his series *A South African Colouring Book*, images like those from children's books state variously: "Colour This Whites Only" and "Colour These People Dead." One print entitled *Colour This Labor Dirt Cheap* shows a woman in serial format cleaning toilets marked for whites only.

His posters, which document such tragedies as the Sharpeville Massacre, recall the poetry of Dennis Brutus speaking of "stubbled graves Expectant, of eternity," or "the bugled dirging slopes," and "panoply/for one whose gifts the mud devours, with our hopes."[26]

A writer as well as visual artist, Jantjes defines art as "the complex expressive heart of a cultural body," and speaks of how Africa has been defined by others: "We were examined, not appreciated. Our cultural body was painstakingly dissected by colonial archaeologists, ethnographers, and anthropologists who studied each segment separately from the other."

Explaining further that African art, like slaves, was used to

. . . enhance the development of other non-African cultures. . . . African art became the catalyst for the most fundamental change in European art history. . . . [a]ppreciation was of our arts' expressive energy, its brilliant use of abstraction and its sheer aesthetic splendour. . . . Our art, both traditional and contemporary, is not the conglomeration of characteristics, curiosities, or things. It is the superstructure, the dynamism and creative potential of a culture that make art possible and nourishes creative expression.

Jantjes also explains that the history of Africa as "published in the fifties or earlier would read to the then contemporary African . . . like a fairy tale."[27]

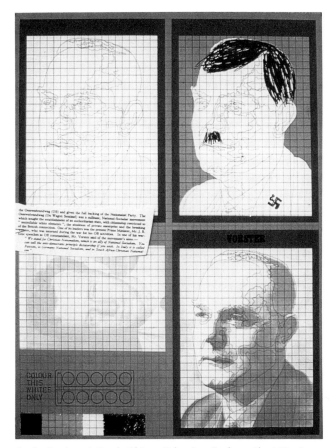

Gavin Jantjes, *A South African Colouring Book — Sheet No. 2*, 1975, screenprint with collage, 23⅝" × 17¾".

He expands on the subject of definition:

Did Picasso, Braque or Brancusi see cubist abstraction as a risk even though its similarities to traditional African sculpture were so clear? No, there is an attitude of mind being laid bare here. An attitude which says "blackman, know your place. Your cultural place below that of the dominant culture."

In his painting *Hot House Nursery Men*, he illustrates the way that a "style" of African art has been "nurtured" by others: "Like prize roses they have pruned African art to fit into their cultural garden."[28] Even the confrontation with oppression has its price. "My early work remains valid for black society yet in another way it was kind of a weird justification for white society," says Jantjes. He goes on to explain that as African artists today:

[We] know who we are, we know what we are about; we are trying to express our future hopes, dreams, aspirations and these are essential things for us. . . . That was basically different from what I was saying a few years previously. So I turned to more essential things in my life.[29]

That we have not lost our sanity or the will to struggle under increased government pressure, demonstrates, not only the government's weakness, but our creative strength.

Creativity is our domain. It is action toward and for fuller humanity. Oppressors have never been creative. Clever, yes, but never creative. Control and maintenance of the status quo are their actions. . . . In the South African situation talent becomes a challenge.[30]

A critic reviewing Jantjes says that his works approach "the density and intricacy of any modern novel, and emerge as broad statements of a society in turmoil. To that extent these paintings are not a respite from the battlefield but a deepening of the struggle and form a part of an ongoing experimentation to come to terms with modern day reality."[31]

Tito Zungu (ca. 1945–) was born in Mapumulo district of Zululand. It is not hard to see connections to environment and tradition in the richly patterned drawings he created on envelopes. A comparison between Ndebele wall decoration and his designs reveals a strong cultural bond. Whether or not he was conscious of this connection, his art clearly bridges the distance between

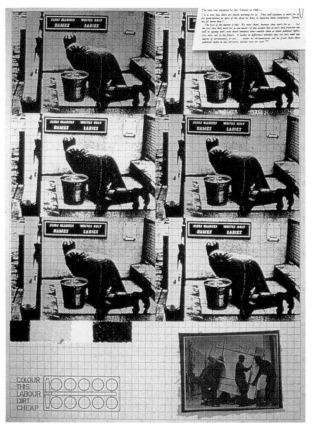

Gavin Jantjes, *A South African Colouring Book — Sheet No. 5 (Colour This Labor Dirt Cheap)*, 1975, serigraph with collage, 23⅝" × 17¾".

Gavin Jantjes, *Anti-Apartheid 1978,* 1978, poster, dimensions unknown.

3 of his designs were selected in 1971 for the exhibition Art: South Africa: Today. In 1972 he won a special award in the annual *African Arts* magazine competition.[33]

Black South African artists are pioneers and social historians, documenting tragedy and tension, pathos and indignity, as well as beauty and endurance in courageous poetic terms. Gavin Jantjes describes how the predicament out of which their art grows still presents barriers, saying that although they "have not lost sight of the essential social role of their traditional art and mirror this role in their art," it is:

frustrating that the words about us have failed to grasp this reflection; failed to put into perspective the crumbling social fabric in which this art was made; failed to recognize the lack of opportunity; failed to perceive the humanity and the human beings; and finally, how upsetting that we have allowed this to happen.[34]

When speaking of the past and future, Jantjes has this to say:

Our forefathers were as aware of social, political, and economic problems as we are. They were as aware of

the indigenous forms—the patterns found in beaded jewelry, in baskets, and on walls—and contemporary expression. The fact that he worked on envelopes is appropriate to the tradition of making useful things beautiful.

Just as the house paintings of the Sotho and Xhosa stress the underlying structure of a building, Zungu's paintings too have an architectural sense, controlled not only by the shape of the envelope but also by the shape of the building or airplane depicted. Rooflines, windows, bricks, and even step patterns, so typical of Xhosa and Ndebele wall paintings, reinforce the overall forms in his designs. Angles dramatize perspective and tiny dots in some areas are organized in strict geometric conformity. The effect is a dazzling mosaic structure of textures and patterns.

Zungu, who had no training, drew such designs on envelopes for "African men working in Durban which they bought to send letters home to their families in the country. He was encouraged by the African Art Centre of the Institute of Race Relations."[32] From 600 entries,

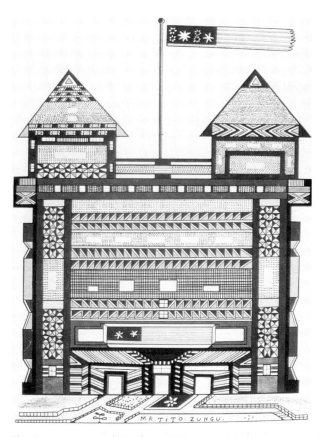

Tito Zungu, *Decorated Envelope,* 1972, colored ballpoint pen and koki pen.

aesthetic, poetic, philosophical, [and] historical problems as we should be, and I think that if we can get that from tradition then we can go somewhere and take the definition out of the hands of the dominant culture and redefine it ourselves. Our definitions could become, should become the foundations to build a contemporary art.[35]

However, the white South African playwright Athol Fugard explains that he is not sure that art can convince disbelievers, "but for the sake of those who believe in human dignity. Let us not desert them. For those who do believe. Art can impart faith."[36]

Jantjes, on the other hand, states:

One makes art with genuine optimism, with the belief that someone is going to understand, is going to accept one's expression as essentially philosophical, political, historical or artistically truthful. If one does not have this belief, why make art? I am addressing humanity in its fullest conceptual meaning which implies its ability to transform the world and make it more human.[37]

South African artists must surely make art, both to address humanity, and to reassure those believers in human dignity. They must also make it to survive, and in so doing they assert their own dignity.

While many other artists such as Ezrom Legae, Judus Mahlangu, Leonard Matsoso, George Msimang, Ephraim Ngatane, Eric Ngcobo, Linda Nolutshungu, Caiphas Nxumalo, G. M. Pemba, Dan Rakgoathe, and Michael Zondi deserve mention, as do others who may be living abroad, there must be, in addition, unknown artists living in remote areas of the country, unremarked and unpraised, who work out of their collective mythologies and local lifeways expressing their talents and delineating their cultures. Perhaps they too will extend our perceptions and speak with eloquence to the moral as well as the aesthetic conscience.

Afterword

Confluences

Sub-Saharan Africa's diversity is impressive. Each country's artists have strong stylistic attributes: the bright architectural shapes of the Nigerians, the orchestrations of color and rhythm of the Senegalese, the subtle lines and forms of the Sudanese, the rich colors and symbols of the Ethiopians, the monumentality of the Zimbabweans, and the pathos and anger of the South Africans. In addition, there are an infinite number of other attributes, many not yet explored. The richness is strength and an important component of the future that is in the making. It is emphatically predicted by the variety and profundity of the present African renaissance.

Just as there is variety in result, so there is variety in origin. This is not to say that the important modern artists are working with past traditions in a self-conscious way. For most of them the past is within and is a natural part of their work syncretized, as it is, with contemporary experience. Traditions enable them to successfully combine seemingly anachronistic elements.

South African writer and scholar Es'kia Mphahlele describes this blending, "Everywhere in Africa we shall for a long time to come continue to commute between tradition and the present. We shall be the vehicle of communication between the two streams of consciousness as they exchange confidences, knowledge, wisdom and dreams." And he states further, "Because not only is the African present seeking out the past, but the past is seeking out the present."[1]

For many artists, getting in touch with sources presents challenges. For Nigerians, rich traditions are close at hand. For others, even though they are far removed from the past, influences of traditions are a distinct presence. This is the case of the sculptors of Zimbabwe, where the last known stone carving is dated ca. 1500. However, in culture after culture many valuable references that might be used to strengthen artistic directions are fast disappearing. Foreign influences are ubiquitous, and much of value is lost in the rush toward modernization. In this delicate situation modern technology entices, and it is the fortunate artist who can come to terms with it and can choose or reject selectively.

Some artists like Ibrahim El Salahi, Skunder Boghossian, Gavin Jantjes, and Francis Nnaggenda have an identification that is as generically African as it is individually indigenous, making use of a variety of African forms as well as those of local traditions. However, the finest expressions—whatever their identification—seem to derive from the living values of the past rather than from a romantic attachment to its classical structures. Drawing on the present as well, as these artists do, they create that vital alchemy. For them, pictorial reproduction of an object is not kinship to tradition; idea, not subject, usually prompts their format. Images may tell a story, but the most interesting and moving works also involve the language of myth, which deals with associations as signposts and leads not so much toward clarification as toward perception.

While some works by African artists can be found to parallel the categories and terms applied to modern

Western art, generally speaking, African artists do not paint the African scene but draw on the world of symbols. Their attachment to symbol and metaphor is shared by African poets, dancers, and musicians. The seminal metaphor is perhaps the most important element in common, but rhythms and repetitions of line, patterns and forms, harmonies and cadences are all familial. Metaphor, a part of every aspect of culture from language to masquerade and religion, combines with these traditional assets to amplify or multiply meaning. Creating symbols by foraging from a wealth of classical lore, African artists add dimensions that enrich and expand.

Topical subject matter embraced by myth and symbol is often overlooked by critics, as is meaning inherent in classical African works. This is due perhaps to their lack of familiarity with the cultures involved. In the case of South African artists, topical subject matter, of course, can not be overlooked. They, as a group, more than others, speak with clear political purpose; their imagery, while also relying on symbol, ranges from poignancy to indictment.

Local aesthetic canons are often ignored by the Western world and canons deemed to be universal are applied. This is not to suggest that one can not enjoy this art without an understanding of other aspects of African culture, but probing further brings rewards. To hear an artist like Twins Seven-Seven tell the story that is inseparable from the painting or to know something about the myths and customs that are intrinsic to Bruce Onobrakpeya's works expands one's visual impressions.

Although artists today sometimes record historical events, they seldom work for shrines and kings. Therefore they need new support. African governments do see their artists as ambassadors of good will, and so sponsor exhibitions. But more patrons at home and centers for contemporary African art at home and abroad, such as Iwalewa Haus in Bayreuth, Germany, are needed. Major museums are just beginning to establish programs to exhibit the works of these artists and to include them in permanent collections. "Rather than spend our time looking backwards and regretting the disappearance of tribal art," says Julian Beinart, who organized some of the first short experimental workshops in Africa, "we should foster and encourage the same imaginations which have certainly not been destroyed by the disappearance of tribal art."[2]

Because Africans have not had equal footing with the West in any realm, they have suffered from a derogatory image. African artists are altering this inequity. They are not committed to a search for "newness," nor are they just reacting to injustice; they are reflecting their own cultural reality, and so expressing the full power of their sensibility. Their work is expository and revelatory. Ideas, concepts, and messages enlighten rather than persuade, and are part of an aesthetic organism.

Therefore, they hold a unique historical position, vital to the understanding of African art and culture as a whole. Many have accepted foreign materials and changed customs and practices to forge their individual identities with national or international reputations. However, at the same time they help to forge the identities of their nation states.

Because their aesthetic opinions, theories, and works are integral to the whole spectrum of African art, they enhance its study. Through them we have a perspective of both past and present, as well as intimations of the future. Many African artists have been overlooked by scholars, collectors, and museums who, by so doing, define the parameters of African culture and suggest the end of creative accomplishment on that continent.

Now one-half century old, despite pressures and prejudices, the new art is mature. Tradition is grist for a creativity that communicates today's passions with humanism and vision. Perhaps future artists who come into their own outside an academic framework, such as those who worked at Oshogbo, Nigeria, and at Inyanga, Zimbabwe, will not be able to survive without ongoing support in the form of enlightened assistance that allows the artist to be selective without vitiating original visions by the imposition of arbitrary formulas and alien standards.

Women artists are few, but more are appearing, and soon they will bring more and different insights. Already the new artists defy the stigmas that label them as ethnic and therefore place them closer to anthropology than art. These new artists wish to abolish stereotypes about Africa. Because artists are the bearers of truth, the voices by which society is measured, they open the doors to cultures about which we know very little. Without them the world is incomplete. They broaden our horizons to include poetic visions which, like the rivers of Africa, run as deep as time.

Notes

Introduction

1. Ulli Beier, *Contemporary Art in Africa* (London: Pall Mall Press, 1968), 59.

1   Sources for Synthesis

1. Simon Ottenberg, "Illusion, Communication and Psychology in West African Masquerades," *Ethos* 10(2) (Summer 1982):151.

2   Image and Metaphor

1. *Presence Africaine: Review Culturelle du Monde Noir* was a quarterly edited by Alioune Diop and published in Paris.

2. *Black Orpheus* was edited by Ulli Beier and issued by Mbari Publications in Ibadan, Nigeria.

3. Daniel Crowley, "Symbolism in African Verbal Art," *African Arts* 1 (4):116.

4. Wole Soyinka, ed., *Poems of Black Africa* (New York: Hill and Wang, 1975), 162.

5. Ulli Beier, ed., *African Poetry: An Anthology of Traditional African Poetry* (London: Cambridge University Press, 1966), 22.

6. Ibid., 39–40.

7. Ibid., 42–43.

8. Gerald Moore and Ulli Beier, eds., *Modern Poetry from Africa* (Harmondsworth, Middlesex, and Baltimore: Penguin African Library, 1963), 38.

9. Ibid., 37.

10. Ibid., 62–63.

11. Ibid., 64.

12. Soyinka, *Poems of Black Africa*, 190.

13. Ibid., 307.

14. Moore and Beier, *Modern Poetry from Africa*, 138–39.

15. Crowley, "Symbolism in African Verbal Art," 116.

16. Soyinka, *Poems of Black Africa*, 14.

3   Bridges: Predecessors in Nigeria

1. William Fagg, *Nigerian Images* (London: Lund Humphries, 1963), 19.

2. Gerald Moore and Ulli Beier, eds., *Modern Poetry from Africa* (Harmondsworth, Middlesex, and Baltimore: Penguin African Library, 1963), 121.

3. Sara Jane Hollis Dickerson, *Benin Artist Idah: Court and Personal Style* (New Orleans: Interdisciplinary Studies Program at Southern University of New Orleans, 1979), 3.

4. Ibid., 47.

5. Ibid., 48, 63.

6. Ibid., 37.

7. Ibid., 50.

8. Philip M. Peek, "Ovia Idah and Eture Egbede: Traditional Nigerian Artists," *African Arts* 18(2):56.

9. Ulli Beier, *Yemi Bisiri: A Yoruba Brass Caster* (Ibadan, Nigeria: Mbari Publications, 1963). In the late sixties Ulli Beier went to live in Ilobu where he was ultimately made a member of the Ogboni cult, a secret organization that once held juridical power in every Yoruba town and village. Beier was able to study the art itself, the process, and the Ogboni cult. He describes his insights in this monograph.

10. Ibid. The larger figures are built around a core of earth, which is always taken from the hard red soil of a termite hill.

11. Ibid. In the case of wood carvings, pressures brought by Christian mores have functioned as a constraint against the purchase or display of sacred objects, resulting in a decline in their production. The same constraints do not apply to these

Edan figures because membership is usually a secret matter. Each member must own a pair, and the pieces are not shown to nonmembers and are not publicly displayed. Moreover, with Ogboni pieces the possibility of mimesis is avoided by a taboo against human likeness, a further distinction between cast Edan figures and wood carvings, which emphasize organic human forms and detail.

12. Ibid.

13. Ibid.

14. Kofi Awoonor, "Introduction," *Night of My Blood* (New York: Anchor Books, 1971), 11.

15. Another copy of the same bronze was given to United Nations in New York.

16. Ulli Beier, "Lamidi Fakeye," *West African Review* 31(391):31.

17. Father Kevin Carroll, *Yoruba Religious Carving* (London: Geoffrey Chapman, 1967), 113, 53. Carroll says, "My conclusion is that the art of the Yoruba carver, at least that with which I am familiar, is a humanistic rather than a deeply religious art, even when directly concerned with the creation of religious objects."

18. Chinua Achebe, *Morning Yet on Creation Day* (Garden City, New York: Anchor Press/Doubleday, 1976), 59–60.

19. Author's notes.

20. Author's notes.

21. *Morning Post,* Lagos (n.d., probably March, 1964).

22. Ibid.

23. "Nigerian Antiquities and the Modern Nigerian Artists" by Yusuf Grillo (Unpublished, n.d.).

24. Daniel Olaniyan Babalola, *The Awo Style: A Synthesis of Traditional and Contemporary Artistic Idioms in Nigeria* (Ann Arbor, Michigan: University Microfilms International, 1982) (Ph.D. diss., Ohio State University), 260.

25. Conversation with author, ca. 1969.

26. Exhibition announcement for "S. Irein Wangboje; June 22–26" (n.d., probably 1970 or 71) at USIS, Lagos.

27. "Solomon Wangboje: Art Forges a Link of Pride with the Past," *Topic Magazine* 36 (Washington, D.C.: United States Information Agency, n.d.:12.

28. Letter to author, April 7, 1971.

29. "Is Art Propaganda?" *Daily Times,* Lagos (n.d.).

30. "Solomon Wangboje: Art Forges a Link of Pride with the Past," 12.

4 Creating a Tradition

Vanguard Sculptors, Printmakers, and Painters of Nigeria

1. David Alade, "Profile: Ben Osawe," *Morning Post,* Lagos (September 27, 1966).

2. Ibid.

3. Quoted in "Ben Osawe," invitation, Exhibition Centre, Marina, Lagos (October 1966).

4. Alade, "Profile: Ben Osawe."

5. Robert Serumaga, conversations with African writers, July, 1965, as quoted by Dennis Duerden in "African Art Today," in *Contemporary African Art,* exhibition catalog (London: Studio International, 1969), 15.

6. Alade, "Profile: Ben Osawe."

7. David Alade, "Profile: Emokpae," *Morning Post,* Lagos (August 30, 1966).

8. Interview with author, February 24, 1988.

9. "About Myself and My Work," by Uzo Egonu (Unpublished descriptive account, 1970).

10. Note to author, December, 1981.

11. Bruce Onobrakpeya, *Notes and Comments No. 7* (April 1982).

12. Unable to locate original source.

13. Bruce Onobrakpeya, *Twenty Deep Etchings* (December 1973), 4.

14. Robert Farris Thompson, "The Rebirth of Power in Break-Pattern Art" in *Who'd A Thought It—Improvisation in African-American Quiltmaking* by Eli Leon (San Francisco: San Francisco Craft and Folk Art Museum, 1987), 17.

15. Lecture: Bruce Onobrakpeya, "Book Illustrations," (1972).

16. Bruce Onobrakpeya, *Print Notes and Comments No. 5* (April 1979), 3.

17. Ibid., 4.

18. Conversation with author.

19. Eli Leon, *Who'd A Thought It—Improvisation in African-American Quiltmaking,* exhibition catalog (San Francisco: San Francisco Craft and Folk Art Museum, 1987), 22.

20. Bruce P. O. Onobrakpeya, *Twenty Deep Etchings* (December 1973), 1.

21. Bruce Onobrakpeya, *Symbols of Ancestral Groves* (Lagos: Ovuomaroro Gallery, 1985).

22. Bruce P. O. Onobrakpeya, *Twenty Deep Etchings* (December 1973), 3.

23. Bruce Onobrakpeya, *Twelve Deep Etchings* (September 1972), 3.

24. As quoted by Juliet Highet in "Nigerian Artists," *African Arts* 2(2):41.

25. Bruce P. O. Onobrakpeya, *Twenty Deep Etchings* (December 1973), 6.

26. "Emergency Commission," in *A Reed in the Tide* (London: Longmans, 1965), 6.

27. Bruce P. O. Onobrakpeya, *Twenty Deep Etchings* (December 1973), 3.

28. Conversation with author, November 8, 1981.

29. Jean Kennedy, "Bruce Onobrakpeya," *African Arts* 5(2):49.

30. Ulli Beier, *Contemporary Art in Africa* (London: Pall Mall Press, 1968), 47.

31. Uche Okeke, *Tales of Life and Death* (Garden City, New York: Zenith Books, Doubleday, 1971), 24.

32. Ibid., xii.

33. Uche Okeke, "The New Nigerian Artist," *Morning Post,* Lagos (March 18, 1965).

34. Ibid.

35. Ibid.

36. He is also the subject of a monograph by Ulli Beier: *Uche Okeke's Drawings* (Ibadan: Mbari Publications, 1965).

37. "A Note on 'Aka,'" *Aka 86—Inaugural Exhibition Catalogue: Aka Circle of Exhibiting Artists* (Enugu: French Centre, Aka Circle of Exhibiting Artists, 1986). Exhibition held at the Ministry of Education, Enugu, April 14–20, 1986, and at the Franco-German Exhibition Hall, Lagos, May 14–31, 1986, 5.

38. Chike Aniakor, "Introduction," *Aka 86—Inaugural Exhibition Catalogue: Aka Circle of Exhibiting Artists,* 9.

39. "A Note on 'Aka,'" *Aka 86—Inaugural Exhibition Catalogue: Aka Circle of Exhibiting Artists,* 5.

40. Ulli Beier, "An Interview With Obiora Udechukwu—Nsukka, 25 September 1980," *Okike* 20 (December, 1981): 59–60.

41. Ibid. 59, 60.

42. Ibid. 62–63.

43. Ibid. 59, 62, 64–65.

44. Ibid.

45. "Chike Aniakor: Poems and Drawings," *African Arts* 8(4):42.

46. Herbert M. Cole and Chicke C. Aniakor, *Igbo Art: Community and Cosmos,* exhibition catalog (Los Angeles: Museum of Cultural History, University of California, Los Angeles, 1984).

47. Ulli Beier, ed., *Neue Kunst in Africa,* exhibition catalog (Berlin: Dietrich Reimer Verlag, 1980), 132. Exhibition entitled Austellung im Mittelrheinischen held at Landesmuseum, Mainz.

48. "Laments for Shola," "August Break," "Native," "Laments for Shola" in *West Africa Verse,* Donatus Nwoga, ed. (London: Longmans, 1967), 89, 91, 85, 90.

49. "Night Rain," in *Modern Poetry from Africa,* Gerald Moore and Ulli Beier, eds. (Baltimore, Maryland: Penguin African Library, 1963), 112.

50. "Water Maid," Ibid., 134.

51. Dennis Duerden, "Sculptures in Light," *West Africa* (June 4, 1984):1163; Chandana Juliet Highet, "Sokari Douglas Camp: Kalabari Sculptress," *Skypower, Nigerian Airways* (June 1984):8.

52. Duerden, "Sculptures in Light," 1163.

53. Correspondence with author, September 19, 1984.

54. Correspondence with author, October 15, 1984.

55. Dore Ashton, *American Art Since 1945* (New York: Oxford University Press, 1982), 165, quoting Al Held.

56. Gerald Moore and Ulli Beier, eds., *Modern Poetry from Africa* (Harmondsworth, Middlesex, and Baltimore: Penguin African Library, 1963), 144–45.

57. Segun Olusola, "The Palm-Wine Drinkard," *Nigeria Magazine* 77 (June 1963):147. A special performance of the play was offered circa June 1963 in honor of the then prime minister Sir Abubakar Tafawa Balewa; it also marked the installation of the Chancellor of the University of Ibadan.

58. David Heathcote, "The Art of Musa Yola," *African Arts* 7(2):35–37.

59. Ibid.

60. Keith Nicklin and Jill Salmons, "Ibibio Metal Work," *African Arts* 10(1):21.

61. Keith Nicklin and Jill Salmons, "S. J. Akpan of Nigeria" *African Arts* 11 (1):30.

62. "Introduction," *Contemporary African Art,* exhibition catalog (London: Studio International, 1969), 5, 6, 7. Exhibition held at the Camden Arts Centre, London, August 10–September 8, 1969.

63. Conversation with Robert Serumaga in "African Art Today" *African Art* by Dennis Duerden (Feltham, Middlesex: Hamlyn Group, 1968), 27.

5 Artists of the Shrines Oshogbo

1. Susanne Wenger Alarape, "Introduction," *The Oshogbo Shrines* (n.p., 1968), 1.

2. Correspondence with author, ca. 1968.

3. Ibid.

4. Ulli Beier and Frank Speed (1964).

5. Correspondence with author, no date, probably 1968.

6. Ibid.

7. "Critic," "Linocuts at Mbari," *Morning Post,* Lagos (June 16, 1964), 13.

8. Ulli Beier, *Contemporary Art in Africa* (London: Pall Mall Press, 1968), 153, 154.

9. Ulli Beier, *The Return of the Gods: The Sacred Art of Susanne Wenger* (London: Cambridge University Press, 1975), 51.

6 The Spontaneous Spirit Oshogbo and Ife

1. *Black Orpheus* was published for the Mbari Club of Ibadan by Longmans of Nigeria, Ltd. *Odu: Journal of Yoruba and Related Studies* was published by the Western Region Literature Committee in Ibadan, Nigeria, and by Thomas Nelson and Sons, in Edinburgh, Scotland.

2. "A Bibliography of Writings by Ulli Beier" with an Introduction by Taban lo Liong (Unpublished, 1975), 1–2.

3. "Indian Issue," guest editor Ulli Beier. *Aspect: Art and Literature* 23 (January 1982).

4. Ulli Beier, correspondence with author, November 11, 1986.

5. Ulli Beier, *Contemporary Art in Africa* (London: Pall Mall Press, 1968), 103. Other similar clubs, one in Benin in Idah's compound and one in Enugu, sprang into being inspired by the Mbari at Ibadan and the Mbari Mbayo at Oshogbo. Lack of financial support forced them to discontinue activities.

6. Ibid., 103, 102.

7. Reverend Samuel Johnson, *History of the Yoruba* (Lagos: Christian Missionary Society, 1921).

8. Quoted in Alan Kriegsman, "Duro Ladipo: Symbol of a Native Culture," *The Washington Post* (February 20, 1975), C1.

9. Wole Soyinka, "Drama and the African World View," *Myth, Literature and the African World* (London: Cambridge University Press, 1976), 64, 42, 65.

10. Alan Kriegsman, "Duro Ladipo: Symbol of a Native Culture," C1.

11. Letter to author, April 25, 1978. In 1987 the Arthur Hall troupe in Philadelphia performed Ladipo's most famous opera, *Oba Koso.*

12. Quoted in *Sbyszek Plocki, Georgina Beier,* exhibition catalog (Adelaide: Andris Lidums Gallery, 1975), 2.

13. Beier, *Contemporary Art in Africa,* 106.

14. Ibid., 110.

15. Transcript of a radio interview with Jenny Zimmer, art historian at the Royal Melbourne Institute of Technology, no date.

16. Tayo Aiyegbusi, "A Mixture of African Mythology and Whimsy," *Georgina Beier,* exhibition catalog (Bayreuth: Iwalewa Haus, University of Bayreuth, 1983).

17. Beier, *Contemporary Art in Africa,* 123.

18. Jean Kennedy, "City as Metaphor," *African Report* (April, 1972):28.

19. Conversation with author, date unknown.

20. Ibid.

21. Sidney Goodsir Smith, "Nigerian Painting Has a Social Function," *The Scotsman,* Edinburgh (February 22, 1967).

22. Muraina Oyelami, *My Life in the Duro Ladipo Theatre* (Bayreuth: Iwalewa Haus, University of Bayreuth, 1982). Oyelami was artist-in-residence with the National Black Theater in New York City's Harlem; at Iwalewa House, University of Bayreuth; and at the Djerassi Foundation in California. He has presented demonstrations in many nations and performed at international arts festivals in Berlin, Edinburgh, Nancy (France), and Singapore (where he was the leader of a group). He recently toured Germany and Austria with his own theatre troupe. A former curator of the Ulli Beier Collection at the Obafemi Awolowo University Antiquities Museum in Oshobgo, Oyelami has created murals at Ori Olokun Cultural Centre and School of Medicine, Obafemi Awolowo University.

23. Conversation with author, date unknown.

24. Conversation with author, date unknown.

25. Conversation with author, date unknown.

26. Ibid.

27. Ibid.

28. Ulli Beier, unable to locate original source.

29. Amos Tutuola, *The Palm-Wine Drinkard* (New York: Grove Press, 1953), 28.

30. Quoted in material printed on the back cover of Grove Press's edition of *The Palm-Wine Drinkard.*

31. Smith, "Nigerian Painting has a Social Function."

32. Conversation with author, date unknown.

33. Dante Alighieri, *The Divine Comedy,* "Inferno," Canto 1.

34. Ademola Onibonkuta, *A Gift from the Gods* (Bayreuth: Iwalewa Haus, University of Bayreuth, 1983). He has several other publications: *The Return of Shango, In Memory of the Duro Ladipo Theater* (Bayreuth: Iwalewa Haus, University of Bayreuth, 1983); one of Yoruba incantations by Mbari Mbayo in Oshogbo and another publication of three plays for children by London University Press. (Unable to locate information about other publications).

35. *The Second Year* (Bayreuth: Iwalewa Haus, University of Bayreuth, 1983), 6.

36. Ulli Beier, correspondence with author, November 11, 1986.

37. *Contemporary Art from the Third World,* exhibition catalog (Port Moresby: Institute of Papua New Guinea Studies, 1975), 9. Exhibition held September 26–29, 1975.

38. Correspondence with author, no date, probably 1971.

39. Ibid.

40. Ulli Beier, correspondence with author, November 11, 1986.

41. John Canaday, "Not for the Airports This Time," *New York Times* (August 16, 1970), Art Section, 17. The review the second major exhibition of works by Oshogbo artists in the United States at the Studio Museum in Harlem; the first at Otis Art Institute in March of 1969. Both were arranged by Jean Kennedy and Miriam Wolford.

42. Ulli Beier, "Gift Orakpo (Nigeria)," *Art in the Third World,* no. 2 (Port Moresby: Institute of Papua New Guinea Studies, 1976), 1. For many of the facts concerning Gift Orakpo, I am indebted to Ulli Beier and Georgina Beier.

43. Ibid., 2.

44. Ibid., 3.

45. Ulli Beier, "Middle Art Talks to Ulli Beier, *Okike* 22:44. Other publications by Ulli Beier on Middle Art include "Naive Nigerian Painting," *Black Orpheus* 19 (March 1966):31; "Signwriters of Nigeria," *African Arts* 4(3):22; "Middle Art: The Paintings of War," *African Arts* 9(2):20; "Populaire Kunst in Afrika," *Neue Kunst in Afrika,* exhibition catalog (Berlin: Deitrich Reimer Verlag, 1980), 69; "Middle Art," *Kunst aus Afrika,* exhibition catalog (Berlin: H. Heenemann GMBH, 1979), 96; and "Laden Schilder und Legenden," *Kunst aus Afrika,* 99.

46. Ulli Beier, "Middle Art Talks to Ulli Beier, *Okike* 22:44.

47. Ulli Beier, correspondence with author, November 11, 1986.

48. Georgina Beier, radio interview with Jenny Zimmer.

49. Ulli Beier, conversation with author, date unknown.

7 New Dynamics The West African Coast

1. Timothy Garrad, "Akan Metal Arts," *African Arts* 13(1):36.

2. George Nelson Preston, "Perseus and Medea in Africa—Military Art in Fanteland, 1834–1972," *African Arts* 8(3):39.

3. Susan Domowitz and Rene Mandirola, "Grave Monuments in Ivory Coast," *African Arts* 17(4):46.

4. Daniel Mato, "History, Style, and the Akan Aesthetic," a lecture given at "Arts of Ghana," symposium, the African Studies Center, University of California. November 5, 1977.

5. Peggy Appiah, "Asante Bird Symbolism," a lecture given at "Arts of Ghana," symposium, the African Studies Center, University of California. November 6, 1977.

6. Interview with author, July 24, 1977.

7. *El Loko,* exhibition catalog (Duisberg-Reinhausen: Stadiche Sammlungen, 1978), unnumbered. Translated from the German by Sigrid Vollerthun and Joyce Carol Thomas.

8. Ulli Beier, *Contemporary Art in Africa* (Pall Mall Press, 1968), 52.

9. Kofi Awoonor, "Lament of the Silent Sister," *Night of My Blood* (New York: Anchor Books, 1971), 75, 76.

10. Vincent Kofi, *Sculpture in Ghana* (Accra: Ghana Information Service, 1964), unnumbered.

11. Beier, *Contemporary Art in Africa,* 52.

12. "Siren Limits" II, *Limits* (Ibadan: Mbari Publications, 1964), unnumbered.

13. Conversation with author, 1974.

14. Interview with author, July 25, 1987.

15. Interview with author, September, 1986.

16. *El Anatsui: Sculptures, Photographs, Drawings,* exhibition catalog (Lagos: Goethe Institute, 1982), 4. Exhibition held February 20–March 5, 1982.

17. *Pieces of Wood, An Exhibition of Mural Sculpture,* exhibition catalog (El Anatsui, 1987), 9.

18. Ibid., 5.

19. David Gardella, "Momodou Ceesay of the Gambia," *African Arts* 7(4):41.

20. Awoonor, "Introduction," *Night of My Blood,* 11.

8 Artists of the Image and Loom Senegal

1. There was an earlier colloquium, "International Congress of African Culture," in Harare (then Salisbury) in the summer of 1962.

2. Léopold Sédar Senghor, "Blues." A poem in which the African living abroad grieves for home. In *Modern Poetry from Africa* by Gerald Moore and Ulli Beier, eds. (Harmondsworth, Middlesex, and Baltimore: Penguin Books, 1963), 47, 48.

3. Opening statement at the Dakar World Festival of Negro Arts. April 1966.

4. "Senegalese Art Today: The African Side of Pan-African Aesthetics" by Peter Mark (Unpublished, n.d.), 77.

5. As described in Senghor's seminal essay, "L'Esthetique Négro-Africaine Liberté 1," *Négritude et Humanisme* (Paris: Editions due Seuil, 1964), 202–17.

6. Peter Mark, "Senegalese Art Today: The African Side of Pan-African Aesthetics," 87, 88.

7. Gerald Moore and Ulli Beier, eds., "Introduction," *Modern Poetry from Africa* (Harmondsworth, Middlesex, and Baltimore: Penguin Books Ltd., 1963), 15, 16.

8. Ibid., "Night of Sine," 48; "Luxemborg 1939," 509; "Totem," 50; "New York," 56.

9. Jack Kroll, *Newsweek* (Date unknown, from quotation in *New Yorker Films* catalog).

10. Informal discussion with author, journalists, and others; San Francisco State University, San Francisco, California, January 8, 1978.

11. Marsha Landy, "*Black Girl* and *Xala*—Ousmane Sembene's Films—Politics and Style in *Black Girl,*" *Jump Cut* 27:24.

12. Ulla Schild, *Exposition Collective, Peintures Sous Verre Dakaroises,* exhibition catalog (Dakar: Allemande Biblioteque, 1983), 1.

13. Jacqueline Delange and Philip Fry, "Introduction," *Contemporary African Art*, exhibition catalog (London: Studio International, 1969), 8. Exhibition held at Camden Arts Centre, August 10–September 8, 1969.

14. Thomas A. Johnson, "A New Black Art Develops in Senegal," *New York Times* (April 23, 1973).

15. Irmila Devgon, translated from "Tapisseries de Thiès," *Topic Magazine* 74. (Washington, D.C.: United States Information Agency, undated).

16. Ibid.

17. Mark, "Senegalese Art Today: The African Side of Pan-African Aesthetics," 81.

18. Ibid., 89–90.

19. Ibid., 85.

20. Gabriel J. Gomis, "Ibou Diouf, Jeune Loup de la Peinture," *Sénégal Carrefour* 6 (May 1968):43.

21. Ibid., 49, 47, 50. Defining the meaning of the symbol, Diouf said, "The black man, at the same time a receptor and a receptacle of the effluviums and the waves of the universe, assimilates, translates, and returns them to the world, magnified and brightened by his human and spiritual grandeur. This is Negro Art." As quoted by Onuora Nzekwu in "Nigeria, Negritude, and the World Festival of Negro Arts," *Nigeria Magazine* (89):84.

22. Gomis, "Ibou Diouf, Jeune Loup de la Peinture," 51.

23. Sol Littman, "Senegalese Native Art Is a Must," *The Toronto Star* (August 19, 1979).

24. Trish Wilson, "Modern Techniques Give African Art a New Face," *The Hamilton Record*, Hamilton, Ontario (August 1979).

25. Littman, "Senegalese Native Art Is a Must."

26. Wilson, "Modern Techniques Give African Art a New Face."

27. *Contemporary Art of Senegal*, exhibition catalog (Washington, D.C.: Corcoran Gallery of Art, 1980), 8. Exhibition traveled from April 1980 to January 1981 beginning at the Corcoran Gallery of Art, Washington, D.C.

28. Léopold Sédar Senghor, "Elegy of the Circumcised," in *Poems of Black Africa*, Wole Soyinka, ed. (New York: Hill and Wang, 1975), 161.

9   Desert Light   Sudan

1. I am indebted to Rene Bravmann for this analysis. Rene Bravmann, "Islamic Patterns," *African Islam* (Washington, D.C.: Smithsonian Institution Press and London: Ethnographica, 1983), 90, 91, 93, quoting Richard Ettinghausen, "The Man-Made Setting" in *The World of Islam*, Bernard Lewis, ed. (London: Thames and Hudson, 1976), 70, 72, 68, 59.

2. Ibid., referring to Jacob Bronowski, "The Music of the Spheres," *The Ascent of Man* (Boston: Little, Brown, 1973), 166.

3. Denis Williams, "A Sudanese Calligraphy," *Transition* (Lusaka, June, 1963), 19, 20.

4. Sondra Hale, *The Vision of Mohamed Omer Bushara*, exhibition catalog (New York: The African-American Institute, 1981), 5. Exhibition held February 20, 1981–May 31, 1981. My gratitude to Sondra Hale for her scholarship, knowledge of, and writings about the Sudanese artists.

5. Ulli Beier, "Without a Tradition," *Contemporary Art in Africa* (London: Pall Mall Press, 1968), 34.

6. Rene Bravmann, "Islamic Patterns," *African Islam* (Washington, D.C.: Smithsonian Institute Press and London: Ethnographica, 1983), 38, 39.

7. Beier, "Without a Tradition," 34.

8. Denis Williams, "A Sudanese Calligraphy," 20.

9. Ibrahim El Salahi, "Interview with Ulli Beier" (University of Bayreuth, September 1983), 23, 24. I am deeply grateful to Ulli Beier for his assiduous gathering and recording of information about, and also for his own views of, Ibrahim El Salahi.

10. Ibid., 25.

11. Ibid., 26, 27.

12. Ibid., 28.

13. Ibid., 28, 29.

14. "Conversation with Ibrahim El Salahi," *Topic Magazine* (Washington, D.C.: United States Information Agency): 14. Conducted by Robert Serumaga of Uganda and first published in *Cultural Events in Africa*.

15. Ibrahim El Salahi, "El Salahi Speaks of His Work," *African Arts* 1(1):26.

16. Ulli Beier, *Ibrahim El Salahi* (Ibadan: Mbari Publications, 1962).

17. El Salahi, "Interview with Ulli Beier," 34, 35, 30.

18. Ibid., 32, 33.

19. "Conversation with Ibrahim El Salahi," 14, 15.

20. Unable to locate original source.

21. "Conversation with Ibrahim El Salahi," 15.

22. Ulli Beier, "Ibrahim El Salahi," *Black Orpheus* 10:50.

23. Ibid., 50.

24. Ibid., 49.

25. Ibid., 50.

26. "Interview with Ulli Beier," 36.

27. Ibid., 37.

28. Ibid., 38.

29. Ibid., 41.

30. "Interview: Amir I. M. Nour on the Place of the African Artist," *Africa Report* (May–June 1974): 16.

31. *Sculpture by Amir Nour*, exhibition brochure (Washington, D.C.: International Monetary Fund, 1976), 2. Exhibition held July 26–September 3, 1976.

32. Lecture by Amir Nour at the George Washington University, Washington, D.C., February, 1975.

33. Ibid.

34. "Interview: Amir I. M. Nour on the Place of the African Artist," 16.

35. Lecture by Amir Nour.

36. Lecture by Amir Nour.

37. "Interview: Amir I. M. Nour on the Place of the African Artist," 14.

38. Lecture by Amir Nour.

39. "Interview: Amir I. M. Nour on the Place of the African Artist," 48.

40. Rene Bravmann quoting Richard Ettinghausen, "The Man-Made Setting" in *The World of Islam*, Bernard Lewis, ed. (London: Thames and Hudson, 1976), 90.

41. *Contemporary African Art*, exhibition catalog (London: Studio International, 1969), 27, 28. I am indebted to J. Hevesi, author of "The Paintings of Kamala Ibrahim," for information on the Zaar cult and Kamala Ibrahim's association with it.

42. Correspondence with artist, July, 1984.

43. Correspondence.

44. Sondra Hale, "Musa Khalifa of Sudan," *African Arts* 6(3):19.

45. Ibid., 15.

46. Ibid., 18, 16.

47. Ibid., 16.

48. Ibid., 18.

49. Ibid., 19.

50. "Bushara at the Slade," *African Arts* 12(3):40.

51. Ibid., 40.

52. Bloke Modisane, "lonely," in *Modern Poetry from Africa,*

Gerald Moore and Ulli Beier, eds. (Harmondsworth, Middlesex, and Baltimore: Penguin African Library, 1963), 211.

53. Hale, *The Vision of Mohamed Omer Bushara,* 8, 10.

54. Sondra Hale and Mohamed Omer Bushara, "In Search of a Face: Salih Abdou Mashamoun—The Sun and the Eclipse," *Ufahamu,* 1976, 6(2):82.

55. Ibid., 87.

56. Ibid., 86.

57. Ibid., 85.

58. Ibid., 85.

59. Ibid., 88.

60. Ibid., 86.

61. Ibid., 86.

62. Kenneth Okwesa, "Abdulla, Sudanese Potter," *African Arts* 3(2):30.

63. Ibid., 31.

10   From a Legacy of Sign and Symbol

1. Sydney W. Head, "A Conversation with Gebre Kristos Desta," *African Arts* 2(4):25.

2. "Traditional African Poetry," *Black Orpheus* 19:8.

3. Michael D. Quam, "*Harvest: 3000 Years*—Sowers of Maize and Bullets," *Jump Cut* 24/25:unnumbered.

4. Françoise Pfaff, "Toward a New Era in Cinema," *Howard University Magazine* (date unknown, unnumbered).

5. Quam, "*Harvest: 3000 Years*—Sowers of Maize and Bullets."

6. Pfaff, "Toward a New Era in Cinema."

7. Conversation with author, June 3, 1984.

8. Pfaff, "Toward a New Era in Cinema."

9. Conversation.

10. Head, "A Conversation with Gebre Kristos Desta," 23.

11. Ibid., 25.

12. Stanislaw Chojnacki, "A Survey of Modern Ethiopian Art," *Zeitschrift für Kuturaustausch,* Special Edition, 1973. Published by Institut für Auslansbeziehungen, Athiopien.

13. Head, "A Conversation with Gebre Kristos Desta," 23.

14. Ibid., 23.

15. Ulli Beier, *Contemporary Art in Africa* (London: Pall Mall Press, 1968), quoting Louise Acheson in the catalog of Skunder's Ibadan exhibition, 35.

16. Janheinz Jahn, *Muntu* (New York: Grove Press, 1961), 141.

17. Chojnacki, "A Survey of Modern Ethiopian Art."

18. Stanislaw Chojnacki, "Skunder: His First Addis Ababa Exhibition, *Ethiopian Observer* 10(3):184.

19. Conversation with author, July 12, 1986.

20. Solomon Deressa, catalog, source unknown.

21. "Other Gods: Containers of Belief," exhibition brochure (Washington, D.C.: Fonda Del Sol, 1986). Exhibition held May 22–July 22, 1986.

22. Acha Debela, correspondence with author, March 29, 1984.

23. Chojnacki, "A Survey of Modern Ethiopian Art."

24. Quoted by Achameleh Debela in *Ethiopian Artists in America,* exhibition catalog (Baltimore: Morgan State College Gallery, 1973). Exhibition held March 4–March 26, 1973; and Acha Debela, correspondence with author, May 10, 1984.

25. Debela, *Ethiopian Artists in America.*

26. Conversation with author, January 10, 1984.

27. Conversation with author.

28. Lincoln F. Johnson, "An Extraordinary Ethiopian Show at Morgan," *Baltimore Sun* (March 23, 1973).

29. Conversation with author, September 5, 1987.

30. Interview with author, November 1987.

31. Head, "A Conversation with Gebre Kristos Desta."

32. Interview with author, July 1985.

33. Catalog, title and date unknown.

34. Interview with author, July 1985.

35. "Overview of My Work," by Alemayehou Gabremedhin (unpublished, 1982).

36. Interview with author, July 1985.

37. Interview with author, July 1985.

11   Between the Natural and Supernatural

1. "What is Paa Ya Paa?" Paa-Ya-Paa Gallery, gallery brochure (Nairobi, 1965).

2. Ibid.

3. Elimo Njau, "Artist's Vision: Wanjau's Long Road to International Fame," *10 Target* (February 26–March 10, 1979).

4. Ibid.

5. Terry Hirst, "Samwel Wanjau: Kenyan Carver," *African Arts* 3(3):48.

6. Ibid., 51.

7. Wole Soyinka, ed., *Poems of Black Africa* (New York: Hill and Wang, 1975) 22, 23.

8. Sidney Kasfir, "Nnaggenda: Experimental Ugandan Artist," *African Arts* 3(1):88.

9. "Owiti: About Himself," by Hezbon Owiti (unpublished, n.d.).

10. Ibid.

11. Hezbon Owiti, "Painting Is a Creation," *African Arts* 2(3):18. Owiti's prints have also been published in *Topic Magazine* 16; *Journal of the New African Literature and the Arts* (Spring 1967); and *Black Orpheus* 20.

12. Don Dodson, "Introducing a Contemporary African Artist: Hezbon Owiti," *Journal of the New African Literature and the Arts,* (Spring 1967): 80.

13. David Cook and David Rubadiri, eds., "Wild Horse of Serengeti," *Poems from East Africa* (London: Heinemann, 1971), 178, 179.

14. Owiti, "Painting Is a Creation," 18.

15. Cook and Rubadiri, *Poems from East Africa,* 67, 68.

16. Lecture given at The Commonwealth Club, San Francisco, California. June 7, 1984.

17. Panel discussion, California College of Arts and Crafts, Oakland, California. January 30, 1984.

18. Julian Beinart, "Malangatana," *Black Orpheus* 10:25.

19. Ulli Beier, *Contemporary Art in Africa* (London: Pall Mall, 1968), 66.

20. Valente Malangatana, "Two Poems," *Black Orpheus* 10:28.

21. Beier, *Contemporary Art in Africa,* 67.

22. Beinart, "Malangatana," 25, 26.

23. Betty Schneider, "Malangatana of Mozambique," *African Arts* 6(2):40.

24. Michael Gibson, "Biazin: Recorder of a Vanishing Africa," *The International Herald Tribune,* Paris, May 23–24, 1981).

25. Michel Leiris, letter to Robert Sève, November 18, 1977.

26. Ibid.

27. Robert Sève, "General Presentation and Judgements (2), Opinions Concerning Biazin" (unpublished) unnumbered.

28. "Text for Information of Stedelijk Museum," by Robert Sève (unpublished, n.d.), 1.

29. Gibson, "Biazin: Recorder of a Vanishing Africa."

12 Sky and Land in Zimbabwe

1. Ulli Beier, *Contemporary Art in Africa* (London: Pall Mall Press, 1968), 88.
2. Correspondence with author, February 14, 1984.
3. Frank McEwen, "Return to Origins: New Directions for African Arts," *African Arts* 1(2):88.
4. McEwen, "Return to Origins: New Directions for African Arts," 25, 88.
5. *New Art from Rhodesia*, exhibition catalog (London: Commonwealth Institute, 1963). Exhibition held at the National Gallery, Salisbury, Rhodesia, February 21–April 1963. Mukarobgwa contributed thirty-one oil paintings to this exhibition.
6. John Reed and Clive Wake, eds., *A Book of African Verse* (London: Heinemann Educational Books, 1964), 63.
7. *African Arts* 1(2): cover and 18.

13 The Sculptors of Zimbabwe
Artists with an Old Legacy

1. Frank McEwen, *The African Workshop School* (N.p., n.d.), unnumbered. Catalog describing school.
2. Frank McEwen, "Return to Origins: New Directions for African Arts," *African Arts* 1(2):25.
3. Unable to locate original source.
4. Michael Peppiatt, "Shona Sculpture: An African Renaissance," *Arts International*, 21.
5. Marion Arnold, "Introduction," *Zimbabwe Stone Sculpture* (Bulawayo: Books of Zimbabwe, 1981), 12.
6. McEwen, *The African Workshop School*.
7. Peppiatt, "Shona Sculpture: An African Renaissance," 21.
8. Ibid., 21.
9. Ibid., 63.
10. Unable to locate original source.
11. Frank McEwen, *New Art from Rhodesia*, exhibition catalog (Salisbury: National Gallery of Rhodesia, n.d.).
12. Unable to locate original source.
13. McEwen, correspondence with author, February 14, 1984.
14. The great variety of type and of color (greens, grays, yellows, reds, and purples) of the often beautifully veined stone enriches the images.
15. "Three Daybreaks," in *A Book of African Verse*, John Reed and Clive Wake, eds. (London: Heinemann Educational Books, 1964), 58.
16. Peppiatt, "Shona Sculpture: An African Renaissance," 63.
17. Frank McEwen, "Shona Art Today," *African Arts* 5(4):11.
18. McEwen, *The African Workshop School*.
19. McEwen, correspondence.
20. Ibid.
21. Ibid.
22. Claire Polakoff, "Contemporary Shona Sculpture at the Musée Rodin, Paris," *African Arts* 5(3):59. McEwen's collection of approximately one hundred pieces represents an important period of the work of the finest artists, including their first paintings and sculptures.
23. Arnold, *Zimbabwe Stone Sculpture*, 40.
24. Peppiatt, "Shona Sculpture: An African Renaissance," 63.

14 South African Artists Speak for The Voiceless

1. Quoted from a theater program for *Sizwe Banzi is Dead*, Arena Stage, Washington, D.C., July 1975.
2. Described by Thomas Matthews in "Mural Painting in South Africa," *African Arts* 10(2):28.
3. David Richards, "The Agony and the Irony: Playwright Athol Fugard and the Sorrows of South Africa," *The Washington Post* (November 8, 1981), M1.
4. Julian Beinart, "Wall Painting: Popular Art in Two African Communities," *African Arts* 2(1):26.
5. Correspondence from Jane Haslem Gallery, Washington, D.C., 1974.
6. K. A. Nortje, "Up Late," in *Modern Poetry from Africa*, Gerald Moore and Ulli Beier, eds. (Harmondsworth, Middlesex, and Baltimore: Penguin African Library, 1963), 216.
7. Dennis Brutus, "Gaily Teetering," in *Modern Poetry from Africa*, 213.
8. Mazisi Kunene, "Farewell," in *Modern Poetry from Africa*, 207.
9. Bloke Modisane, "lonely," in *Modern Poetry from Africa*, 211.
10. William Kgositsile, *Places and Bloodstains* (Oakland, California: Achebe Publications, 1975), 10.
11. William (Keorapetse) Kgositsile, "The Air I Hear," in *Modern Poetry from Africa*, 215.
12. "1972 Prizewinners," *African Arts* 6(2):8.
13. Dan Rakgoathe, "Cyprian Shilakoe: In Memoriam," *African Arts* 7(1):68.
14. Hal Eads in Rakgoathe, "Cyprian Shilakoe: In Memoriam," 69.
15. Conversation with author, January 2, 1985.
16. Ibid.
17. E. J. De Jager, *Contemporary African Art in South Africa* (Cape Town: C. Struik, 1973), 25; Esme Berman, *Art and Artists of South Africa* (Cape Town and Rotterdam: A. A. Balkema, 1983); *African Arts* 6(2):13.
18. Ulli Beier, "Rabearivelo," *Black Orpheus* 11:14.
19. Conversation with author, January 2, 1985.
20. Lionel Ngakane, "Dumile: A Profile," *African Arts* 3(2):10.
21. "1971 Prizewinners," *African Arts* 4(2):10–11.
22. E. J. De Jager, "Five South African Artists," *African Arts* 2(2):55.
23. Ngakane, "Dumile": A Profile," 10.
24. Conversation with author, February 27, 1988.
25. *Gavin Jantjes: Graphic Work 1974–1978*, exhibition catalog (Stockholm: Kulturhuset, 1978), 8. Exhibition held October 27–November 26, 1978.
26. Dennis Brutus in *Modern Poetry from Africa*, 212.
27. Gavin Jantjes, "The Words About Us," *Art Libraries Journal* (Winter 1983): 17, 16, 17.
28. Gavin Jantjes, "Critical Perspective," *Artrage* 2 (February 1983): 3.
29. "From a Conversation between Gavin Jantjes and Rasheed Araeen 26 November 1983," in *Gavin Jantjes: Paintings and Drawings*, exhibition catalog (Nottingham: The Midland Group, 1984), 10, unnumbered. Exhibition held January 10–February 1, 1984.
30. Jantjes, "Critical Perspective," 3.
31. Errol Lloyd, "Gavin Jantjes' Recent Exhibition," *Artrage* 2 (February 1983): 4.
32. "1972 Prizewinners," *African Arts* Vol. 6(2):12.

33. Ibid.

34. Gavin Jantjes, "The Words About Us," 21, 22.

35. "From a Conversation between Gavin Jantjes and Rasheed Araeen, 26 November 1983," in *Gavin Jantjes: Paintings and Drawings.*

36. Athol Fugard, *Notebooks 1960–1977* (New York: Alfred A. Knopf, 1984), 59, 60.

37. "From a Conversation between Gavin Jantjes and Rasheed Araeen, 26 November 1983," in *Gavin Jantjes: Paintings and Drawings.*

Afterword Confluences

1. Ezekiel Mphahlele, *Voices in the Whirlwind—And Other Essays* (New York: Hill and Wang, 1967) 151.

2. "Popular Art of Africa," *Morning Post,* Lagos (March 4, 1965), Review 13.

Bibliography

General

African Artists in America: An Exhibition of Work by Twenty African Artists Living in America. New York: African-American Institute, 1977.

African Contemporary Art. Washington, D.C.: The Gallery of Art, Howard University, 1977. Catalog of an exhibition held April 30–July 31, 1977.

Awoonor, Kofi. "Contemporary Art Forms." In *The Breast of Earth: A Survey of the History, Culture, and Literature of Africa South of the Sahara,* 337–46. Garden City, Anchor Press/Doubleday, 1975.

Beier, Ulli. *Contemporary Art in Africa.* London: Pall Mall, 1968.

Bennett, George. "BBC Art Competition 1970." *African Arts* (Los Angeles) 5(1):36–39 (Autumn 1971).

Benson, Peter. *Black Orpheus, Transition, and Modern Cultural Awakening in Africa.* Berkeley, Los Angeles, London: University of California Press, 1986.

Black Art—Ancestral Legacy: The African Impulse in African-American Art. Dallas: Dallas Museum of Art, 1989.

Brown, Evelyn S. *Africa's Contemporary Art and Artists.* New York: Harmon Foundation, 1966.

Contemporary African Artists: Changing Traditions. New York: The Studio Museum in Harlem, 1990.

Donahue, Benedict. *The Cultural Arts of Africa.* Washington, D.C.: University Press of America, 1979.

Duerden, Dennis. *African Art.* Feltham, Middlesex: Hamlyn Group, 1968.

———*Cultural Events in Africa.* London: Transcription Centre. Monthly publication begun in 1964.

"Harmon Foundation Collection." Section 313 in *Guide to Federal Archives Relating to Africa,* 127–30. Waltham, Mass., Crossroads Press, 1977.

Leyten, Harry, and Paul Faber. *Moderne Kunst in Afrika.* Amsterdam: Tropenmuseum, 1980.

Liyong, Taban lo. *A Bibliography of Writings by Ulli Beier.* Port Moresby: University of Papua New Guinea, 1975.

McEwen, Frank. "Modern African Painting and Sculpture." In *Colloquim on Negro Art,* vol. 1, 427–37. Dakar, 1966.

Modern Kunst aus Afrika. Berlin: Das Festspiele, 1979.

Mount, Marshall Ward. *African Art: The Years Since 1920.* Bloomington: Indiana University Press, 1973.

Ofori-Ansah, Kwaku. "The Growth of African Contemporary Art: The Howard Connection." *New Directions* (Washington, D.C.) 10 (3–4):36–39 (July–October 1983).

Ouevres Africaines Nouvelles Recueillies au Nigeria et Dans l'Est de l'Afrique. Collection Ulli Beier et Musée Náprstek, Prague. Paris: Musée de l'Homme, 1972.

Von D. Miller, Judith. *Art in East Africa.* London: Frederick Muller, 1975.

Willett, Frank. *African Art.* New York: Praeger Publishers, 1971.

World Print Four: An International Survey. San Francisco: World Print Council, 1983.

Nigeria

Adekeye, Adeyemi. "Uzo Egonu of Nigeria." *African Arts* (Los Angeles) 7(1):34–37 (Autumn 1973).

Adepegba, Cornelius O. Introduction to *Bruce Onobrakpeya: Twenty-five Years of Creative Search.* Lagos: Ovuomaroo Gallery, 1984.

Aiyegbusi, Tayo. *A Mixture of African Mythology and English Whimsey.* Bayreuth: Iwalewa Haus, 1983.

Ajala. "Museum of Popular Art in Oshogbo." *Nigeria Magazine* (Lagos) 86:231–32 (September 1965).

Aka 86—Inaugural Exhibition Catalogue: Aka Circle of Exhibiting Artists. Enugu: Aka Circle of Exhibiting Artists, 1986. Catalog of exhibition held April and May 1986.

Aniakor, Chike C. "Contemporary Nigerian Artists and Their Traditions." *Black Art* (Jamaica, N.Y.) 4(2):40–55 (1980).

Armstrong, Robert G. "On 'The Myth of Oshogbo'." *African Arts* (Los Angeles) 15(1):8 (November 1981).

Armstrong, Robert Plant. "Aesthetic Continuity in Two Yoruba Works." *African Arts* (Los Angeles) 4(3):40–43, 68–70 (Spring 1971).

Arneson, Jeanette Jensen. *Tradition and Change in Yoruba Art.* Sacramento: E. B. Crocker Gallery, 1974.

Barde, Robert. "Bruce Onobrakpeya." *Black Art* (Jamaica, N.Y.) 4(3):49–58 (1981).

Beier, Georgina. "Bruce Onobrakpeya," "Tijiani Mayakira," "Valente Malangtana." In *Contemporary Art from the Third World.* Port Moresby: Institute of Papua New Guinea Studies, 1975.

———*Design Workshop.* Ife, Nigeria: Institute of African Studies, University of Ife, 1973.

———*Outsider Art in the Third World.* Port Moresby: Institute of Papua New Guinea Studies, 1977.

———*Patchwork Paintings.* Bayreuth: Iwalewa Haus, 1983.

———"Wyckom and Gilbert." *African Arts* (Los Angeles) 10(1):5 (October 1976). A response to allegations of the sameness of Oshogbo and Papua New Guinea artists associated with Georgina and Ulli Beier.

Beier, Ulli. *Art in Nigeria, 1960.* Cambridge: Cambridge University Press, 1960.

———"Asiru Olatunde." In *Modern Konst I Afrika* (Modern Art in Africa), 96–99. Lund: Kalesdoskop, 1978.

———"Contemporary Art in Africa." *Tendenzen* (Munich) 59:106–7 (July 1969).

———"Experimental Art School." *Nigeria Magazine* (Lagos) 86:199–204 (September 1965).

———*Gift Orakpo.* Port Moresby: Institute of Papua New Guinea Studies, 1976.

———"Glucklose Kopfe: Malerei von ver-ruckten aus Nigeria-Lucklessheads:" Painting by Deranged Nigerians. Bremen: Edition CON, 1982.

———"Ladenschilder und Legenden." *Tendenzen* (Munich) 37:2–11.

———*Middle Art.* Bayreuth: Iwalewa Haus, 1982.

———"Middle Art: The Paintings of War." *African Arts* (Los Angeles) 9(2):20–23 (January 1976).

———"Moderne Kunst in Afrika," "Vincent Akweti Kofi," "Buraimoh Gbadamosi," "Valente Malangatana," "Ibrahim el Salahi," "Adebisi Akanji," "Moderne Architektur in Afrika," "Populare Kunst in Afrika." *Tendenzen* (Munich) 49:104–51 (1967).

———"Moderne Kunst in Einer Afrikanischen Stadt." *Tendenzen* (Munich) 32:47–55 (May 1965).

———*Moderne Kunst in Einer Afrikanischen Stadt—Katalog 14.* Munich: Der Dennoch-Verlag/Neue Münchner Galerie.

———*Neue Kunst in Afrika.* Berlin: Dietrich Reimer Verlag, 1980.

———"Obiora Udechukwu." Bayreuth: Iwalewa Haus, n.d., but after 1981.

———*The Return of the Gods: The Sacred Art of Susanne Wenger.* Cambridge: Cambridge University Press, 1975.

———"Seven-Seven." *Black Orpheus* (Ibadan) 22:45–48 (August 1967).

———"Signwriters Art in Nigeria." *African Arts* (Los Angeles) 9(2):20–23 (January 1976).

———"Three Zaria Artists." *West African Review* (London) 31:37–41 (October 1960).

———*Yemi Bisiri: A Yoruba Brass Caster.* Ibadan, Nigeria: Mbari Publications, 1963.

Beier, Ulli, and Denis Williams. "Experiment in Art Teaching." *Black Orpheus* (Ibadan) 12:43–47 (1961).

Ben Amos, Paula. "Ben Osawe: A Modern Nigerian Sculptor." *Nigeria Magazine* (Lagos) 94:248–50 (September 1967).

Bohrer, Stanley, and Susanne Wenger Alarape. "Gods and Myths in Susanne Wenger's Art: The Example of a Batik Cloth." *Nigeria Magazine* (Lagos) 120:1–12 (1976).

Brokensha, David. "Ori Olokun: A New Art Center." *African Arts* (Los Angeles) 2(3):32–35 (Spring 1969).

Buraimoh, Jimoh. "Painting With Beads." *African Arts* (Los Angeles) 5(1):116–19 (Autumn 1971).

Carroll, Kevin. *Yoruba Religious Carving: Pagan and Christian Sculpture in Nigeria and Dahomey.* New York: Praeger, 1967.

Cole, Herbert M. *Icons: Ideals and Power in the Art of Africa.* Washington, D.C.: Smithsonian Institution Press for the National Museum of African Art. Exhibition held October 25, 1989–September 3, 1990).

Cole, Herbert M., and Chike C. Aniakor. *Igbo Art: Community and Cosmos.* Los Angeles: Museum of Cultural History, University of California, 1984.

"Competition 1974: Isaac Ojo Fajana." *African Arts* (Los Angeles) 8(2):12–13 (Winter 1975).

Contemporary African Art: Painting, Sculpture, Drawing, Graphics, Ceramics, Fabrics. Los Angeles: Otis Art Institute of Los Angeles County, 1969. Catalog of an exhibition held March 13–May 4, 1969.

Crowder, Michael. "Nigeria's Artists Emerge." *West African Review* (London) 33(417):30–36 (1959).

———"Patronage and Audience in Nigeria." *Black Orpheus* (Lagos) 4(1):68–74 (1981).

Dean, Roy. "Oshogbo Art in London." *Nigeria Magazine* (Lagos) 95:288–89 (December 1967).

Dickerson, Sara Jane Hollis. *Benin Sculptor Idah: Court Art and Personal Style.* New Orleans: Interdisciplinary Studies Program at Southern University of New Orleans, 1979.

Duerden, Dennis. "Sculptures in Light." *West Africa* (London) 3485:1163 (June 4, 1984). On Sokari Douglas Camp.

Duro Ladipo. Produced by National Educational Television. Edited by Henry Dore. 16mm, 30 minutes. 1967. Distributed by Indiana University, Bloomington, IN.

Ekom, Ernest. "The Two Mbaris." *Nigeria Magazine* (Lagos) 89:160–62 (June 1966). On Mbari centers in Nigeria.

Harper, Peggy. "Gift Orakpo." *African Arts* (Los Angeles) 12(2):62–64 (February 1979).

Heady, Victor, and Jeanette Arneson. "Yinka Adeyemi." *Black Art* (Jamaica, N.Y.) 1(2):38–43 (Winter 1976).

Heathcote, David. "The Art of Musa Yola." *African Arts* (Los Angeles) 8(2):34–37 (Winter 1974).

Hendrickse, Begum. "The Mbari Story." *African Forum* (New York) 1(1):109–11 (1965).

Highet, Juliet. "Five Nigerian Artists." *African Arts* (Los Angeles) 2(2):34–41 (Winter 1969).

Kennedy, Jean. "Bruce Onobrakpeya: An Art of Synthesis." *Print News* (New York) 6(5):8–9, 11 (September/October 1984).

_____"Bruce Onobrakpeya, Artist for Nigeria." *Topic Magazine* (Washington, D.C.) 161:42–46 (1985).

_____"I Saw and I Was Happy: Festival Oshogbo." *African Arts* (Los Angeles) 1(2):8–16, 85 (Winter, 1967).

_____"Muraina Oyelami of Nigeria." *African Arts* (Los Angeles) 6(3):32–33, inside back cover (Spring 1973).

_____"Printmaking in Nigeria." *Artist's Proof* 3 (1964).

_____"Renaissance in Oshogbo I: The Shrines, A Developing Art Form." *West African Builder and Architect* (Lagos) 8(3):71–74, n.d.

_____"Renaissance in Oshogbo II: Ten Artists, Ten Styles." *West African Builder and Architect* (Lagos) 8(5):126, n.d.

_____"Senabu Oloyede, Kikelomo Oladepo: New Heirs to Talent in Oshogbo." *African Arts* (Los Angeles) 4(4):24–27 (Summer 1971).

_____"Speaking of Myths." *African Arts* (Los Angeles) 14(4):78–80 (August 1981). Rejoinder to Steven Naifeh's "The Myth of Oshogbo." *African Arts* (February 1981).

_____"The City as Metaphor." *African Report* (Washington, D.C.) 17 4):27–29 (April 1972).

_____"Two Nigerian Artists." *Nigeria Magazine* (Lagos) 96:2–11 (March 1968). On Asiru Olatunde and Jimoh Buraimoh.

"Lagos Art Galleries." *Nigeria Magazine* (Lagos) 92:2–18 (March 1967).

Lawal, Babatunde. Introduction to *Symbols of Ancestral Groves: A Monograph of Prints and Paintings, 1978–1985,* by Bruce Onobrakpeya. Lagos: Bruce Onobrakpeya, 1985.

_____"The Mythical Realism of Bruce Onobrakpeya." *Nigeria Magazine* (Lagos) 120:50–59 (1976).

Lawrence, Wendy. "Bruce Onobrakpeya: The Spirit in Ascent." In *Bruce Onobrakpeya: Nigeria's Master Printmaker,* 2–7. Toronto: Best of Africa, 1978.

Maiden Catalogue of Works in Nigeria's National Gallery of Modern Art—The Nucleus. Lagos: Federal Department of Culture, 1981.

Middle Art. "Middle Art Talks to Ulli Beier." *Okike* (Nsukka) 22:42–46 (September 1982). Interview by Ulli Beier.

Modern Konst I Afrika. Modern Art in Africa. Lund: Kalesdoskop, 1978.

Moderne Kunst aus Oshogbo, Nigeria. Munich: Neue Münchner Galerie.

Moses, Sybil E. "Simon Obiekezie Okeke." *African Arts* (Los Angeles) 10(4):86–87 (July 1977).

Mundy-Castle, A. C., and Vicky Mundy-Castle. "Twins Seven-Sevens." *African Arts* (Los Angeles) 6(1):8–13 (Autumn 1972).

Mundy-Castle, Vicky. "Adebisi Fabunmi of Nigeria." *African Arts* (Los Angeles) 7(3):36–37, inside back cover (Spring 1974).

Naifeh, Steven W. "The Myth of Oshogbo." *African Arts* (Los Angeles) 14(2):25–27, 85–86 (February 1981).

Nevadomsky, Joseph. "The House That Idah Built." *African Arts* (Los Angeles) 19(2):8 (February 1986). On Chief Ovia Idah.

New Culture. Vol. 1, no. 1. Ibadan: New Culture Studios, 1978.

New Images: Art in a Changing Society. Produced by Frank Speed and Ulli Beier, 1964. Distributed by Colour Film Services, Ltd., London.

"A New Sanctuary at Oshogbo." *Nigeria Magazine* (Lagos) 81:98–105 (June 1964).

Nicklin, Keith. "Ibibio Metalwork." *African Arts* (Los Angeles) 10(1):20–23, 98, inside front cover (October 1976).

Nicklin, Keith, and Jill Salmons. "S. J. Akpan of Nigeria." *African Arts* (Los Angeles) 11(1):30–34 (October 1977).

Nigerian Sculpture at the 269th Exhibition of the Royal Society of British Artists. Enugu: New Africa Centre, 1986. Catalog of an exhibition held at the Mall Galleries, The Mall, London, July 11–13, 1986.

"1972 Prizewinners." *African Arts* (Los Angeles) 6(2):11–12, 16, front cover (Winter 1973).

Okeke, Uche. *Drawings.* Ibadan, Nigeria: Mbari Publications, 1961.

Olatunde, Asiru. *Asiru: A New Yoruba Artist Introduced by Ulli Beier.* Oshogbo: Mbari Mbayo Productions, 1965.

Onibonkuta, Ademola. The Return of Shango. Bayreuth: Iwalewa Haus, 1983.

_____*Mbari Mbayo.* New York: Studio Museum of Harlem, 1970.

Onobrakpeya, Bruce. *Bruce Onobrakpeya: Poems and Lithographs.* Lagos, Nigeria: Ovuomaroro Gallery, 1989.

_____"An Interview with Bruce Onobrakpeya." Interview by Obiora Udechukwu. *Okike* (Nsukka) 21:61–66 (July 1982).

_____*Forty-six Prints.* Lagos: Bruce Onobrakpeya, 1978.

_____*Nine Deep Etchings.* Lagos: Bruce Onobrakpeya, 1971.

_____*Portfolio.* Lagos: Bruce Onobrakpeya, 1982.

_____*Print Notes and Comments No. 5.* Lagos: Bruce Onobrakpeya, 1979.

_____*Print Notes and Comments No. 6* Lagos: Bruce Onobrakpeya, 1982.

_____*Print Notes and Comments No. 7.* Lagos: Bruce Onobrakpeya, 1982.

_____*Sabbatical Experiments, 1978–1983.* Lagos: Bruce Onobrakpeya, 1983.

_____*Sahelian Masquerades.* Lagos, Nigeria: Ovuomaroro Gallery, 1988.

_____*Symbols of Ancestral Groves: A Monograph of Prints and Paintings, 1978–1985.* Lagos: Bruce Onobrakpeya, 1985. Introduction by Babatunde Lawal.

_____*Twelve Deep Etchings.* Lagos: Bruce Onobrakpeya, 1972.

_____*Twenty Deep Etchings*. Lagos: Bruce Onobrakpeya, 1973.

"Our Authors and Performing Artists-I." *Nigeria Magazine* (Lagos) 88:57–67 (March 1966). On Ben Enwonwu, Erhabor O. Emokpae, Felix Idubor, Demas Nwoko, Christopher Uchefuna Okeke, Bruce Onobrakpeya, Solomon Irein Wangboje.

Oyelami, Muriana. "Mbari Mbayo and the Oshogbo Artists." *African Arts* (Los Angeles) 15(2):85–87 (February 1982).

Oyelami, Muraina. *My Life in the Duro Ladipo Theatre*. Bayreuth: Iwalewa Haus, 1982.

Oyelola, Pat. "The Modern Scene." In *Everyman's Guide to Nigerian Art*, 62–141. Lagos: *Nigeria Magazine*, 1976.

Plocki, Z. "Ulli and Georgina Beier." *African Arts* (Los Angeles) 9(4):7–8 (July 1976).

Richards, Margaret. "Changing Art in Africa. *Nigeria Magazine* (Lagos) 95:290–92 (December 1967).

Scott, Victoria. "FAB Art." *Black Art* (Jamaica, N.Y.) 4(30:22–32 (1980). On Adebisi Fabunmi.

_____"Nike Olaniyi." *African Arts* (Los Angeles) 16(2):46–47 (February 1983).

Sokari Douglas Camp: Kinetic Sculptures and Drawings. London: The October Gallery, 1985. Brochure from an exhibition held July 3–August 3, 1985.

"Susanne Wenger." "Tribal Eye" television series. Part 2 of No. 7 of 90100. 52 minutes. 1976.

Today and Before Yesterday. Produced by Frank Speed. 1978.

Udechukwu, Obiora. "An Interview with Obiora Udechukwu." *Okike* (Nsukka) 20:53–66 (December 1981). Interview by Ulli Beier.

_____*No Water: An Exhibition of Drawings, Watercolors, and Prints*. Nsukka: Odunke Publications, 1981.

_____"Obiora Udechukwu, Towards Essence and Clarity." *Nigeria Magazine* (Lagos) 132–33:43–46 (1980).

_____"Observations on Art Criticism in Nigeria." *Nigeria Magazine* (Lagos) 126–27:35–43 (1978).

_____*Obiora Udechukwu: Selected Sketches, 1965–83*. Lagos: National Council for Arts and Culture, 1984.

Wenger, Susanne, and Gert Chesi. *A Life With the Gods in Their Yoruba Homeland*. Wörgl, Austria: Perlinger, 1983.

_____*Susanne Wenger: Batiks and Oil Paintings*. Lagos: Goethe Institute, 1984. Catalog of an exhibition.

_____*The Timeless Mind of the Sacred: Its New Manifestation in the Osun Groves*. Ibadan, Nigeria: Institute of African Studies, Ibadan University, 1977.

Williams, Denis. "A Revival of Terra-Cotta at Ibadan." *Nigeria Magazine* (Lagos) 88:4–13 (March 1966). On Demas Nwoko.

Zimmer, Jenny. The *Art of Georgina Beier*. Bayreuth: Iwalewa Haus, 1983.

Gambia, Ghana, and Ivory Coast

Anatsui, El. *Sculptures, Photographs, and Drawings*. Enugu: SNAAP Press, 1982.

Anatsui, El, and Liz Willis. *Walls and Gates—Exhibition Catalogue*. Kaduna: Avant-Garde Gallery, 1988.

"Christian Lattier." In *Écrivains, Cinéastes et Artistes Ivoriens*, 121–22. Abidjan-Dakar: Nouvelles Éditions Africanes, 1973.

Gardella, David. "Momodou Ceesay of the Gambia." *African Arts* (Los Angeles) 7(4):40–41 (Summer 1974).

Grah-Mel, F., and J. James Houra. "Les Ficelles de la Gloire: Hommage à Christian Lattier." *Social* (Abidjan): 9–21 (1980?).

Grobel, Lawrence. "Ghana's Vincent Kofi." *African Arts* (Los Angeles) 3(4):8–11, 68–70, 80 (Summer 1970).

Kofi, Vincent Akwete. *Sculpture in Ghana*. Accra: Ghana Information Services, 1964.

Sculptures in Wood: "Thoughts and Processes" by El Anatsui and Ndubisi Onah. Lagos: Italian Cultural Institute, 1988. Catalog of an exhibition held November 12–25, 1988.

Senegal

Art Sénégalais d'Aujourd'hui. Paris: Galeries Nationales du Grand Palais, 1974.

Contemporary Art of Senegal: Art Contemporain du Sénégal. Hamilton, Ontario: The Art Gallery of Hamilton, 1979. Catalog of an exhibition held August–September, 1979.

Contemporary Art of Senegal. Washington, D.C.: Corcoran Gallery of Art, 1980. Catalog of an exhibition held February 22–April 6, 1980.

Gomis, Gabriel J. "Ibou Diouf—Jeune Loup de la Peinture." *Sénégal Carrefour* (Dakar) 6:43–51 (May 1968).

Mark, Peter. "Senegalese Art Today: The African Side of Pan-African Aesthetics." Chapter 4. Unpublished article.

Pataux, Bernard. "Senegalese Art Today." *African Arts* (Los Angeles) 8(1):26–31, 56–59, 87 (Autumn 1974).

Polakoff, Claire. "Iba Ndiaye." *African Arts* (Los Angeles) 10(3):72–74 (April 1977). Exhibition review.

"Tapisseries de Thiès." *African Arts* (Los Angeles) 3(2):61–63 (Winter 1970).

Sudan

"Ancestor." *African Arts* (Los Angeles) 2(2):10–11 (Winter 1969). On Amir I. M. Nour.

Beier, Ulli. "Ibrahim El Salahi." *Black Orpheus* (Ibadan) 10:48–50, n.d.

_____*Ibrahim El Salahi*. Bayreuth: Iwalewa Haus, 1982.

"Bushara at the Slade." *African Arts* (Los Angeles) 12(3):36–41 (May 1979). On Mohamed Bushara.

Donovan, Alan. "Salih Mashamoun." *African Arts* (Los Angeles) 12(2):60–61 (February 1979).

El Salahi, Ibrahim. "Portfolio: Paintings and Drawings by El Salahi." *African Arts* (Los Angeles) 1(1):16, 26, 40–43, 65, 70, 71, 74 (Autumn 1967).

_____ "Ibrahim El Salahi: Kalligraphie ist nicht Selbstzweck; Gespräch mit Ulli Beier." *Tendenzen* (Munich) 146:44–51 (April/June 1984).

Hale, Sondra. "Art in a Changing Society." *Ufahuma* (Los Angeles) 1(1).

_____"Musa Khalifa of Sudan." *African Arts* (Los Angeles) 6(3):14–19 (Spring 1973).

_____*The Vision of Mohamed Omer Bushara.* New York: African-American Institute, 1981.

Hale, Sondra, and Mohamed Omer Bushara. "In Search of a Face: Salih Abdou Mashamoun—The Sun and the Eclipse." *Ufahamu* (Los Angeles) 6(2):82–105 (1976).

Ibrahim El Salahi: Drawings. Ibadan: Mbari Publications, 1961.

Kennedy, Jean. "Mohammad Omer Khalil Pays Homage to Miro." *Print News* (San Francisco) 8(1):19–20 (Winter 1986).

Mohammad Khalil. Washington, D.C.: Alif Gallery, 1986. Brochure from an exhibition held March 11–April 4, 1986.

"New Sculpture From Amir I. M. Nour." *African Arts* (Los Angeles) 4(4):54–57 (Summer 1971).

Nour, Amir I. M. "Interview: The Place of the African Artist." *Africa Report* 20(3):12–16, 48 (May–June 1974).

Okwesa, Kenneth. "Abdulla: Sudanese Potter." *African Arts* (Los Angeles) 3(2):29–31 (Winter 1970).

Serumaga, Robert. "Conversation with Ibrahim El Salahi." *Topic* (Washington, D.C.).

Soghayroon, A. Z. "El Salahi: A Painter From the Sudan." *African Arts* (Los Angeles) 1(1):16–26 (Autumn 1967).

Ethiopia

Benjamin, Tritobia H. "Skunder Boghossian: A Different Magnificence." *African Arts* (Los Angeles) 5(4):22–25 (Summer 1972).

Boghossian, Skunder. *Skunder.* Athens, Ohio: The Trisolini Gallery. Catalog of an exhibition sponsored by the Center for Afro-American Studies and the Trisolini Gallery of Ohio University; held March 31–May 3, 1980.

Chojnacki, Stanislaw. "The Art of Gebre Christos Desta." *Ethiopia Observer* (Addis Ababa) 7(2):104–13 (1953).

_____"Gebre Christos Desta: Impressions of His Recent Exhibition." *Ethiopia Observer* (Addis Ababa) 14(1):10–24 (1971).

_____"Skunder: His First Addis Ababa Exhibition." *Ethiopia Observer* (Addis Ababa) 10(3):184–91 (1966).

Head, Sydney W. "A Conversation with Gebre Kristos Desta." *African Arts* (Los Angeles) 2(4):20–25 (Summer 1969).

Kennedy, Jean. "Wosene Kosrof of Ethiopia." *African Arts* (Los Angeles) 20(3):64–67 (May 1987).

Talbot, David. "The Art of Gebre Kristos Desta," *Ethiopia Observer* (Addis Ababa) 9(4):271–85 (1966).

Tribute to Ethiopian Artists. Introduction by Kwaku Ofori-Ansah. Washington, D.C.: Ethiopian Community Center, 1984.

Central African Republic, Kenya, Mozambique, Tanzania, Uganda, and Zaire

Beinart, Julian. "Malangatana." *Black Orpheus* (Ibadan) 10:20–27, n.d.

Bowen, Donald. "Exhibitions at the Commonwealth Institute," *African Arts* (Los Angeles) 6(2):42–45 (Winter 1973).

Dodson, Don. "Introducing a Contemporary African Artist: Hezbon Owiti." In *New African Literature and the Arts,* 332–39. New York: Crowell, 1970.

Kasfir, Sidney. "Nnaggenda: Experimental Ugandan Artist." *African Arts* (Los Angeles) 3(1):8–13, 88 (Autumn 1969).

Kennedy, Jean. "A Profile of Artist Kiure Msangi." *The Daily Californian* (Berkeley) February 11, 1986. Black History Month: The Special.

Lawrence, Mike. "Francis Nnaggenda." *African Arts* (Los Angeles) 11(1):78 (October 1977). Exhibition review.

M'Puanga, Liyolo Limbé, *Liyolo.* n.p., 1977.

Miller, Judith von D. *Art in East Africa: A Guide to Contemporary Art.* London: Frederick Muller, 1975.

Msanji, Francis. "I Opened My Eyes to The World." *African Arts* (Los Angeles) 3(4):28–31 (Summer 1970).

Owiti, Hezbon Edward. "Painting Is a Creation." *African Arts* (Los Angeles) 2(3):8, 17 (Spring 1969).

Povey, John. "Francis Nnaggenda." *African Arts* (Los Angeles) 8(3):75 (Spring 1975). Exhibition review.

Schneider, Betty. "Malangatana of Mozambique." *African Arts* (Los Angeles) 5(2):40–45 (Winter 1972).

Sève, Robert. *Clément-Marie Biazin.* Amsterdam: Stedelijk Museum, 1978. Catalog of an exhibition.

Zimbabwe

African Workshop School. Salisbury: National Gallery of Rhodesia, (1967?).

Commonwealth Institute, London. *New Art from Rhodesia.* Salisbury: National Gallery, 1963. Catalog of an exhibition held February 21–April 15, 1963.

McEwen, Frank. "Shona Art Today." *African Arts* (Los Angeles) 5(4):8–11, front cover (Summer 1972).

_____"Return to Origins: New Directions for African Arts." *African Arts* (Los Angeles) 1(2):18–25, 88 (Winter 1968).

Polakoff, Claire. "Contemporary Shona Sculpture at the Musée Rodin, Paris." *African Arts* (Los Angeles) 5(3):57–59 (Spring 1972).

Povey, John. "Nicholas Mukomberanwa, Gallery 10, London." *African Arts* (Los Angeles) 17(4):83 (August 1984). Exhibition review.

Rhodes National Gallery. *New African Talent: Salisbury.* Salisbury: Rhodes National Gallery, 1962. Catalog of an exhibition held May–June 1962.

Sculpture Contemporaine des Shonas d'Afrique, Musée Rodin, Paris, 1971. Paris: Musée Rodin, 1971.

Southern Africa

Arnott, B. *John Muafangejo.* Cape Town: C. Struik, 1977.

Art in South-West Africa. Pretoria: J. P. Van der Walt, 1978. On John Muafangejo.

Battiss, Walter. "ELC Art and Craft Centre at Rorke's Drift." *African Arts* (Los Angeles) 11(1):38–42 (October 1977).

Black/South Africa/Contemporary Graphics and Tapestries. Brooklyn, N.Y.: The Brooklyn Museum, 1976.

DeJager, E. J. *Contemporary African Art in South Africa.* Cape Town: C. Struik, 1973.

————"Contemporary African Sculpture in South Africa." *Fort Hare Papers* (University of Fort Hare, South Africa) 6(6):421–58 (1978).

————"Five South African Artists." *African Arts* (Los Angeles) 11(2):50–55 (January 1978). On Julian Motau, Lucky Sibiya, Dan Rakgoathe, Lucas Sithole, and Mslaba Dumile.

————"Township Arts in Southern Africa." *Fort Hare Papers* (University of Fort Hare, South Africa) 7(6):407–17 (1984).

Gavin Jantjes: Graphic Work 1974–1978. Stockholm: Kulturhuset, 1978.

Haenggi, F. F. *Lucas Sithole.* Johannesburg: Haenggi Foundation Museum, 1980.

Jantjes, Gavin, and Edward Kamau Braithwaite. *Korabra.* London: Edward Totah Gallery, 1986.

Levinson, Olga. "The Life and Art of John Muafangejo." *S.W.A. Annual* (Windhoek): 107–10 (1981).

Ngakane, Lionel. "Dumile: A Profile." *African Arts* (Los Angeles) 3(2):10–13 (Winter 1970).

"1972 Prizewinners: Cyprian Shilakoe, Louis Maqhubela, and Tito Zungu." *African Arts* (Los Angeles) 6(2):8–13, inside front cover (Winter 1973).

Rakgoathe, Dan. "Cyprian Shilakoe: In Memoriam." *African Arts* (Los Angeles) 7(1):68–69 (Autumn 1973). See also Hal Eads, "Tribute to Cyprian Shilakoe" in same article.

Scholz, Ute, ed. *Phafa Nyika: Contemporary Black Art in South Africa, with Special Reference to the Transvaal.* Pretoria: University of Pretoria, 1980.

Tambo, Oliver. "Der Kunstler und die Revolution." *Tendenzen* (Munich) 132:6–9 (October/November 1980).

Watter, Lola. "Louis Maqhubela." *The Classic* (Johannesburg) 3(2):25–28 (1969).

Williamson, Sue. *Resistance Art in South Africa.* New York: St. Martin's Press, 1990.

Younge, Gavin. *Art of the South African Townships.* New York: Rizzoli, 1988.

Index

My mother, Jean Kennedy Wolford, was a great woman
with beautiful energy, who dedicated her life to encouraging and empowering people with self-confidence and
a sense of themselves. She gave fully of herself, and she
was loved deeply by those she touched. Her rich and
varied interests were an inspiration, a beacon that drew
people to her, and their lives were heightened because
of it. As unfair and premature as her death was, we all
will stand in awe of her accomplishments—magical
assemblages, poignant poetry, exhibitions assembled,
and this book.

Miriam Kennedy Wolford
April 1992